Huddersfield & district road transport history series, no 4

HANSONS of HUDDERSFIELD and their NEIG

a further look at bus operations in the Colne & Holme va

Peter Cardno and Stephen Harling

ROBIN HOOD
PUBLISHING

CONTENTS

Designed and Published by

ROBIN HOOD PUBLISHING

Attenborough, Notts.
NG9 6AP
mail@robinhood publishing.co.uk
www.robinhood publishing.co.uk

Title Page
AEC Regal 55 (VH 4576) was new in 1932 with an AEC 8.8 litre diesel engine and a Brush body. In this January 1941 view it had just been rebodied by Burlingham; the white paint on the mudguards was to aid visibility in the blackout. The bus is pictured in Slades Lane, Helme en route from Meltham to Huddersfield. [Omnibus Society collection]

Front Cover
Roe bodied AEC Reliance rebuild 390 (ECX 887C) was "new" in April 1965, constructed using running units from a 1956 Bottomleys coach. Here it is turning out of Thorncliffe Street to reach the Lidget Street, Lindley terminus of the inter-suburban routes to Newsome. From October 1969 it survived long enough with Huddersfield Corporation to become 4090 in the West Yorkshire PTE fleet. [Photobus]

Back cover left
One of the May 1976 delivery of Volvo/Plaxton 49 seaters, 1509 (LUB 509P), displays the Metro Hanson fleetname at the present Huddersfield Bus Station on 16 September 1978. All the Volvo coaches were disposed of by the PTE in March 1979 prior to its sale of the Hanson business. [H.J. Black]

Back cover upper right
The final (1965) batch of Ford Thames Traders consisted of four Plaxton bodied examples, one of which was delivered in Bottomleys livery, although by this time all coaches were licensed to Hansons. 392 (ECX 110C) is seen in St John's Road on 8 September 1971; it was withdrawn and sold in the following month. [H.J. Black]

Back cover lower right
A few years after the native ex-Huddersfield Corporation Seddons had disappeared from the town, Seddon RU/Seddon RHG 312K, new to Burnley, Colne & Nelson Joint Transport in 1972, was being used by SKJ on tendered route 319 from Huddersfield Bus Station to Storthes Hall Hospital via Penistone Road on 24 April 1987. Of the two Yorkshire Rider Atlanteans on the left, one is still in West Yorkshire PTE livery while the other carries Huddersfield JOC livery applied to commemorate the centenary of municipal public transport in 1983. [H.J. Black]

ISBN 978 0 948854 20 0
© January 2010 Peter Cardno & Stephen Harling

INTRODUCTION

This fourth volume in our series of books on Huddersfield area bus services takes as its major theme the passenger transport operations of Hansons, for years the district's premier coaching business. Hansons were equally well known for their buses, remembered crawling up Lockwood Scar or engaging low gear on some testing approach to a windswept eminence such as Scapegoat Hill or Blackmoorfoot.

You will find accounts of several prewar Holme Valley omnibus proprietors, not least Wilson Haigh, who was prepared to serve destinations such as Holme, Parkhead and Honley village, whose residents had been ignored by Huddersfield Corporation. We have also included some supplementary material on Baddeleys not available when Baddeleys of Holmfirth was published in 2002.

Finally a modern parallel is described in the form of Holme Valley Parish Council's pioneering development of a minibus network during the early and mid 1980s.

ACKNOWLEDGEMENTS

The authors are particularly grateful to the following individuals for assistance: John Bennett, Mike Bennett, Marjorie Bewick, John Black, Amanda Booth, Stephen Carter, Tony Garrood, Tony Hanson, Evelyn Harrison, Paul Hilton, Liz Hirst, Geoff Hodgson, Jim Holmes, Geoff Lumb, Roy Marshall, Gordon Pitt, John F. Sharp and G. Stadden.

Sources consulted include the Huddersfield Daily Examiner, Huddersfield Weekly Examiner, Holmfirth Express and Colne Valley Guardian newspapers; minutes of the county borough, urban district and parish councils of Huddersfield, Colne Valley, Golcar, Holmfirth, Honley, Linthwaite, Meltham and Holme Valley; Notices and Proceedings of the Yorkshire Traffic Area and fleet records of the PSV Circle.

The following libraries, archives, museums and other organisations provided access to material of interest and we thank their staff for the help given: The Geoff Lumb Transport Archive, Holme Valley Parish Council, Huddersfield Examiner Library, Huddersfield Local Studies Library, Kirklees Image Archive and the Omnibus Society Library.

We apologise to any individuals or organisations inadvertently omitted. Any errors or misinterpretations in the text are of course the authors' responsibility.

Right
In March 1963 concern was being expressed about the narrow roads around Helme. Hansons AEC Regent/Roe rebuild 349 (MVH 837) demonstrates in Slades Lane.
[Kirklees Image Archive Ke19034]

GW Castle's Upperthong route was very popular on its first day. Plaxton bodied Leyland Tiger coach 9 (GWR 790), bought new in September 1947, wears a lucky horse shoe on its radiator in Victoria Street, Holmfirth on Sunday 18 January 1953. Loadings were such that a duplicate was required; Bedford OB 8 (FWU 584) can just be seen tucked in behind. Unfortunately patronage was not sustained so the service survived for fewer than four months. [Kirklees Image Archive Ke08485]

PART 1
TRAVEL THE HIGHWAY THE HANSON WAY:
HANSONS BUSES OF HUDDERSFIELD

1: CARRIERS AND CHARABANCS (1830-1923)

As far back as the 1830s Mary Hanson started a horse drawn carriers business to supplement the income from her husband Joseph's farm in the Colne Valley. At first they carried textiles for the local mills, leaving Longwood at 3.00pm on three days each week for the Cherry Tree Inn, Huddersfield, but later they were able to handle machinery used in the mills and by 1846 were carrying goods to Leeds and Manchester. The eldest son, Joseph, took over as head of the business in 1854 following Mary's death and his name was to remain part of the firm's title until 1948. Joseph Hanson moved to Botham Hall Farm in 1880 and also managed to combine farming with running the haulage business. Joseph's son, James William, took over in 1896 and ran the firm from its headquarters under the railway arches in Milnsbridge until his death in 1911. Two of his sons, Robert and Joseph, then shared the running of the firm until Joseph's untimely death in 1919 from influenza.

The first motor charabancs to be owned by Hansons appeared in 1919 and the first motor "chara" outing to Blackpool was achieved with a legal top speed of only 10 mph. Mr Holmes (senior) was later booked for doing 12 mph at Preston by a policeman on a push bike. Until 1920 steam wagons were also used for excursions; bodies with seats were fitted at weekends, as was the case with some of the earlier motor charabancs. It was the job of Mr Holmes (senior), as chief engineer, with his mechanics every summer Friday night to remove the cabs and bodies from lorries and drop on replacement bodies with seats for thirty passengers. The resulting "chara" would then run excursions to places such as Blackpool, Buxton, Harrogate and Scarborough. On Sunday night these charas had to be converted back to lorries ready for Monday morning.

The firm suffered a disastrous fire at the Savile Street (Milnsbridge) depot on 18 August 1919 when two charabancs and four steam wagons as well as 130 van loads of furniture with a total estimated value of £50,000 were destroyed. The fire was particularly fierce because a large quantity of petrol, which had been stored in drums in a shed adjacent to the warehouse, ignited. Robert and his other brother Donald (an auctioneer) appeared undaunted and it was hoped to have new charas on the road within two weeks; vehicles were probably hired from other firms to allow existing bookings to be honoured.

Throughout 1920 Hansons claimed in advertisements that they were the oldest road transport contractors in the West Riding, with a reputation for reliability dating back to pack horse days. They had a fleet of new purpose built Leyland charabancs for private parties seating 22, 28 or 33. Hansons would, it was said, never be booked up and could supply any number of vehicles at any time. They even boasted that their drivers knew every main road in the country! A weekly service to Blackpool started on Whit Saturday 1920 and on Sundays in June day trips were offered to the general public and private parties. The first advertised destinations were Louth, recently inundated by flood waters, Harrogate and Knaresborough and of course Blackpool. On 9 September 1920 it was claimed that a record 21 (mostly hired?) charas were despatched to six different destinations from the office at 32 John William Street, which had been opened on 5 July 1919. The new Leyland chara Kitchener was available for private hire, joined a week later by a 12 seater chara aptly named Midget. Most of the charabancs were given patriotic names such as Pride of the Ridings and Number Ten.

Before the fire the warehouse and vehicles had been properly insured but, under the storage agreements signed by customers, it was the clients' responsibility to insure their furniture. On 30 July 1920, however, Mrs Minerva Fox of London sued J Hanson and Son at Leeds Assizes for negligence resulting in her losing furniture worth £683. The judge was astonished to hear from the superintendent of Huddersfield Fire Brigade of the quantity of petrol stored near the furniture repository and awarded a total of £500 damages to Mrs Fox. Robert Hanson was ordered to pay £200 immediately and given three weeks to pay the rest. As this judgement also resulted in further claims against the firm, he decided that the best course of action was to sue for bankruptcy. To this end, the company's remaining assets were auctioned by his brother Donald, raising £11,000.

A new limited company (Joseph Hanson and Son Ltd) was formed on 20 September 1920 with an authorised capital of £12,000. The directors were Donald Hanson, Charles Holdsworth (who along with his brother Oliver was later to own the Hebble bus company in Halifax) and WH Robinson. Robinson, a scrap dealer, and the Holdsworths had bought the Hanson company's assets and now paid Robert Hanson £7 a week to manage it.

Robinson was succeeded in 1923 by Dyson Bradley who would in turn give way to Robert Hanson in 1928 after he had been discharged from bankruptcy. The formation of the new company was noted by the official receiver at Huddersfield County Court who on 29 December 1920 expressed dissatisfaction at the way in which Hanson had conducted his affairs and set up the limited company; as we have seen, the Hansons charabanc business had continued to trade through this period of insolvency, sale of assets and bankruptcy. Robert Hanson maintained that he had been harshly treated and was not discharged from bankruptcy until 1927.

Daily throughout August and September 1921 Hansons charabancs were to be seen along the road to Blackpool but competition was intense. Albert Schofield of Marsden, whose business was eventually to be bought by Hansons, advertised excursions to different destinations each day during the Colne Valley September holiday week. Huddersfield & District Charabanc Owners' Association had 23 members in 1920. No doubt many Huddersfield people were among the 100,000 lined up along the seafront at Blackpool on 11 September to witness a spectacular fire at the end of the North Pier when the wooden Italian pavilion was totally destroyed and its charred remains fell into the sea. The fire brigade were hampered by having to run their hoses 1215 yards down the full length of the pier. Much of the pier decking was lost and some of the iron framework buckled as a result of the intense heat.

In June 1922 an advertisement in the Huddersfield Examiner promised that charas would leave at 7.30am every Saturday and Sunday for Blackpool; the fare was 7/6d single or 11/6d return with luggage conveyed free of charge. The following summer (1923) trippers were exhorted to "Follow the crowd and ride in comfort with Joseph Hanson and Son Ltd". During the holiday weeks charas ran to Blackpool on Mondays and Wednesdays and for the first time trips were advertised to all the popular resorts including Scarborough, where the local territorial batallions were at camp. In 1923 the Leyland charas were again said to be mostly new and all passengers were fully insured against all risks.

Excursions usually started from St George's Square where about six stands had to suffice for all the local operators. The drivers used to arrive in the square before 7.00am to draw lots (using a driver's cap) to see who would pull up at the stands first. The lucky Hansons driver would place a board by the front wheel of his chara, showing not only his own destination but those of all the other Hansons drivers who had not been lucky in the draw. These drivers parked in St Peter's Street and relied on the first driver to direct passengers to them. When a chara was full and left the stand, it would be replaced by another from the same firm.

2: LOCAL BUSES IN THE COLNE VALLEY (1924-1930)

Before starting to run local bus services, Hansons purchased new buses in 1924. These were obtained through the Holdsworths, whose own buses ran in Halifax under the Hebble fleetname. Leyland SG7 CX 6914, which was no. 6 in the Hansons fleet, carried both Hanson and Hebble fleetnames. This single decker with 38 seat dual doorway (separate entrance and exit) Leyland bodywork had the highest seating capacity in the fleet at the time and was affectionately known as "Big Bertha".

The first bus route was started on Saturday 22 November 1924 and ran from Golcar (Town End) to Linthwaite Church via Leymoor, Wood Street, Royd Street, Milnsbridge, Pickford Street and Cowlersley Lane. An advertisement in the Colne Valley Guardian shows that an hourly service was operated by one bus, with first departures at 6.40am and 7.10am from Golcar and Linthwaite respectively. The last trip (10.40pm from Golcar) ran to the Milnsbridge garage only. Public demand was so great on the first day that the bus carried 824 passengers. All buses from Golcar connected with the Corporation tram to Huddersfield on the hour at the Queen Hotel in Manchester Road. Trams from Town also connected at Cowlersley on the hour for Linthwaite and at 15 minutes past each hour for Golcar.

The new service apparently had the approval of Linthwaite council but not of Golcar council. At this period Milnsbridge and Cowlersley were not yet in Huddersfield so the whole route lay outside the borough boundary. Previously Linthwaite residents had had no alternative to a steep walk from the tram route along Manchester Road; Robert Hanson's wife Louisa was a native of Linthwaite. Golcar was a different matter as Huddersfield Corporation already ran motorbuses from Paddock Head (for trams to and from Town) to Town End via Milnsbridge and Scar Lane, hence the unwillingness of Golcar Urban District Council to upset the Corporation by expressing support for the private operator. Yet the Hansons service avoided the route of the municipal buses as much as possible.

Hansons' next move was to apply to operate a service partly within Huddersfield borough from the town centre to Golcar via Heaton Road, Paddock Head and Milnsbridge. Unsurprisingly this application was rejected by the Watch Committee in December but a week later Robert Hanson retaliated and on 23 December 1924 he started unlicensed services from Huddersfield to both Golcar and Linthwaite Church. These ran from the yard of the Sun Inn (now the Minstrel) on Cross Church Street (access was via Venn Street) on the return ticket system. The Holdsworths started a Hebble bus service to Halifax from the same yard on the same day. On this first day the two Hansons buses are reported to have carried 2,162 passengers. The Golcar route ran hourly from Town from 9.15am with one bus via Manchester Road, Milnsbridge and the existing route through Leymoor. Return fares to Huddersfield were: 5d from Milnsbridge; 7d from Albert House and 8d from Golcar Town End. At first only an afternoon service was provided to Linthwaite Church on Monday to Friday, the first (hourly) departure from Town via Manchester Road, Milnsbridge and Cowlersley Lane being at 1.45pm. The round trip took one hour so one vehicle sufficed. On Saturdays a morning service began at 8.45am. Return fares to Huddersfield were: 5d from Milnsbridge; 7d from Storth and 9d from Linthwaite Church.

These separate Golcar and Linthwaite services replaced the shortlived Golcar-Linthwaite tramway feeder and were popular with passengers who no longer had to complete their journeys to Town by tram. There were soon reports of overcrowding on the Linthwaite buses and the Hansons Golcar service was so convenient that from the following month Huddersfield Corporation were obliged to extend all journeys on their Golcar-Scar Lane-Paddock route into Town via Heaton Road.

Attempts to license the Golcar service in 1925 failed even though a 3d minimum fare was charged to Milnsbridge to protect the Corporation trams. The Tramways Committee claimed that a 3d fare was inadequate protection and that the area was well enough served. Similarly licence requests for both the existing Linthwaite Church service and for a new route to Slaithwaite were rejected. An appeal to the Minister of Transport by Robert Hanson, supported by Linthwaite UDC, also failed.

A circular service proposed in February 1925 (Huddersfield-Milnsbridge-Wellhouse-Slaithwaite-Manchester Road-Huddersfield and vice versa) came to nothing too but a Huddersfield-Milnsbridge-Scar Lane-James Street-Wellhouse route is thought to have started on 6 March 1925: hourly from Wellhouse from 1.25pm and returning

from Town thirty minutes later. Unfortunately this had been withdrawn by September owing to poor patronage; Huddersfield Corporation would later serve Wellhouse.

A more permanent facility was a new service from Slaithwaite Market Place to Huddersfield via Manchester Road which started on 29 May 1925. Previously Slaithwaite folk had had to walk to the main road, where they could catch a tram. At first Monday to Friday departures were just hourly from 2.00pm from Slaithwaite and 2.30pm from Huddersfield; a morning service was provided only on Saturdays. As the service was again unlicensed, passengers boarding the bus within Huddersfield borough had to be in possession of a return ticket. Return fares to Huddersfield were : 8d from Slaithwaite; 6d from Victoria; 5d from Jovil or Cowlersley and 4d from Pickford Street. The new route was enthusiastically received; a letter from "Well Wisher" to the editor of the local newspaper is interesting. He pointed out that the tramway system through the Colne Valley had long been considered inadequate, especially at meal times, and judged that the buses would probably be well patronised. He also outlined many ways in which he thought buses had the advantage over trams; they were quicker and could more easily negotiate the traffic on busy Manchester Road, not being restricted to tracks. They could penetrate outlying districts which would otherwise remain isolated and they required less capital outlay. When running they made much less noise than the trams and, particularly in winter, they offered a much warmer ride.

James Coulburn of Milnsbridge was a regular driver on the Slaithwaite route who had started working for Hansons in April 1925 after having already driven buses for over five years. Although an experienced driver, he was involved in a fatal accident at Slaithwaite terminus at 10.30pm on 17 November 1925. Harry and Randolph Beaumont had just left the Commercial Hotel as the bus began to reverse; there was no conductor on the 26 seater to supervise the manoeuvre. Neither hearing the horn nor seeing the bus, the brothers were both knocked down at the back of the bus. Harry died two days later from his injuries in the Huddersfield Royal Infirmary. The driver was criticised for not using side streets to turn the bus round without reversing in the absence of a conductor. The Slaithwaite service had quickly attracted more passengers and by January 1926 two buses were needed to provide a half hourly frequency; even this was not always sufficient.

From 4 March 1927 the Linthwaite Church service was extended to Heights and according to the Colne Valley Guardian after this the overcrowding was even worse. Hansons conductors were sometimes in trouble with the police for allowing their buses to become overcrowded. On 16 December 1927 Percy Pickering was fined 20/- for carrying 48 passengers on a 32 seater bus and John Hall was fined 40/- for carrying 38 passengers on a 26 seater bus; that fine was heavier because the driver had deviated from the normal route in an attempt to avoid being seen by Constable Boothroyd! These were considerable sums of money, given the level of wages of the time. A driver earned 50/- and a conductor 35/- per week in shifts from 6.00am to 2.00pm and from 2.00pm to the end of the day's service. Drivers could earn an extra 2/6d by driving a taxi or hearse in addition to their shift. In another incident the police allegedly found Big Bertha (Leyland SG7 6) so overcrowded at Golcar that the

driver even had two [small?] young ladies in his cab.

It is said that, in order to force the authorities to grant Hansons their first legal bus stand in the town centre, Robert Hanson instructed driver Frank Brook to set down and pick up his passengers outside the police station in Peel Street. No doubt this was meant to block the police station entrance and generally cause chaos. Inspector Moore threatened to arrest the driver who in turn pleaded that he would be sacked if he disobeyed his gaffer. The result, as anticipated by Mr Hanson, was that the chief constable had allotted Hansons a stand in Lord Street for all their services by May 1927. The Golcar route was finally licensed by Huddersfield Watch Committee on 20 December 1927 but Hansons still had to run their other services on the return ticket system.

From 7 January 1928 the basic service on the Slaithwaite route was extended from the Market Place to Hill Top via Crimble Corner, Crimble Bank and Royd Street and on Saturday afternoons a 15 minute frequency was operated, with alternate buses running through to Hill Top. Just before reaching Crimble Corner, buses had to turn round using a side street and then reverse beyond the junction; they could then move forward and ascend Crimble Bank. The same manoeuvre was still required at this sharp corner on the last day of operation in 1969.

Manchester Road was a busy thoroughfare even in 1928 and many drivers had minor accidents, some caused by dangerous driving as they competed with other operators to pick up passengers. Neither were tram drivers always blameless. On 30 January 1928 a Hansons bus returning from Slaithwaite passed a tram and then stopped at the Bath Hotel to allow two passengers to alight. The bus had only moved off a distance of five yards before the tram crashed into the back of it. The rear panelling of the bus was damaged, several windows were broken and one passenger in the bus received spinal injuries. In court the Hansons version of the accident was accepted and the Corporation had to pay £75 in damages to the injured passenger.

The extension of the Huddersfield-Heights (Linthwaite) route to Meltham via Blackmoorfoot and Helme took place during the last week of December 1928. Leyland PLSC1 Lion 19 (VH 1703) was equipped with especially low gears because of the hills encountered on this route.

Towards the end of 1928 passengers were experiencing difficulties in identifying the bus they wished to board along Manchester Road in the dark. The problem was worse for people not familiar with the various departure

times. "Traveller" wrote to the Colne Valley Guardian, suggesting that Hansons buses should display a coloured light at the front, just as Walter Bower's Blue and White buses on his Marsden route showed a blue light. It was proposed that a green light be used for Linthwaite Church buses and a red light for Slaithwaite and Hill Top. This did not happen but perhaps it led to better illumination of destination displays.

Walter Bower had been providing stiff competition for the Corporation's Marsden trams as well as along the Manchester Road section of the Hansons Slaithwaite and Hill Top route. From 11 January 1929, however, the Corporation and Hansons jointly purchased his Blue and White Huddersfield-Marsden bus service for £5,400 and the first coordination of services between Hansons and Huddersfield Corporation took place. Both parties agreed to share the Marsden bus route on a 50:50 basis but that was not all as also into the shared pool went the Hansons services from Huddersfield to Heights and Slaithwaite/Hill Top. In return the Corporation granted Hansons the necessary licences so that all their services (including the recently introduced Meltham via Linthwaite and Helme route, which remained outside the scheme) could operate on a fully legal basis and the return ticket system was no longer needed.

Walter Bower's fleet of four buses was auctioned by the firm of Harold Hanson and realised about £700 for the joint vendors. Leyland Lion WW 3672 was actually purchased by Hansons, becoming no. 20 in their fleet. A maximum of two buses from each of the Corporation and Hansons fleets were required for the Slaithwaite/Hill Top service. The Marsden route needed three buses but Heights only one so in alternate weeks Hansons operated either two buses on the Marsden service or one on Marsden and one on Heights.

The Marsden service ran every 30 minutes as far as the centre of Marsden from the first departure from Huddersfield at 6.25am. After noon alternate buses were extended to Hemplow (later Hard End) and six ran to Warehouse Hill. Three daily journeys also ran as far as the Great Western Hotel, Standedge. The Heights route, which ran via Milnsbridge, was hourly. Buses ran to Slaithwaite half hourly from 6.00am to 1.00pm and every 15 minutes for the rest of the day. Buses arriving at Slaithwaite on the hour and also on the half hour in the afternoon ran through to Hill Top.

Hansons issued a notice to the effect that all their return tickets bought before 11 January would have to be used before 1 February on any bus or be exchanged for cash at the Savile Street office, as they would be invalid after that date. Under the pooling arrangement return tickets were interavailable between the two operators and balancing cash payments were made at three monthly intervals.

Hansons were keen to expand their bus network. In January 1929 they were granted licences for new routes to Oldham and Leeds which they did not attempt to operate immediately but were also refused the following services during the year:

Huddersfield-Crimble via Heaton Road, Paddock Head and Milnsbridge

Huddersfield-Stainland via Halifax Old Road, Grimescar and Outlane

Huddersfield-Nont Sarah's via Grimescar and Outlane

On Monday 6 January 1930 one of the two new Leyland Lion LT1 single deck buses (26/7) entered service on the Marsden route and, much to the amusement of passengers, a hefty three pound mallet was fixed inside the saloon. Speculation as to its purpose was rife. One individual suggested that it was for the conductor to "nobble them as wants to get on when the bus is full"; another thought it was for dealing with rowdy late night revellers and a third thought it could be used to give the driver a tap on the head if he nodded off! The official use was to break windows in an emergency such as fire but, to quote one loquacious passenger, "a boot would have done just as well".

Hansons were not the first operator on the route over the Pennines to Oldham. As far back as 8 April 1925 the Stockport based North Western Road Car company had started a daily service from Oldham to the Fountain Inn at "Linthwaite" via Lees, Uppermill and Marsden. The Fountain Inn was in Manchester Road near the then Huddersfield borough boundary, four minutes journey time beyond its junction with Cowlersley Lane in the Huddersfield direction. This terminus was used because Huddersfield refused to issue a licence. Six return journeys were operated at two hour intervals on Saturdays and Sundays with a running time of 106 minutes. From Monday to Friday a service of three return journeys was also provided but these weekday journeys had been withdrawn by April 1926. What had become service 61 was accelerated to 84 minutes' running time by 2 October 1927 (with Monday to Friday operation restored – only to be withdrawn again on those days by 15 August 1928). From 28 March 1929, however, North Western started a daily express service between Manchester and Huddersfield via Oldham and Uppermill on a temporary licence. This did not permit the carriage of local passengers between the Great Western Hotel (Standedge) and Huddersfield (served by Huddersfield Corporation and Hansons); the Oldham-"Linthwaite" service was not immediately withdrawn. From 15 May 1929 the express service was extended to Leeds and Newcastle on Tyne. It initially used the same route number as the Oldham-"Linthwaite" service and soon became part of the Limited Stop pool long distance express services later

JOSEPH HANSON & SON, LTD.
Huddersfield - Marsden - Uppermill - Oldham
TIME-TABLE.

DEPART	a.m.	First Bus Sundays	p.m.					
HUDDERSFIELD (Market St.)	6-55	8-55	10-55	12-55	2-55	4-55	6-55	8-55
Great Western	7-27	9-27	11-27	1-27	3-27	5-27	7-27	9-27
Uppermill	7-40	9-40	11-40	1-40	3-40	5-40	7-40	9-40
OLDHAM (Mumps)	7-55	9-55	11-55	1-55	3-55	5-55	7-55	9-55
Uppermill	8-10	10-10	12-10	2-10	4-10	6-10	8-10	10-10
Great Western	8-23	10-23	12-23	2-23	4-23	6-23	8-23	10-23
HUDDERSFIELD	8-55	10-55	12-55	2-55	4-55	6-55	8-55	10-55

FARES.

Huddersfield
9d. Thornton Lodge
9d. 9d. Pickford Street
9d. 9d. 6d. Jovil
9d. 9d. 6d. 6d. 5d. Varley Road
9d. 9d. 6d. 6d. 5d. 3d. Olive Branch
9d. 9d. 6d. 6d. 5d. 3d. 2d. Marsden
9d. 9d. 6d. 6d. 5d. 3d. 2d. 1d. Warrington Terrace
9d. 9d. 6d. 6d. 5d. 3d. 2d. 1d. 1d. Coach and Horses
10d. 9d. 7d. 7d. 6d. 5d. 3d. 1d. 1d. Great Western
10d. 9d. 8d. 7d. 6d. 5d. 4d. 3d. 1d. 1d. Floating Light
11d. 10d. 9d. 8d. 7d. 6d. 4d. 3d. 2d. 1d. 1d. Horse and Jockey
1 1 11d. 10d. 10d. 9d. 7d. 6d. 5d. 4d. 3d. 2d. 2d. Ambrose (or Navigation Inn)
1 2 1 1 11d. 11d. 10d. 10d. 9d. 8d. 6d. 5d. 4d. 4d. 4d. Greenfield Station
1 3 1 3 1 1 1- 1- 11d. 10d. 10d. 9d. 8d. 6d. 5d. 4d. 4d. Grasscroft
1 4 1 4 1 2 1 1 1 1 1- 1- 11d. 10d. 9d. 7d. 6d. 5d. 5d. Station Road
1 5 1 5 1 3 1 2 1 2 1 1 1/- 11d. 10d. 9d. 8d. 7d. 6d. 6d. County End Lees
1 6 1 6 1 4 1 3 1 3 1 2 1 1 1/- 11d. 10d. 9d. 8d. 7d. 7d. Oldham

Special Return Fares.

Huddersfield to Lees Tram Terminus ... 2 6	Uppermill to Oldham ... 9d.	
Huddersfield to Uppermill ... 2 -	Navigation Inn to Oldham 11d.	

Workmen's Return Fares are issued at fare-and-one-half the ordinary single journey on all Omnibuses arriving at their destination on or before 9 a.m.

Lenny Halstead & Co., Ltd., Printers, Dowker St., Milnsbridge, Huddersfield.

JOSEPH HANSON & SON, LTD.
Huddersfield - Marsden
TIME TABLE.

OUTWARD				INWARD			
Depart HUDDERSFIELD	Marsden	Hardend	Warehouse Hill	Warehouse Hill	Hardend	Marsden	Depart Slaithwaite for Hudd.
				8-20			
6-20	6-50					6-27	6-32
6-50	7-20					6-50	6-55
7-20	7-50					7-50	7-25
7-50	8-20					8-20	7-55
8-50	8-50					8-50	8-25
8-50	9-20					9-20	8-55
9-20	9-50					9-50	9-25
9-50	10-20					10-20	9-55
10-20	10-50					10-50	10-25
10-50	11-20					11-20	10-55
11-20	11-50					11-50	11-25
11-50	12-20					12-20	11-55
12-50	12-50					12-50	12-25
a1-20	1-20					1-20	12-55
1-50	1-50	2-0				a1-50	1-25
2-20	2-00					2-20	1-55
2-50	2-50	3-0				2-50	2-25
	3-20		c3-27 c5-43			3-20	2-55
3-50	3-50	4-0				3-50	3-25
4-20	4-20		c4-27 c4-43			4-20	3-55
4-50	4-50	c5-0	Weekdays 5-5 Marsden: 5-10 Slaithwaite to Marsden	c5-10		5-20	4-25
4-50	5-20					5-20	4-55
5-20	5-50	6-0				5-50	5-25
5-50	6-20		6-27	6-43	6-10	6-20	5-55
6-20	6-50	7-0				6-50	6-20
6-50	7-20		7-27	7-43	7-10	7-20	6-55
7-20	7-50	8-0				7-50	7-25
7-50	8-20		8-27	8-43	8-10	8-20	7-55
8-20	8-50	9-0				8-50	8-55
9-20	9-20				9-10	9-30	9-25
9-50	10-20	10-0				10-20	9-55
10-50	11-20		10-27	10-43	10-10	10-50	10-25
b11-20	11-20	11-0			11-10	11-20	d11-25
	11-50					11-50	11-55

a First Bus Sundays   b Saturdays only   c Saturdays & Sundays only.   d To Milnsbridge only.

SATURDAYS ONLY.

Huddersfield	Marsden	Slaithwaite	Marsden	Great Western	Marsden	Warehouse Hill	Marsden	Hard End
11-55	12-5	12-15	12-25	12-40	12-55	1-0	1-5	1-15
			1-25	1-40	1-50	1-50		

FARES.

Huddersfield
2½d. Thornton Lodge
2½d. 2½d. Pickford Street
3d. 3d. 1d. Spurn Point
3d. 3d. 1d. 1d. Jovil
3d. 3d. 2d. 1d. 1d. Bargate
3d. 3d. 2d. 2d. 1d. 1d. Hoylehouse
3d. 3d. 3d. 2d. 1d. 1d. Victoria Hotel
4d. 3d. 3d. 3d. 2d. 1d. 1d. Linthwaite Steps
4d. 4d. 3d. 3d. 2d. 1½d. 1d. 1d. Varley Road
5d. 4d. 4d. 3d. 3d. 2d. 2d. 1d. 1d. Blue Bell
5d. 4d. 4d. 4d. 3d. 2d. 2d. 1d. 1d. 1d. Olive Branch
6d. 5d. 4d. 4d. 4d. 3d. 2d. 2d. 1d. 1d. Council Houses
6d. 5d. 4d. 4d. 4d. 3d. 3d. 3½d. 2d. 1d. 1d. Marsden
7d. 6d. 5d. 4d. 4d. 4d. 4d. 3d. 2d. 2d. 1d. Warehouse Hill or Hardend

WORKMEN'S RETURN FARES are issued at fare-and-one-half the ordinary single journey on all Omnibuses arriving at their destination on or before 9 a.m.

Lenny Halstead & Co., Milnsbridge.

known as the "Tyne-Tees-Mersey", the development of which is beyond the scope of this account. The Oldham-"Linthwaite" service was still running in July 1929 but was withdrawn shortly afterwards. In its final form it ran Saturdays and Sundays only with four departures from Oldham at three hour intervals from 10.00am, returning 90 minutes later from "Linthwaite". Further requests for a licence to extend the service into Huddersfield had been regularly refused by Huddersfield Watch Committee between 1926 and 1929. The final faretable between Saddleworth Station and Linthwaite is as shown below:

Saddleworth Station									
3	Bleak Hey Nook								
4	2	Floating Light Inn							
6	3	2	Great Western Inn						
7	4	3	2	Coach and Horses Inn					
9	6	5	3	2	Marsden Tram Terminus				
10	7	6	4	3	1	Olive Branch			
11	8	7	5	4	2	1	Star Hotel		
1/-	10	9	7	6	4	3	2	Cowlersley Lane	
1/1	11	10	8	7	5	4	3	1	Linthwaite

Hansons had first been refused a licence for a Huddersfield to Oldham service in June 1928. Even though a licence was granted by Huddersfield Watch Committee in January 1929 doubtless as part of the Bower takeover agreement, according to the Colne Valley Guardian the service did not commence until 21 March 1930, running from Macaulay Street via Marsden, Standedge, Uppermill and Lees. The first departure from Huddersfield was at 6.55am; the morning frequency was every two hours but from 12.55pm the buses ran hourly. The scattered inhabitants of the bleak moorland section would stop the buses as near to their homes as possible. Conditions in winter were often atrocious when drivers had to contend with both ice and fog. Accidents were not unknown and, on one occasion when the hourly frequency was in operation, Leyland Tiger TS2 vehicles 21 and 22 were involved in a head on collision near the Floating Light Hotel. On another day the sun's reflection from the windscreen temporarily blinded Fred Haigh as his bus was ascending Standedge from the Marsden side with the result that the bus ran off the nearside of the road and came to rest in a trench leaning over on its side. Windows were broken and the radiator damaged but the four passengers and conductor were unhurt. Very near the scene of the accident at Flint Pit there was a deep well covered over merely by wooden boards. Hansons never owned a breakdown vehicle as they always used the associated firm of Oswald Tillotson of Bradford instead.

Conductors were never well paid and when times were hard there was always the temptation to take something out of the cash bag. In need of extra money to pay for repairs to his motorcycle, a conductor from Marsden succumbed to temptation on more than one occasion. On Sunday 16 November 1930 his waybill showed initial and final entries for 3d tickets as 1204 and 1371 respectively. He falsified the subtraction to show that only 67 instead of 167 tickets had been sold and pocketed the difference (£1-5s). The clerk spotted the discrepancy a week later and in court it transpired that the conductor had previously defrauded Hansons in connection with fifty 6d tickets.

Leyland Lion LT1 27 (VH 2851) with Leyland 30 seater bodywork was delivered to Hansons in March 1930. It is seen on the bus stand on the east side of Market Street, Huddersfield awaiting departure for Meltham via Milnsbridge and Helme, a stand shared with the [Linthwaite] Heights route (joint with Huddersfield JOC), plus the North Western Oldham route (from 1932) and, after the war, Hansons' own Oldham route. Buses would reach this stand via Upperhead Row and Dundas Street and on departure would run direct via High Street. 27 was withdrawn in 1939 and later worked for Boddy of Bridlington. [G. Hodgson collection]

A 30 seater Leyland bodied LT1 Lion of 1929/30, this is believed to be 23 (VH 2215) of 1929. Note the early style of fleetname without enlargement of the initial H and final N.
[British Commercial Vehicle Museum]

Leyland Lion LT1 25 (VH 2728) was new in January 1930 with 30 seater Leyland bodywork. It was withdrawn by Hansons in 1940.
[British Commercial Vehicle Museum]

3: BUS OPERATION UNDER THE NEW TRAFFIC COMMISSIONERS' REGIME (1931-1937)

During 1931 the old system of licensing bus and coach operations by local authorities was swept away and replaced by the uniform and nationwide network of traffic commissioners. Robert Hanson appeared before the Yorkshire Area Traffic Commissioners in Huddersfield Town Hall in June 1931 and was permitted to continue his existing services:

Huddersfield-Manchester Road-Milnsbridge-Leymoor-Golcar

Huddersfield-Manchester Road-Marsden-Uppermill-Oldham

Huddersfield-Manchester Road-Milnsbridge-Linthwaite-Helme-Meltham

Huddersfield-Manchester Road-Milnsbridge-Linthwaite (Heights)

Huddersfield-Manchester Road-Slaithwaite-Hill Top

Huddersfield-Manchester Road-Marsden-Hard End or Warehouse Hill or Great Western

The last three were by now jointly operated with the Huddersfield Joint Omnibus Committee, an undertaking owned by both Huddersfield Corporation and the LMS Railway which had taken over Huddersfield Corporation's motorbus operations in the previous year.

The Oldham, Hill Top and Marsden routes started from Macaulay Street while the Meltham and Heights stand was in Market Street almost opposite Macaulay Street. The Golcar stand was moved from Market Street to Macaulay Street around this time. Buses entered town via Outcote Bank, which had recently been improved, and Upperhead Row; they left via High Street and Buxton Road.

Robert Hanson was less successful with other applications made to the commissioners. Huddersfield Watch Committee had granted him a licence for a service to Leeds in January 1929 but unfortunately the Leeds authorities had refused permission for passengers to be picked up within their boundaries. The service could have been operated on the return ticket system from that date but Mr Hanson declined to do so and instead waited to apply to the commissioners for a licence. There were already at least 75 daily trips between Huddersfield and Leeds with the fastest journey taking almost an hour and a quarter; Hansons wanted to operate a half hourly service running direct via the A62 and taking only 45 minutes. This would have required three buses and Robert Hanson was prepared to charge a protective

North Western Dennis Lancet/Dennis 206 (JA 2880) had been new in July 1932 as a test vehicle. It was known to the crews as Leaping Lena, doubtless on account of a "savage clutch". The bodywork is of a style introduced on the Lancet but usually finished as a coach. The bus stands on the A62 opposite the Great Western Hotel, Standedge. This new Oldham-Delph-Huddersfield route had started (as 115) on 3 December 1932 and the photograph dates from late 1932 or early 1933. 206 was withdrawn and scrapped in 1939. [S.T. Harling collection]

fare in and out of Huddersfield, charging the same fares as the other operators over the rest of the route. There may have been some plan eventually to link part of the service with the Oldham buses to provide a through facility from the Colne Valley to Leeds but this was denied at the time. Had the licence been granted, which it was not, this service could have been used as a means of connecting with Wallace Arnold holiday tours in Leeds, just as the Oldham service connected there with Yelloway express services to Devon.

There was still no public transport to the Lowerhouses district at the beginning of 1932. A bus service via Somerset Road and Longley Road proposed by CB Senior of Moldgreen had been refused a licence in 1926 and more recently, in connection with a tramway replacement service of trolleybuses to Almondbury, the Tramways Committee had considered the possibility of running trolleybuses to Lowerhouses. Nothing had happened by April 1932 when Hansons made an application to run motorbuses over the same route. The traffic commissioners did not grant Hansons a licence but Huddersfield Joint Omnibus Committee then put forward an alternative application which was successful.

All was not gloom, however, as (at the second attempt) a licence was surprisingly granted for a cross suburban service which would soon lie completely within the Huddersfield borough as a result of boundary changes: Lockwood to Lindley via Park Road West, Milnsbridge, Paddock Head, Reinwood Road and Acre Street. The terminal stand at Lockwood was in Meltham Road near the end of Neale Road. Coming from Crosland Moor, buses turned right from Swan Lane into Bentley Street, then left into Meltham Road. The triangle was completed on the return journey by turning left from Meltham Road to regain Swan Lane. At Lindley, from Lidget Street buses turned in a clockwise loop via Brian Street, Thorncliffe Street and Thomas Street to reach a stand in Lidget

Street near the chapel. This new service covered part of a route which Walter Bower had tried to start in 1926 and initially an hourly timetable was advertised to commence on Wednesday 15 June 1932. One bus was required, taking up service at Lockwood at 6.30am and departing from Lindley 30 minutes later. The minimum fare from Lindley was $1^1/_2$d to give protection to the Corporation trams (later trolleybuses). Similarly, to protect Huddersfield JOC, at first the same passenger could not be both picked up after Milnsbridge and set down before Paddock Head (or vice versa) and the fare between these two points was $1^1/_2$d, compared with the 1d fare charged on the JOC's buses. On the first day the bus is said to have carried 1,065 passengers and from 11 September this popular service was doubled in frequency.

Meanwhile Robert Hanson had applied to the traffic commissioners for licences for a further two services, both entirely within the Huddersfield borough boundary. The first was for a route from the town centre via Birkby to Lindley. Hanson explained that there was a demand for such a service from 30 employees of Hopkinsons who lived at Lindley and also from many others living along the proposed route (there was no public transport in the area between the West Vale and Birkby tramlines). The application was of course opposed by the Corporation even though Hanson was willing to give the usual fare protection to the Birkby trams. The Corporation did, however, offer to withdraw their opposition if the route was curtailed to omit the Birkby to Huddersfield section.

In due course the commissioners perhaps unexpectedly granted a licence for the full route. From 8 October 1932 a service was operated every 30 minutes between John William Street (opposite the Empire cinema) and Lindley (Thomas Street) via St John's Road, Blacker Road, Birkby Lodge Road, Birkby Road and East Street. The journey took 15 minutes each way so only one bus was needed, starting from Lindley at 6.30am. The faretable was as shown:

Huddersfield
2						Blacker Road
2	1					Birkby Hall Road
2	1	1				Stanwell Avenue
2	1	1	1			Inglewood
3	1	1	1	1		Cavalry Arms
3	2	1	1	1	1	Lindley

Not long after 4 August 1933 the Town terminus was moved to a more convenient location on the west side of Byram Street, reached via St Peter's Street, where passengers were generally set down. Outward bound buses returned to John William Street via Northumberland Street. The route was also extended for a short distance at the other end in Lindley via West Street to Weatherhill. This would of course be the only route to pass the postwar depot in St John's Road.

The other interesting route proposal, which did not come to fruition, was for a service to Oakes via Paddock and Quarmby. The precise route from Town was to have been via Manchester Road, Longroyd Lane, Brow Road, Upper Brow Road, Victory Avenue, Quarmby Road and Oakes Road South. The traffic commissioners regarded this application as unnecessary and undesirable in the public interest despite the fact that it would have given a direct link to Town from Quarmby Fold and also for the residents of the new housing estate between Paddock Head and Quarmby. The town clerk, who had accused Robert Hanson of deliberately trying to filch tram passengers, had pleaded from the outset for the rejection of the application.

With the expansion of routes the size of the bus fleet grew from two in 1924 to six in 1926, 10 in 1928 and 20 by 1930. During this period the miles run and numbers of passengers carried increased each year. In 1932 on the stage carriage (local bus as opposed to express) routes alone, the buses ran over 650,000 miles and carried over 2.5 million passengers.

The first vehicle delivered with a "high speed compression ignition" (diesel) engine was probably AEC Regal 55 of 1932. Keen to show the public that they were a progressive firm, Hansons exhibited a diesel engine in their travel offices in John William Street and thousands of people came to see the demonstration.

North Western started a new Huddersfield-Oldham service on 3 December 1932, this time operating every two hours direct via Delph and Waterhead as route 115 (renumbered 160 from January 1936) instead of through Uppermill. The service was coordinated (but not jointly operated) with the existing Hansons service to provide an hourly frequency over common sections.

On the joint route to Marsden, although some timings were duplicated, buses were often overcrowded and there had been several prosecutions. This and the increasing use made of double deckers in general by Huddersfield JOC probably led to the decision to purchase the first double deckers for the fleet. These were all Leyland Titan TD2s (60/3) with H24/24R bodies which entered service in January and April 1933. From 19 June 1933 eight trips daily on the joint Hill Top route were extended to the hamlet of Wilberlee.

Hansons 59 (VH 4873) was new in January 1933. An AEC Regal with 32 seat Brush bodywork, it had an AEC diesel engine from new. Photographs taken before delivery to Hansons show the exterior from the front nearside and the interior. This bus was later rebodied by Burlingham. [Omnibus Society collection]

In January 1933 Leyland Titan TD2/Leyland 60 (VH 4875) was the first double decker for Hansons, one of two placed in service in that year. A highbridge 48 seater, 60 had aLeyland 8.1 litre diesel engine. After the Marsden route was withdrawn in September 1939, 60 was sold to an old established Essex bus operator Moores of Kelvedon. [British Commercial Vehicle Museum]

Hansons AEC Regal/Brush 61 (VH 4874) was also new in January 1933, with an AEC 8.8 litre diesel engine, and is pictured here in Market Street, Milnsbridge soon after entering service. It lasted with Hansons until 1947, albeit rebodied by Burlingham around 1941. [Omnibus Society collection]

This February 1933 scene illustrates typical wintry operating conditions on the Oldham route. New in the previous month, AEC Regal/Brush 59 (VH 4873) was photographed below New Farm near Diggle. [S.T. Harling collection]

Hansons Leyland TS4/Leyland 62 (VH 5138) was new in April 1933 with a Leyland 8.1 litre diesel engine. This Leyland Tiger later regularly operated the Lindley-Newsome routes with their fearsome ascent of Lockwood Scar. It was withdrawn in 1945. [British Commercial Vehicle Museum]

Quarmby was to be served by Hansons after all from shortly after 1 September 1933 when they were granted modifications to the cross suburban Lockwood-Lindley route. Additional journeys leaving Lockwood at 45 minutes past the hour followed the existing route to Paddock Head then ran via Luck Lane, Reed Street and Occupation Road to Lindley. New journeys leaving Lockwood at 15 minutes past the hour again used the established route to Paddock Head then served Longwood Road, Quarmby Road, Oakes Road South and Plover Road en route to Lindley. These two additional services made 17 return trips during the three peak periods (lunchtime was a peak in those days) on Monday to Thursday. On Friday, Saturday and Sunday both these new routes ran all day [pm only on Sunday] except for a short mid morning

Lindley												
-	Highgate Oakes											
1½	-	Bottom Occupation Road										
1½	-	-	Bay Horse									
1½	-	1½	-	Croppers Arms								
-	1	-	-	-	Quarmby Village							
1½	1	-	1	-	1	Reinwood Road						
2	1½	1½	1½	1	1	1	Paddock Head					
2½	2	2	2	1½	1½	1½	1½	Milnsbridge				
3	2½	2½	2½	2	2	2	1½	1	Whiteley Street			
3	2½	2½	2½	2	2	2	2	1	1	Blackmoorfoot Road		
4	3	3½	3	3	3	2½	2	1½	1	1	Lockwood Bar	
5	4	4½	-	4	4	3½	3	2½	2	2	1	Newsome

break, offering a regular 15 minutes frequency between Lindley and Lockwood.

During the financial year ending March 1934 Hansons had been operating six diesel engined buses (AECs 55/9/61 and Leylands 60/2/3). Fuelled by Shell light oil these buses averaged twice the number of miles per gallon managed by their petrol engined counterparts. They clocked up a total of 410,000 miles with the highest individual mileage being 100,000 by Regal 55 on the Oldham route.

JOSEPH HANSON & SON, Ltd.
Lindley - Birkby - Huddersfield
TIME-TABLE.

HUDDERSFIELD	...	6-45 a.m.	and	10-45 p.m.
Blacker Road	...	6-47 a.m.	every	10-47 p.m.
Birkby Hall Road	...	6-50 a.m.	30	10-50 p.m.
Stanwell Avenue	...	6-52 a.m.	minutes	10-52 p.m.
Inglewood	...	6-53 a.m.	until	10-53 p.m.
Cavalry Arms	...	6-56 a.m.		10-56 p.m.
LINDLEY (Weather Hill)	...	6-30 a.m.		11-0 p.m.
Cavalry Arms	...	6-33 a.m.	and	11-3 p.m.
Inglewood	...	6-36 a.m.	every	11-6 p.m.
Stanwell Avenue	...	6-37 a.m.	30	11-7 p.m.
Birkby Hall Road	...	6-39 a.m.	minutes	11-9 p.m.
Blacker Road	...	6-42 a.m.	until	11-12 p.m.
HUDDERSFIELD	...	6-44 a.m.		11-14 p.m.

1st Bus Sundays. From Lindley 1-30 p.m.
From Huddersfield 1-45 p.m.

FARES.
Huddersfield
2d. Blacker Road
2d. 1d. Birkby Hall Road
2½d. 1d. 1d. Stanwell Avenue
2½d. 1½d. 1d. 1d. Inglewood
3d. 1½d. 1d. 1d. 1d. Cavalry Arms
3d. 2d. 1½d. 1d. 1d. 1d. Lindley (Weatherhill)

Workmen's Return Tickets are issued at fare-and-one-half the ordinary single journey all Omnibuses arriving at their destination on or before 9 a.m.

Leroy Halstead & Co., Ltd., Printers, Dowker St., Milnsbridge, Huddersfield.

From 19 March 1934 two further daily journeys were extended from Hill Top to Wilberlee and the remaining "Slaithwaite turnbacks" were extended from Market Place to Hill Top.

The Oldham service had operated at two hourly intervals between 6.55am and 12.55pm, then hourly until 9.55pm. From May 1934 the journeys from Huddersfield at 55 minutes past the odd hour were discontinued except on Summer Saturdays and Sundays and Bank Holidays. On this route the minimum fare out of Huddersfield was 9d (later reduced to 6d); there was a 7d minimum out of Oldham. The single through fare was 1/6d. Return fares were also available between certain points: Huddersfield to Uppermill 2/-; Huddersfield to Oldham 2/6d; Oldham to Uppermill 9d; Oldham to Marsden 1/8d. With fares ranging from 1d to 2/6d a special ticket rack was needed with two rows of punch tickets on each side. North Western also applied to halve their winter service at the same time. Their receipts were 1½d per bus mile less than their operating costs on a monthly mileage of 13,910.

On the other hand the frequency of the Golcar service was increased to three per hour on Monday to Saturday from September 1934; this had already been the case on Friday and Saturday afternoons. The 17 minutes past the hour departure from Huddersfield was routed via Dale Street between Milnsbridge and Leymoor whereas the other journeys used the existing route via Wood Street and Royd Street.

In the traffic courts in March 1935 Robert Hanson applied to extend the Lindley-Lockwood routes a distance of 0.7 miles up Lockwood Scar to Newsome. The application was of course opposed by Huddersfield JOC. Many people had recently moved from Lockwood into new housing at Newsome and were faced with a very steep walk up Lockwood Scar from work. A census taken in Lockwood Scar had revealed that 142 people

walked downhill and 42 uphill on their way to work between 6.00am and 7.00am whereas after work between 5.00pm and 6.00pm 52 walked downhill and 151 walked uphill. The commissioners did not dispute the need for a bus service but were concerned about the 1 in 8 gradient where the road climbed 300 feet. Despite claims by Robert Hanson that his haulage vehicles climbed the Scar safely each day the commissioners were not convinced that the route was safe for buses; the hearing was adjourned until they had tested the route personally.

The Hansons application was successful and the Luck Lane and Quarmby variants were the first to be projected to Newsome, from 29 March 1935; the journeys via Reinwood Road were not extended until 1 July 1936. Buses running through to Newsome ran via Swan Lane in both directions and no longer served Bentley Street. Crews working the Quarmby and Luck Lane duties often had to work a double split shift to accommodate the three peaks. The original Newsome faretable is interesting, showing the 1½d minimum fares from Lindley and between Paddock and Milnsbridge mentioned earlier but with penny fares over other sections.

Two significant events took place in 1935. On 15 April a new company, Hanson's Buses Ltd, was incorporated with an authorised capital of £20,000 to take over the passenger transport business of Joseph Hanson and Son Ltd. Robert and Donald Hanson were the only directors of the new company, which owned a fleet of 33 buses and coaches. Of the authorised capital, only 10,600 of the £1 shares were issued. On 3 June a syndicate of haulage contractors, including Charles and Oliver Holdsworth and Robert and Donald Hanson, purchased the firm of Oswald Tillotson which in turn controlled the Burnley firm of Bouts-Tillotson. The deal, involving 300 haulage vehicles, was worth £100,000. The Holdsworths and Hansons were now also directors of the Queen Car-

A third double decker for Hansons arrived in August 1935. Leyland Titan TD4 76 (VH 8081) was fitted with a Leyland 8.6 litre diesel engine. In this photograph 76's original Leyland 52 seat highbridge body is featured.
[British Commercial Vehicle Museum]

impediment for the Lindley-Newsome services, as if the severe gradient of Lockwood Scar was not enough (double deckers would later be used as duplicates on the section between David Browns and Lindley). Other routes were in general insufficiently busy in the 1930s to need double deckers; they would never be needed on the Weatherhill service, which passed through an affluent district where Robert Hanson's family had recently taken up residence in a mansion.

Robert Hanson had come to regard local bus routes as useful generators of cash to fund the establishment of other business activities. Up to the early part of 1935 he had been relatively successful in obtaining new licences from the traffic commissioners but was constantly at loggerheads with Huddersfield Corporation and the Joint Omnibus Committee. In June 1935 he had four applications turned down for separate routes from Huddersfield which he had hoped to run hourly daily:
Crimble via Manchester Road, Scar Lane and Wellhouse
Scapegoat Hill via Manchester Road, Leymoor, Golcar and Bolster Moor
Golcar (Station Road) via Manchester Road and Leymoor
Golcar (Station Road) via Manchester Road and Britannia Road
A licence for a Summer Sunday service from Milnsbridge to Nont Sarah's Hotel via Leymoor, Golcar and Waller Clough was also refused. The traffic commissioners granted an increase in the Saturday Golcar frequency to four journeys per hour but were keen to introduce greater timetable coordination of the Golcar services operated by Hansons (via Manchester Road and Leymoor) and Huddersfield JOC (via Paddock and Scar Lane).

This outcome did not meet with Robert Hanson's approval and a public inquiry followed in the Town Hall on 23 November 1935. Hanson, represented by his solicitor JD Eaton Smith and supported by the chairman of Golcar UDC, Mr H Garside, justified the need for a service from Scapegoat Hill on the basis that it would have served Leymoor and Manchester Road, which were not on the JOC Scapegoat Hill route. Eaton Smith claimed that his client had always had to beg Huddersfield Corporation to grant licences, despite the fact that Robert Hanson claimed to be the original operator in the Milnsbridge/Golcar area and the first to run a through bus to Huddersfield. [The Corporation were actually the first to operate in Milnsbridge and Golcar and had run for four years before Hansons appeared on the scene]. Eaton Smith absurdly proceeded to describe the Corporation as

In about 1946 Leyland TD4 76 (VH 8081) was fitted with this new Massey lowbridge body. The resulting combination waits at the Meltham via Helme stand in Market Street, Huddersfield. 76 was withdrawn in 1949 and later ran for well known Scottish independent bus operators Baxter's of Airdrie and Paton of Renfrew.
[W.J. Haynes]

riage Company of Huddersfield which had once been a rival charabanc operator.

The third and final prewar double decker appeared in August 1935 as no. 76, another Leyland Titan, the last Leyland bus to be purchased by Hansons. In this period the double deckers were used mainly on the Marsden and Hill Top/Wilberlee routes. They could not be used on the Golcar route because buses had to pass under part of a mill in Grove Street while the low railway bridge in Swan Lane near Lockwood Station provided a similar a "greedy, devouring colossus" that was intent on diminishing the operating area of his clients. Not surprisingly the Corporation/JOC won the day and Hansons achieved nothing. All the corridors on the proposed routes were already served by the JOC or Hansons.

For several years departure times on the Hansons' Meltham via Helme route and the joint service to Heights (merely the inner section of the Meltham route) had not been fully coordinated; this was achieved in June 1936. The running time to Heights was 20 minutes and that to Meltham 30 minutes so, in order to achieve balanced headways, each Heights bus had for some time had a 20 minutes layover at Heights, where the crews enjoyed tea brewed by Emma at the village shop. Morning departures from Huddersfield were at 10 minutes past the hour to Meltham and 40 minutes past to Heights; later buses left Town for Meltham at 10 and 30 minutes past the hour and at 50 minutes past for Heights. From as early as July 1934 Meltham and Linthwaite UDCs had been suggesting that the Hansons and JOC (via Netherton) routes to Meltham should be combined and operated as a circular service.

Following the successful replacement of the Almondbury, Waterloo, Lindley and Outlane trams during 1933/34 by faster, modern and efficient Corporation trolleybuses, Robert Hanson realised that a future conversion of the Marsden tram route would pose a real threat to his own bus services in the Colne Valley. The Hill Top/Wilberlee route and, in particular, the Marsden service carried many passengers, especially outside the Huddersfield boundary, who chose not to use the trams but might defect to a new trolleybus service. [These routes were of course jointly operated with Huddersfield JOC, half owned by the tramway operator with which they competed.] To introduce trolleybuses, however, the Corporation would need royal assent for a further Trolley Vehicle Act.

During the first half of 1936, through his solicitors Robert Hanson engaged in a prolonged campaign in both the House of Commons and the House of Lords to prevent the spread of trolleybuses in the Huddersfield area. He claimed that the new bill sought by Huddersfield Corporation would give them an unfair advantage in carrying passengers over certain former tramway routes. Leading counsel were engaged to oppose the bill and petitions were brought before both houses. The cost to Hansons was a not inconsiderable £775.

At the time the joint Colne Valley routes yielded about £10,000 in revenue per annum to each operator. The tram

fare to Marsden was only 3d compared with 6d charged on the faster bus service. Mr Hanson was only prepared to withdraw his objections to the introduction of trolleybuses if he was granted control of the coordination of the fares on the two services. He pointed out that, since the introduction of the Lindley trolleybus service, the revenue on his Huddersfield-Birkby-Lindley(Weatherhill) route had fallen by $1\frac{1}{2}$d per mile and the two routes did not even parallel each other. All his other routes either ran on or crossed Manchester Road in the Colne Valley and he predicted very considerable loss of revenue if short distance passengers chose to travel at a lower fare on the faster trolleybuses. Indeed he suggested that some of the services would have to be taken off as they would no longer be financially viable. When asked by the chairman of the Select Committee of the House of Commons, Annesley Sommerville, if he was willing to sell his share of the joint Colne Valley bus routes to Huddersfield JOC, it was revealed that he had offered to sell the whole of his local bus undertaking to the JOC a year earlier for £65,000 but that no agreement had been reached. The chairman accepted that in the past the Hansons buses had served the local community well and expressed the hope that in future the Corporation would deal with him in a fair and generous manner.

The Huddersfield Corporation Trolley Vehicle Act finally received royal assent on 14 July 1936 and became the basis for all remaining tramway conversions. It was, however, not until 10 April 1938 that Karrier trolleybus 69 made the first journey to Marsden. Possibly to placate Robert Hanson, the Corporation increased their through fare to 4d but, just as he had predicted, the trolleybuses soon made an impact on the motorbus route's profits. [The jointly operated Marsden motorbus service was to remain in competition with the trolleybuses for little over a year, conveniently expiring with the outbreak of war.]

On all Hansons services at this period extra buses were needed to cater for shift changeover times at the various textile mills which were served. Extensive use was made of all the services on Sundays and public holidays and a wet day could reduce takings by 25%. Special late night buses could also be run over the normal routes for people returning home from dance halls at the request of the organisers, with charges per person of 9d for a journey up to three miles or 1/- for longer journeys. Various clubs, halls and institutes were served in Huddersfield and the Colne Valley.

During the mid 1930s and up to the outbreak of war about 18 vehicles were needed to operate the basic ser-

vices. Jim Holmes recalled that some vehicles seemed to be associated with particular routes:

Blackpool:	2 coaches
Golcar:	2 single decks
Heights:	1 single deck
Hill Top:	1 double deck and 1 single deck
Lindley-Newsome	4 single decks, often Leyland Lions 18, 23, 24, 25 or 27
Weatherhill	1 single deck
Marsden	2 double decks
Meltham	2 single decks, often Leyland Lion 19 and AEC Regals 59 or 61
Oldham	2 single decks, often Leyland Tiger 30 and AEC Regal 55

At Christmas the single deckers would be decorated with coloured paper "trimmings" fastened with drawing pins and hung from one window post to the next. This tradition, unique among Huddersfield bus operators, was maintained through the war and for a few years afterwards.

4: PREWAR AND WARTIME COACHING (1927-1942)

On 29 June 1927 a total eclipse of the sun was expected and, as viewing conditions were predicted to be best in the north, the Astronomer Royal, Sir Frank Dyson, set up a camp at Giggleswick to make official observations. Thousands of people were expected to descend on Giggleswick and the surrounding area. Seeing this as an additional source of revenue, Hansons announced that their saloon buses would leave the Savile Street garage at 2.30pm on the Wednesday afternoon, picking up 15 minutes later in St George's Square. The total eclipse was in fact visible at 6.23pm. During this period Hansons were keen to point out that all their vehicles were fully insured, licensed by the Huddersfield police and driven by competent drivers, the implication being that this was not always the case with some of the small rival firms. Safety must often have been in the minds of many potential passengers as in those days there were regular newspaper reports of horrendous charabanc and coach crashes.

At Whitsuntide 1928 Hansons began their daily service to Blackpool, although it was actually the end of July before they were granted an express licence for this service by Huddersfield Watch Committee. The route was via Elland, Halifax, Todmorden, Burnley and Preston with three daily departures, at first leaving both Huddersfield and Blackpool at 8.30am, 1.30pm and 6.00pm. There were two regular drivers and the two Lancias (3 and 5) were the usual vehicles. Mr Burley drove 3 on the 8.30am from Huddersfield and Mr Nunn, who lived in Blackpool, drove 5 on the 8.30am from Blackpool. On the evening journeys the drivers exchanged their passengers at the Petrie Arms near Whalley so that both of them returned to their home town each night.

From Whitsuntide 1928 Hansons also advertised in the Huddersfield Examiner on an almost daily basis, particularly for the Blackpool express. No doubt this was done as a response to the competing Progress Motors service run by William Armitage (formerly of Huddersfield but by then resident in Blackpool), unlicensed by the Huddersfield authorities but from May 1928 operated from the new Progress garage in Venn Street. With the delivery of two "all weather saloon coaches" (Leyland Lion 4 and Lancia 9) Hansons made the dubious claim that their fleet was now one of the best in the north of England.

By the end of October 1928 the world's largest airship, the R100, was nearing completion in Howden airship sheds. Such was the novelty that even in cold November weather excursions were run to view the progress. It was so huge that it had to be tethered by cables embedded in cement and it was estimated that 500 men would be required for manhandling prior to the launch.

Although Hansons vehicles were traditionally red, more new Leyland coaches began to arrive during 1929/30 in a very impressive livery consisting of a black roof and a mainly white body relieved by a black waist band. Just what the public thought on being asked if they had seen the new Lion and Tiger coaches is not known. After 1933 a red flash and red mudguards further enhanced their appearance. A former AEC Regal demonstrator was an exception when it was purchased in 1933 and numbered 66 as it ran in cream with green mudguards before repainting. Coaches were later painted red with white relief, as were the buses.

Under the new licensing system Robert Hanson had to appear before the traffic commissioners in Huddersfield Town Hall in June 1931 to support applications for the renewal of existing licences. The Blackpool express service had been operating for twelve years and 10 per cent of its passengers were day trippers; on ordinary summer days up to 12 buses were used but at special holiday times extra buses had to be hired in and it was claimed that as many as 30 could be on the service. Before the Hansons route had been started, the railways were carrying 78,900 passengers annually from Huddersfield to

Driver Joe Baxter stands alongside a Hansons Leyland Tiger TS2 coach. Although this vehicle has been quoted as 22 (VH 2067), it is probably 21 (VH 2066), also new in February 1929. The bodywork has been recorded as Ramsden of Liversedge but it is thought to be by Burlingham. [W. Holmes]

In May 1930 this fine Leyland bodied Leyland Tiger TS2 joined the Hansoms fleet. 30 (VH 3015) was withdrawn in 1942 and later used as a canteen at the depot. [British Commercial Vehicle Museum]

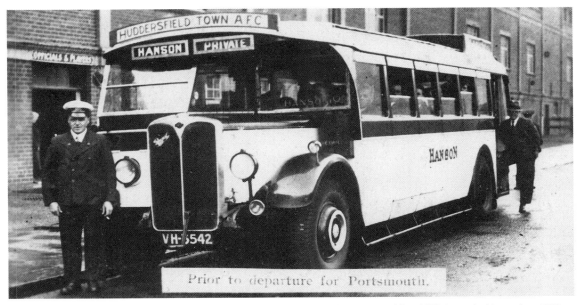

Hansons AEC Regal/Burlingham coach 37 (VH 3542) was one of a pair (Hansons' first AECs) new in November 1930. Originally ordered by a Blackpool operator they were diverted to Hansons, previously a largely Leyland firm – and Leylands continued to be purchased for a number of years. Acting as the Huddersfield Town AFC coach, 37 waits in Bradley Mills Road (off Leeds Road) before departing for Portsmouth. [S.T. Harling collection]

Blackpool but by 1929 this figure had fallen to 57,000 so naturally the LMS Railway opposed this application. Other objectors were Ribble Motor Services and Todmorden Corporation. Nevertheless Hansons obtained a Huddersfield to Blackpool licence.

One of the largest excursions organised in the early days was for the workers of John Crowther and Sons Union Woollen Mill at Milnsbridge on Thursday 2 July 1931, to celebrate that firm's part in creating a world record. On 24 June twelve fully coated Southdown sheep had been herded into Crowthers' mill where shearers from Derbyshire removed the fleeces, weighing 20 pounds in all. Weaving was begun only 47 minutes after the shearing had started and was completed after a further 43 minutes. The suit length was then hastily conveyed by runner to Prices Tailors, who produced the finished suit in marginally less than 30 minutes. From sheeps' backs to finished garment had taken just under two hours and ten minutes; this was the new world record which had to be celebrated in style.

Hansons were called upon to organise the transport from Milnsbridge to Blackpool. Some 50 coaches were needed to transport over 1500 people, the Crowthers workers and their spouses. Mrs Holmes, daughter in law of the Hansons chief engineer, was one of them; his son Jim had also been a Hansons mechanic since leaving school in 1928. The Hansons coaches used probably comprised Leyland Tigers 21/2/30, Leyland Lions 25 and 40 (the rebodied and renumbered 4) and AEC Regals 36/7. The remaining 40 or so coaches were hired in from other operators with whom Hansons enjoyed good relations, many in the Barnsley area.

The first coaches left Milnsbridge at 6.30am and, to prevent traffic chaos, not all the coaches followed the same route. The plan was not to arrive in Blackpool before 11.30am so that the men were less likely to be inebriated before lunchtime. Dinner and tea were provided free for all participants, as was entry to the Tower and Winter Gardens. A good day was had by all and a very good day by some who did not arrive home until late the following day, having either missed the coach home or been thrown off for disorderly behaviour. The coaches arrived back in Milnsbridge at intervals between 10.30 and 11.15pm; as many people had by then missed their last buses home, Hansons ran special buses to the outlying districts.

Crowthers organised annual trips to Blackpool for their employees and spouses and Hansons always provided the transport. Probably the largest of these took place on

17

Leyland TS6 coach 65 (VH 5335), new to Hansons in 1933, was parked outside what is believed to be one of the public houses patronised by travellers to and from the Yorkshire coast. The bodywork seems to be English Electric to Leyland style. Withdrawn in 1942, 65 worked for several owners before ending its days as a mobile shop in Liverpool. [R. Brook]

21 June 1934 to commemorate the 60th birthday of Mr D Stoner Crowther when 62 coaches were required for 1900 participants. All the coaches were numbered and each passenger had a ticket for a specific coach; they were despatched in small convoys under the supervision of both Robert and Donald Hanson, such was the importance of the event.

Joe Kaye of Moorbottom Road, Thornton Lodge, who had originally traded as the Conqueror Motor Company, formed a partnership to run the Thornton Lodge Chara Company in July 1919. By the time his partner withdrew in 1926 the firm was a well established if small competitor of Hansons. The value of adequate insurance was clearly demonstrated when he suffered a disastrous garage fire on the evening of 30 August 1929. His chara and two nearly new coaches were lost in the inferno and only the office was saved. This could easily have been the end of the road for Joe, who had also operated a visitors' service to Bradley Sanatorium since 1923. The insurance claim was insufficient to clear his debts and he was found to be insolvent but the business effects were purchased by his mother in law for £400 and she employed him as manager of the business for a weekly wage of £5. By October 1930 he was advertising weekend trips to Blackpool illuminations in new coaches. All was not well and increasing competition during 1932 caused him to cut his fares and to operate some excursions without a licence. When he applied to renew his licences in January 1933 his application was opposed by Hansons and he was admonished by the traffic commissioners. Following further infringements the commissioners revoked all Kaye's licences in January 1934.

What was left of the business passed to Hansons and Kaye was declared bankrupt later in the year.

The first Mersey tunnel, linking Liverpool with Birkenhead, was opened by the king (George V) on 18 July 1934. The 2.13 miles long tunnel soon became a magnet for coach operators with the final destination usually being the Wirral resort of New Brighton.

Coaching activities tend to be highly seasonal but Hansons had one all year contract for many years. Jesse Lumb, woollen manufacturers of Folly Hall, employed over a hundred workers who lived in the Barnsley area and four coaches were needed to transport them to and from work. To save empty running, three coaches were regularly out-stabled overnight at Wombwell where driver Fred Bullock lived. One coach left Huddersfield every morning with two drivers on board and similarly brought them back in the evening.

The Hansons Huddersfield to Blackpool express coach service was another all year activity but modest loadings out of season resulted in the competing operators' routes being coordinated. From 1 February 1935 the Hansons service became jointly operated in winter with that of the Yorkshire-Blackpool Pool operators (Yorkshire Traction and four other major companies), whose stand in Huddersfield was moved from Kirkgate to Venn Street later in the year. In summer (and over Christmas and Easter) Hansons continued to run independently from the west side of Springwood Street, outside the Parochial Hall between George Street and Westgate. The Hansons stand remained there when Huddersfield JOC's Halifax, Golcar/Scapegoat Hill and Crimble stands in front of it were moved across the road to Sparrow Park on 20 April 1936 after complaints from shopkeepers about waiting passengers blocking doorways and problems with deliveries. Meanwhile from 1 November 1935 B & S (Bullocks of Featherstone), who ran Wakefield-Huddersfield-Blackpool, also became part of the winter joint operation between Huddersfield and Blackpool.

Many operators in seaside resorts were in the habit of exhibiting their newest coach in the booking office. Arthur Audsley, who came from Standerwicks at Blackpool, persuaded Robert Hanson to adopt this practice. A well known photograph shows AEC Regal coach 89, delivered in March 1937, parked with its front end protruding from the front of the travel office as an advertisement. The floor of the building had previously been strengthened. At night the coach was reversed inside the building. This practice was not resumed after the war.

Audsley was employed as the coach tout in St George's Square; it was his job to persuade intending passengers to travel with Hansons rather than with any of their competitors. People always wanted to travel in the newest coach; one way in which they were tricked, it is recalled, was that just when the new coach had filled up on the stand and was seemingly ready to leave, an older coach would pull up at its side and the passengers, who of course had already parted with their money, were requested to transfer on some pretext or other to the older vehicle. The tout could then use the new coach to attract a fresh load of customers. Apparently this dodge was common to many firms in this period.

There was also considerable competition with the LMS Railway for excursion traffic. During 1937 the LMS introduced a save to travel scheme, whereby potential passengers were urged to buy 1/- savings stamps and 10/- vouchers, for which they were paid interest at 5% at a time when the Huddersfield Building Society was paying only $2^1/_2$%. The LMS also offered very cheap evening trips to the Lancashire coast which could be reached for as little as 2/3d. To compete, Hansons introduced a series of evening tours for 2/6d to places such as Hollingworth Lake, Newmillerdam, Denholme, Cawthorne and Dunford Bridge. Hardly as attractive as the longer rail trips, they did at least guarantee a return to Huddersfield in good time to catch the last buses and trams. The trains had a bad habit of getting shunted into sidings and not returning until the small hours of the morning.

Before the war Robert Hanson, besides his other activities, was Master of Rockwood Hunt. He used to take his hunting friends to the Grand National at Aintree in one of the firm's coaches. A viewing platform with collapsible wooden sides was specially constructed so that it could be secured to the roof of 30, a Leyland Tiger TS2 of 1930. On arrival at Aintree, the viewing platform was assembled and the dignitaries climbed a ladder to reach the roof; additional support was provided by props inside the vehicle. This proved such a success that viewing platforms were eventually fitted to four vehicles. Each year the parties consisted of local mill owners and their families and friends, managers of chemicals companies and other influential people with whom Hansons did business.

Before the start of these outings, large hampers containing packed lunches from Whiteleys Cafe and crates of champagne were stowed away in the boot of the vehicle. The wealthy clients tipped well and Jim Holmes reckoned that he received about £1 from each couple. On one occasion he did much better when the wife of a

Milnsbridge mill owner wanted to place a bet on a horse called "Lovely Cottage" (because she and her husband had seen a lovely cottage near Cambridge). The odds were 33 to 1 and driver Jim placed the bet for her with a bookmaker on the course. The horse won and the good lady gave her winnings to Jim. The practice of using viewing platforms ended after the war but in more recent times open top double deck buses (not a feature of the Hansons fleet!) have served the same purpose.

Jim Holmes's usual coach before the war was AEC Regal 78 but on one occasion after he had upset Mr Hanson he was told to take Leyland Lion 72 to Morecambe instead. Lions 72 and 73 had a reputation for boiling over on long hilly runs and at regular intervals Jim had to use his watering can to refill the radiator. Needless to say the other coaches overtook him on the outward journey. Not to be outdone, for the return trip Jim had his passengers on board a good 15 minutes before the normal departure time and so made sure that his coach was the first back in Huddersfield. The next day, knowing what the answer would be, Robert Hanson asked Jim if he had passed any coaches on the way to Morecambe. Jim replied in the negative, adding that none had passed him on the way back.

It is worth mentioning that, unlike their rivals Baddeleys or Schofields of Marsden, Hansons never ran extended holiday tours on their own account after the summer of 1921. That year five-day tours to the Lakes, North Wales and London were advertised, costing seven guineas. Over 400 miles of motoring was to be personally conducted and only first class hotels were promised. Presumably the venture was not a success and Robert Hanson believed that booking hotels was not worth the bother. Obvious advantages would have been that customers paid in advance and that the tour took place

irrespective of the weather. For day excursions, if the weather was bad some coaches would not turn a wheel as in those days many people turned up and booked on the day only if the weather was good.

Each year some Hansons drivers and their coaches were hired by Wallace Arnold for the Leeds holiday week at the beginning of August. They would drive empty to Leeds on the Saturday morning, pick up their passengers at The Calls and often take them via Ilkley, Skipton and Clitheroe to Blackpool. Another set of passengers would then be brought back to either Huddersfield or Leeds. A second round trip would be started late in the afternoon. The arduous day's work would be worth 23/- to the driver and his meals would be provided by Mr and Mrs Denby at the Park Gate public house between Whalley and Preston, used by many of the drivers as a halfway house. If the coach was required for an early start from Leeds the following day, the driver would probably spend the night on the back seat of his coach at The Calls; for this he received an extra 5/- expenses.

Hansons themselves often had to hire in buses and coaches at busy periods, particularly for the Blackpool express service and for important rugby league matches when Fartown were playing away. Many a Hansons driver had to make his way to Leeds Road depot to collect a Huddersfield JOC bus; he would then drive it to Wakefield or Wigan with claret and gold scarves hanging out of the windows. Before the war this was worth an extra 5/- and free entry to the match.

Huddersfield Town reached the final of the FA cup in 1938 and played Preston North End who unfortunately won. Many of the fans, sporting the blue and white colours, travelled to the event in Hansons coaches and one decorated coach was exhibited in St George's Square on the Saturday evening with a large painting of

captain Alf Young at the front. The Town team were given a civic reception at the Town Hall on the following Monday (2 May). Hansons provided four vehicles to transport the team and the invited guests to the Town Hall. Leading the cavalcade was the newest coach (AEC Regal 113) with sun roof open and suitably decorated in the club's blue and white colours while following behind in numerical fleet order were the newest buses, AEC Regals 110-2. Large crowds gathered to greet the team which, despite its Wembley setback, at least managed to win the remaining two games of the season and so avoid relegation.

During the 1938 summer season two new series of Sunday tours were promoted. A group of seven half-day tours was operated, one each week in rotation, costing no more than 6/- and including: How Stean Ravine and Nidderdale; Ashopton, the quaint Derbyshire village about to be submerged by a new reservoir; Castleton via Grindleford and Hathersage; and Kettlewell. Shorter evening trips priced at 2/6d visited the still popular Golden Acre amusement park at Otley Road, Leeds and a selection of local beauty spots.

As early as October 1938, fearing that poison gas would be used in any future war, the Air Raid Precautions authorities set up a gas chamber in the basement of the Hansons John William Street booking office. Visitors wearing respirators walked through a chamber in which tear gas had been released; it was hoped that this would convince the civilian population of the usefulness of respirators or gas masks as they were called.

Despite or possibly because of the threat of war the 1939 summer season was a record for Hansons. Whit Monday was the busiest so far, with 12 Huddersfield JOC AEC Regal buses hired for the afternoon trip to Ripon. The reconstruction of John William Street throughout June meant that coaches could not start from St George's Square and had to use St Peter's Street instead. On Saturday 12 August coaches were hired in from Barnsley area operators as well as 20 AEC Regal single deck buses from Huddersfield JOC (mainly from the series 46-73 bought in 1938/39). The first bus left Huddersfield for Blackpool at 6.30am, followed by others at regular intervals until 9.00am. Most vehicles performed a second return trip in the afternoon. For those who stayed at home, a wide variety of day excursions was operated during the week, ranging from Boston Spa and Brimham Rocks to Whitley Bay and Gretna Green, the latter being two of the longest trips operated so far.

One of the last advertised excursions ran to York for

In March 1937 Hansons placed in service three Burlingham bodied AEC Regal coaches, running them until 1947. This is 89 (ACX 368). [P.J. Cardno collection]

In the late 1930s Hansons regularly hired newish single deckers from Huddersfield Joint Omnibus Committee in busy periods. Not long after entering service in May 1939, the JOC's AEC Regal/Park Royal 64 (BVH 164), a 32 seater with Gardner 6LW engine, on hire to Hansons awaits custom for a 2/6d Moorland Drive in St George's Square, then the main picking up point for excursions in Huddersfield. [S.T. Harling collection]

the races on 24 August 1939 before the declaration of war in September officially brought coaching operations to a halt. All crude oil was imported by sea and supplies could no longer be guaranteed while existing stocks of petrol and diesel had to be conserved; supplying the war effort was naturally given priority. Excursions were at first suspended but a limited number of trips was later permitted during certain phases of the war.

It is claimed that Hansons obtained what was described as "washed colliery oil" which could be mixed with ordinary diesel and used to fuel some of the haulage vehicles. The fuel saved in this way allowed coaches to be run to Blackpool after other firms had stopped running but Ministry of Transport inspectors soon became aware of the scheme, which had to stop. This of course left Hansons with a surplus of buses and coaches which could be requisitioned by the Minister of War Transport for transportation of troops and essential war workers. There was no guarantee of return and any compensa-

tion was dependent on the outcome of the war. In the event Leyland Lions 38 and 120 and AEC Regal 66 were requisitioned and not returned whereas Lions 23/4/6/72/3 and Regals 87/8/121 were requisitioned but subsequently returned. Robert Hanson held a senior position in the Road Haulage section of the Ministry of War Transport.

The four diesel coaches, Lions 72/3 and Regals 87/8, were sent with their Hansons drivers to Stoke on Trent where they were used for transporting female munition workers in the Wem, Burslem, Stone and Stafford areas. The four drivers returned home each weekend. Royal Ordnance Factories also had residential wings attached housing up to 1000 girls, many of whom were recruited from the West Riding, and they might have been able to use the Hansons coaches when they returned home for a weekend visit. Other coaches, including AEC Regals 78-80, were stripped of their engines and stored in the mews of Norwood Grange at Edgerton, the Hanson family home. The engines were classified as under repair for the

duration of the war and in this way the coaches avoided requisition.

On Friday 10 May 1940 (the day before Whit Saturday) the government made a last minute announcement as a result of the German invasion of Belgium and Holland. It was decreed that the situation made it essential for people to continue working for the war effort and to forgo their Whitsuntide holiday; all unnecessary travel was to be avoided. In Huddersfield the engineers carried on working but the textile mills were closed. The LMS Railway special trains to Blackpool which were already fully booked were cancelled, as were the bulk of the Yorkshire Traction excursions. Hansons had already advertised their excursions programme, based on the fuel allocation granted by the authorities at a time when it was obviously thought that Whitsuntide excursions would be a boost to public morale likely to be reflected in higher productivity levels in the factories. All advertised trips were run and bookings cancelled by people who found that they were required to work were avidly taken up by those who had failed to reserve seats before. Every available coach in the district was hired and about 80 bus loads were taken to Blackpool on the Saturday. 30 coaches were on the road on Monday, many of them bringing back the weekend trippers. It was noted that many passengers now carried their gas masks with them.

Throughout 1941 the fuel situation became more serious and fewer passengers could be carried to Blackpool for holidays or taken on day trips to the west coast resorts, which were still thought to be safe from enemy bombing. Securing transport was not the only problem for would be holidaymakers. Blackpool was bursting at the seams with evacuees, troops and civil servants displaced from their London offices and a Huddersfield Examiner reporter warned people not to travel unless they had booked accommodation in advance, laid in a good stock of unrationed foodstuffs and secured their emergency ration cards.

With the war situation becoming ever more grave there were no excursions to Blackpool during the summer of 1942. A Holidays at Home programme was organised by Huddersfield Corporation Entertainments Committee, centred largely on Greenhead Park for the traditional July and August holiday weeks. The Regional Transport Commissioner allowed Hansons to run a very limited number of short distance excursions to local beauty spots on Wednesdays, Saturdays and Sundays throughout the period.

5: BUSES IN WARTIME AND A SECOND COORDINATION SCHEME (1938-1945)

As early as October 1935 the traffic commissioners had drawn up a scheme for the coordination of the services of Hansons and Huddersfield JOC in the Golcar area but nothing came of it. By March 1938 the JOC were convinced of the necessity of either outright purchase of the Hansons services or the extension of the existing Colne Valley coordination scheme to cover the Golcar area as well. They had estimated that the Hansons routes could provide an annual revenue of £33,200 and that mileage economies of 62,500 per annum should be possible. They then resolved to offer a sum not exceeding £85,000 for the purchase of the Hansons routes; in the event of this being unacceptable to Hansons, a further scheme of coordination was to be drawn up.

Robert Hanson's lowest price was £125,000, based on the assumption that the JOC would be able to operate the Hansons services at a cost of 8.62d per mile and should therefore pay him accordingly. Furthermore Mr Hanson was prepared to operate the JOC's Colne Valley services himself and guarantee the JOC a fixed income. After general discussion it was agreed to proceed with the extended coordination scheme which finally came to fruition at a meeting held on 14 July 1938 between members of the JOC and Robert and Donald Hanson. The main points of the new agreement were:
(1) The scheme would cover the services in the Colne Valley already being operated on a 50:50 basis together with those services of both operators then being provided in the Golcar area.
(2) Buses of both parties would operate on any of the coordinated routes as might be best for convenient operation.
(3) Timetables, sufficient for public requirements, would be printed as economically as possible.
(4) Tickets and waybills would be common to both parties.
(5) Inspectors employed by either party would check and supervise the buses of both parties on the coordinated routes.
(6) Road service licences were to be jointly obtained from the traffic commissioners with the full timetable being shown on the application of each party.
(7) The basic year's traffic returns and accounts of each party were to be verified and agreed by the other party. Both parties were to accept the audit of the Borough Treasurer's Department.

(8) The mileages operated by both parties on the routes in question for 1937 were to be used to calculate the percentage of miles to be operated by each party over the coordinated routes. The gross revenues from the co-ordinated services were to be pooled and divided in this same proportion. The new mileages to be run would also be in this proportion. Adjustments would be made to the operating schedules every three months to allow either party to balance any shortages or excesses of mileage in the previous quarter. In carrying out the percentage mileage calculation, it was agreed to credit Hansons with the whole of the miles operated by the JOC on the Heights service and with 25% of the miles run by the JOC on their Crimble via Wellhouse service.

The revised agreement was supposed to start on 1 June 1939 if possible and was initially to be in force for ten years. Either party could terminate the agreement after this date by giving one year's notice. The agreement was signed on 6 September 1939 but introduction of the new services was delayed until 23 September 1939 as, after the declaration of war, it was necessary to draw up and produce emergency timetables. Hansons were to operate 41.515% of the mileage and take 40.75% of the combined receipts. The following routes were then jointly operated as the Colne Valley Services:
Huddersfield-Paddock Head-Scar Lane-Golcar-Leymoor-Manchester Road-Huddersfield
Huddersfield-Manchester Road-Leymoor-Golcar-Scar Lane-Paddock Head-Huddersfield
Huddersfield-Paddock Head-Scar Lane-Golcar-Bolster Moor-Scapegoat Hill
Huddersfield-Manchester Road-Leymoor-Golcar-Bolster Moor-Scapegoat Hill
Huddersfield-Britannia Road-Golcar-Bolster Moor-Scapegoat Hill
Huddersfield-Paddock Head-Scar Lane-Wellhouse-Crimble
Huddersfield-Manchester Road-Scar Lane-Wellhouse-Crimble
Huddersfield-Manchester Road-Slaithwaite-Hill Top
Huddersfield-Manchester Road-Slaithwaite-Hill Top-Wilberlee
[From 1943 the JOC would number these routes 1 to 9 respectively but Hansons never used route numbers.]

The Marsden route was completely withdrawn and not reinstated after the war; the Corporation trolleybuses had been victorious. As there was no longer an immediate need for three double deckers, Leyland Titan 60 was prematurely withdrawn and sold in 1940 to Moore's of

Kelvedon, Essex. Also permanently withdrawn was the Heights route; Linthwaite would henceforth be served only by Hansons buses on the Meltham via Helme route, which remained outside the coordination scheme. Buses on the Hill Top/Wilberlee services would no longer be allowed to compete with the trolleybuses for passengers, as protective fares would be charged as far as Manchester Road, Slaithwaite. Circular operation across Golcar Town End was a useful new feature for passengers, as were direct journeys between Scapegoat Hill or Crimble and sections of the existing Hansons route between Golcar and Town. Hansons buses could now be seen running to the formerly JOC only Scapegoat Hill and Crimble via Wellhouse destinations and along the Paddock-Milnsbridge-Scar Lane corridor. The Golcar/Scapegoat Hill/Crimble buses used a common terminus in Huddersfield at the existing JOC stands in Sparrow Park on the east side of Springwood Street. Buses for these destinations leaving Town via Manchester Road also served the former Hansons Golcar route terminus in Macaulay Street.

Drastic frequency cuts were also made on all Hansons' other routes in order to comply with instructions from the Minister for War Transport to save fuel. The Newsome-Lindley routes were particularly badly hit, possibly because no intending passengers lived or worked very far from a Corporation trolleybus route. In the early morning, lunchtime and teatime peaks the 15 minutes frequency was maintained but off peak only an hourly service was provided using just one bus which left Lindley on the hour and Newsome 30 minutes later. The last through journeys of the day left Lindley at 9.00pm and Newsome at 9.30pm. On Sundays the services via Luck Lane and Quarmby were completely suspended and a half hourly frequency was operated via Reinwood Road, starting at 1.14pm from Milnsbridge.

On the Weatherhill via Birkby route the normal 30 minutes frequency operated during the three peaks and an hourly service at other times during the week. During Monday to Friday off peak periods a bus arriving at Weatherhill at one minute to the hour did not appear to leave until 30 minutes past the hour; perhaps the regular crew lived in Lindley. The Newsome bus arrived in Lindley at around the same time so it is also possible that crew changeovers took place. The Saturday/Sunday frequency was unchanged at 30 minutes so the situation did not arise then.

The long Oldham service was severely pruned and there was only one morning departure from Huddersfield, at 6.55am for workpeople. From 12.55pm a two hourly frequency was operated until the last bus at 6.55pm. On Sundays there was no morning service at all. North Western route 160 to Oldham via Delph was completely withdrawn for the duration of the war. By 1943 the Hansons Oldham stand had been moved from Macaulay Street to the Meltham via Helme stand in Market Street which North Western 160 had used before the war.

On the Meltham via Helme service from Monday to Thursday a basic hourly frequency was offered until the last departure from Town at 10.10pm. During morning and teatime peaks two or three extra journeys were made. On Friday, Saturday and Sunday afternoons the prewar 30 minutes frequency was maintained.

By comparing the weekly numbers of journeys made before the war with those made during the war it is possible to estimate the percentage cut to each service. This is shown in the table below.

Route	Prewar	Wartime	% Cut
Newsome-Lindley	418	240	43
Weatherhill	213	172	20
Meltham	200	160	20
Oldham	64	34	47

By taking into account the length of each route it appears that approximately 33% of the prewar mileage was saved on these routes as a whole. This of course ignores any duplication - much overcrowding was the order of the day, particularly in Milnsbridge at times of shift changes in the various mills.

Similarly for jointly operated Colne Valley Services:

Route	Prewar	Wartime	%Cut
Scapegoat Hill	249	203	19
Golcar via Leymoor/Scar Ln	542	301	44
Crimble via Wellhouse	197	156	22
Hill Top/Wilberlee	373	159	57
Marsden	225	0	100

In comparison with the combined Hansons and Huddersfield JOC prewar mileages on these routes the emergency coordinated timetables gave an almost 50% reduction in mileage, not allowing for duplication.

For operation in the blackout, it was vital that any illumination from the saloon lights was not visible to enemy aircraft, so windows were painted with semi opaque paint. Sometimes neither passengers nor the conductress knew exactly where the bus was. On one occasion a lady boarded a bus at Golcar to travel to Town. She settled herself in one of the front seats and, as she could see little or nothing through the window, contented herself

with studying the timetable. She paid little heed to the frequent stops but, when the bus came to a standstill for quite a time, became a little concerned and asked one of the passengers who had just boarded the bus why it was waiting so long. The bus had of course reached its terminus in Springwood Street without her realising and was almost ready to depart for Golcar again.

Early on in the war Hansons converted a bus into a mobile first aid post to carry a staff of 20 first aid workers. This was presented to the Corporation, who already had three buses on day and night standby for emergency ambulance duties.

During the weekend of 27/28 January 1940 Huddersfield and district had its heaviest falls of snow for several years and many of the outlying areas were cut off for days by drifts up to 20 feet deep. The Corporation Highways Department were severely handicapped in their efforts to clear the roads by a shortage of labour. Normally much snow clearing would have been done at night but this was impossible in the blackout. Also fuel rationing reduced the number of vehicles that could be used to carry away the snow and ice. Buses could only crawl along the rutted icy roads, with great strain being placed on springs and axles. The Oldham route was completely suspended for ten days and for several days the Meltham service terminated at Heights. On the joint services most of the outer termini could not be reached; Crimble buses turned round at Golcar Town Hall, the Hill Top/Wilberlee service terminated in Slaithwaite and Scapegoat Hill buses only managed to reach Bolster Moor from 10 February onwards.

At the end of the first 48 weeks period of the operation of the revised coordination agreement total receipts were £25,873-5s; as the Hansons portion of £10,638-10s-6d slightly exceeded their allotted 40.75% they had to make a payment of £95-3s-5d to Huddersfield JOC. After the next 48 weeks period the JOC had to make a balancing payment of £144-13s-11d to Hansons.

By 1943 Huddersfield's municipal platform staff had become so dissatisfied with their rates of pay and wartime working conditions that against the advice of their union they took strike action on 14 May. Most of the Hansons conductors and some of the drivers supported their municipal colleagues by not turning up for work. An emergency service was provided for workmen, who collected their own fares and gave them to the driver who was unable to issue tickets. Later in the day office staff took over as temporary conductors while on the following days Robert Hanson's wife and some of her

friends acted as emergency conductresses. It was said that no workmen were left behind at stops so the buses must have been crammed to capacity. The strike ended on the 18 May with much bad publicity for the municipal workers but with praise for Hansons who had managed to keep going.

The difficulty of obtaining new buses during the war and in the immediate postwar years caused many prewar buses to enjoy an extended lifespan and record unusually high mileages. One such Hansons vehicle was AEC Regal 55 of 1932 vintage. This Brush B32F bodied single decker powered with an 8.8 litre diesel engine had worked mainly on the Oldham route until the end of 1940 when it was often on the road from 7.00am until 11.00pm. According to the AEC Gazette, it had clocked over 600,000 miles by December 1940. The chassis was then reconditioned and fitted with a 7.7 litre engine and a new Burlingham B35F body; in this form 55 was put to work mainly on the arduous Meltham route. Before withdrawal in 1947 it had completed a record of over a million miles. Two sister vehicles of 1933, 59 and 61, also lasted until 1947 with new Burlingham bodies fitted in about 1941 but their mileages are not known.

The first Albions (151/2: CCX 446/7) arrived in 1941; these were of the CX13 type with Burlingham B35F bodies to utility specification and were disposed of in 1950. No further vehicles were delivered until 1945 when Hansons received some typical utility buses: 176/7 (CCX 762/3) of the famous Bedford OWB type with B32F bodies by Duple (downseated to 28 before being sold in 1946); and a solitary Guy Arab II, 183 (CCX 810) .The Guy's utility Roe L27/28R body was delivered with wooden seats upstairs; these were upholstered later to the relief of Oldham bound passengers. This vehicle, which survived until 1955, restored the double deck complement to three; Colne Valley UDC had been complaining in 1944 about many passengers on the Hill Top route being left behind by single deckers in the peak periods. The two remaining prewar Leyland Titan double deckers performed throughout the wartime period. 63 received a new Burlingham L27/27R body in 1946 and ran in this form until 1949, after withdrawal joining the fleet of J Clark and Sons of Glencaple. Late in the war Leyland Titan 76 was also rebodied but this time with a L27/24R Massey body. After withdrawal in 1949 it saw further service with two other Scottish independents, Baxters of Airdrie and Patons of Renfrew.

Also new in 1945 were 186-9 (CCX 880-3), Albion CX13 bodied to utility standards by Pickering (B34F).

New in May 1945 was the only utility double decker of Hansons, Roe lowbridge bodied Guy Arab II 183 (CCX 810). 183 is standing in the parking ground east of Manchester Street and the bus stations; the houses on the right are in South Parade. To anyone aware of the Colne Valley's rugged terrain, "Heights" may seem a rather vague destination. The heights in question tower above Linthwaite just before you reach Blackmoorfoot, here a short working on the Meltham route but until 1939 also enjoying a separate service joint with the JOC. [R. Marshall collection]

These Scottish buses were sold in 1950 to yet another Scottish independent, Carmichael of Glenboig, near Airdrie (trading as Highland!). Another batch of these buses delivered in 1946 (196-9; CVH 226-9), also with bodies to utility specifications, were kept for only four years before being sold to Birkenshaw Mills, be-

tween Birstall and Bradford.

From or by 8 January 1945 certain journeys on the Meltham via Helme service were extended to or from Meltham Mills via Mill Bank Road to serve the David Browns works, later well known for tractor production but at that time engaged on other vital war work. The

Guy Arab 183 (CCX 810) waits on the Hill Top and Wilberlee stand in Upperhead Row Bus Station in the 1949-52 period. 183 was scrapped in 1955. [P.J. Cardno collection]

fare from Meltham Market Place was 1½d and all other fares were a penny higher than the fare to Meltham.

6: POSTWAR COACHING AND EXPRESS REVIVAL (1945-1950)

Following the end of hostilities in Europe (May 1945), a relaxation in fuel rationing allowed a limited number of day excursions to be advertised for the August Huddersfield holiday week. These were fully booked in advance but some half day trips were announced later for which there was to be no advance booking. After the travel restrictions of the war years people were only too keen to make up for lost time. A rival firm, Chapman's Ivy Coaches (eventually to be taken over by Hansons), sensing an upturn in business, opened a new booking office at Palace Mansions on 7 August.

In 1946 Robert Hanson was vice chairman of the Yorkshire branch of the Passenger Vehicle Operators' Association and Huddersfield was also represented on the area committee by G Chapman of Ivy Coaches and Leonard Baddeley. When excursions were resumed at Easter 1946, Blackpool as usual proved the most popular destination. On the Monday a total of 41 coaches were despatched and the people left behind in the queues outside the booking office could have filled another 50.

An excursion postponed from 1939 because of the war finally took place on 9 September 1946. It had originally been planned to celebrate the silver wedding of Mr and Mrs Dyson Mallinson by taking 700 past and present workers from the George Mallinson and Sons Ltd woollen and worsted mills at Linthwaite on an outing to Blackpool. 22 coaches were provided for the event.

In the prewar years as already mentioned, Hansons had bussed in mill girls from Darfield and Wombwell. In November 1946 this operation was extended under a "Clothe Britain" scheme devised by Huddersfield Labour Exchange. Besides the girls, former miners were now brought in from Barnsley to train as spinners and drawers at the Broadfield Mills of Kaye and Stewart Ltd at Lockwood. At first three coach loads were carried daily and a night shift later proved popular for the miners who were of course used to nocturnal working.

A pantomime party from the Wappy Springs Inn at Lindley Moor taken to the Manchester Palace got more than they bargained for one winter night in March 1947. On the return journey the coach got as far as Delph before the police advised them that a snow blizzard had blocked all roads from Lancashire to Yorkshire, eventu-

Burlingham bodied AEC Regal 111 (AVH 901), which had been new in March 1938, was rebodied with this new Duple "dual purpose" semi-coach body in February 1947 and renumbered 244. Withdrawn by Hansons in 1952, it later served with a variety of smaller coach operators and a military unit until 1962. [W.J. Haynes]

St George's Square was the main loading point for excursions from Huddersfield before the parking ground adjacent to the new bus stations in Manchester Street and Upperhead Row was brought into use in May 1948. The latest Hansons coaches, two Maudslays on the left and five Bedford OBs (centre and right) are in the care of immaculately turned out drivers. The building to the right was the head office of the Corporation's Passenger Transport Department until 1973. [P.J. Cardno collection]

ally arranging overnight accommodation for the party at the Oldham hospital. On the following morning the 17 mile journey to Huddersfield took four hours and in places flood water from the melting snow came into the driver's cab.

An air pageant at Squires Gate Airport during July was an added attraction for day trippers to Blackpool. The latest civilian and RAF aircraft and equipment were on display as well as captured German fighters and "V" weapons. On certain days flying displays featured fighters and bombers of both the RAF and the Royal Navy.

On Sunday 12 October 1947 over 200 drivers and other members of the Hansons haulage and passenger transport staff were taken by coach on a day's outing to Blackpool in recognition of an excellent year's trading. These drivers had carried over 5 million passengers and 200,000 tons of merchandise throughout the length and breadth of the country. Some members of this party had been present on a trip almost 26 years earlier when Hanson charabancs had taken local chara drivers on an excursion to Blackpool. It has been claimed that this was the origin of the phrase "a busman's holiday". There were still no illuminations at Blackpool owing to the electricity shortage but excursions to Blackpool and the other resorts continued on Sundays and Wednesdays until the end of October.

By the end of February 1948 there was still no petrol allowance for "pleasure" for private motorists and it was anticipated that the Minister for Fuel and Power, Hugh Gaitskell, would make an allowance for 90 miles per month only from June at the earliest. Thus when Han-

sons announced that they would start booking for excursions and summer holiday period returns on 28 February 1948 it was hardly surprising that on a cold foggy morning a queue formed at 6.30am outside the John William Street booking office. When the doors opened, six clerks were on duty and two policemen had arrived to regulate the queue. Thousands of tickets were sold and, because of the 12½% cut in fuel supply, it was learned that there would be no coaches available for private hire at Easter. As from Saturday 22 May all advertised excursions

departed from the new Upperhead Row coach park, on ground adjacent to the bus stations still under construction, but the Blackpool express service coaches continued to start from Springwood Street.

Sunday day trips tended to depart at either 8.00 or 8.30am which made it rather difficult for many would be trippers to catch a trolleybus to Town. An innovation in the June Travel Bulletin was the printing of times of connecting trolleys from outlying districts. The list was incomplete, giving the false impression that there was no

This Hansons Bedford OB/Plaxton, 224 (DCX 627), was new in July 1947 but passed to EB Broadbent of Penistone as early as August 1948. Many OBs spent only a short period in the fleet and some were sold for more than their original purchase price. [R. Marshall]

1948 AEC Regal III/Duple coach 243 (DVH 311) is seen here in its original half-cab form. This was one of the vehicles later rebuilt by Plaxton with a full front to make it look more modern, when it became 322. A more drastic change of identity occurred in 1957 when its chassis formed the basis of double deck rebuild 350.
[P.J. Cardno collection]

Maudslay Marathon 3 248 (DVH 682) was new in June 1948 and is seen parked in Scarborough, appropriately for a coach bodied in the resort by Plaxtons. Note the pre-1952 Hansons livery incorporating white relief. 248 was withdrawn at the end of the 1950 season.
[W.J. Haynes]

This full width front on Hansons AEC Regal III/Duple coach 295 (EVH 805), new in May 1950, retains the exposed radiator and as a result fails to make the coach look much more modern than an ordinary half-cab. In 1961 the chassis was reconstituted as part of double deck rebuild 361.
[Omnibus Society/S.N.J. White]

bus from Outlane, and also served to emphasise that there were no suitable early buses from Fixby, Lindley, Sheepridge or Woodhouse. This idea was not repeated.

A new licence had been obtained for an express service to Llandudno for the 1948 summer season. This was for one coach only to operate on Saturdays but picking up points were sanctioned along the Oldham bus route as far as Uppermill and passengers could book to the holiday resorts of Rhyl, Abergele, Colwyn Bay, Rhos on Sea and Llandudno.

For the Engineers holidays in July 1948 each day a full programme of excursions was offered, varying in length from Ilkley & Bolton Woods to Gretna Green and the coaches were filled to capacity. In contrast British Railways cancelled advertised trains from Huddersfield to Belle Vue and Blackpool owing to lack of advance bookings, claiming that so many people had left the town for a week's holiday that day excursions were superfluous. The Hansons traffic manager, Frank Brook Dyson, made the most of this, saying that on each of the first three days of the holiday they had operated 40 coaches carrying a total of 3,600 passengers. In his words the shortage was of fuel and not of passengers. He claimed that passengers had deserted the postwar railways in favour of road transport which was cheaper, more comfortable and above all guaranteed a seat. The Holidays with Pay Act was passed in 1948 which guaranteed all workers two weeks paid annual holiday; this in itself was bound to create a greater demand for transport.

From early summer 1949 Hansons certainly stepped up their newspaper advertising with a series of "your pleasure pin ups" aimed largely at the holiday weeks. Full page length advertisements three columns wide exhorted patrons to book early in order to "travel the highway the Hanson way". From the start of the rugby football season advertisements aimed at private party organisers actually included a booking form. It was suggested that, as it cost no more for "door to door" travel, organisers might like to hire a private coach for all 17 away matches en bloc. Hansons of course provided the official Fartown team coach which carried a headboard in the club's familiar claret and gold colours. The famous Blackpool illuminations were switched on for the first time after the war in September 1949 and no doubt this was welcomed by all Huddersfield coach operators. The Tower alone was bedecked with 10,000 bulbs and a further 300,000 bulbs shone over six miles of the promenade.

Immediately after the war most of the new coaches obtained by Hansons (from June 1946 onwards) were the

In 1949 Hansons AEC Regal/Burlingham 112 (AVH 902), new in March 1938, was fitted with this new Duple dual purpose body and renumbered 283.
[Omnibus Society/S.N.J. White]

small 29 seater Bedford OBs. During the period 1947-50 Hansons purchased no fewer than 35 of these. Bodies were supplied by Duple, Plaxton and SMT as shown below.

	Duple	Plaxton	SMT	Total
1947	2	9	2	13
1948	6	3	0	9
1949	7	1	0	8
1950	5	0	0	5

At first it was the policy to run these coaches for only two summer seasons. Then, fitted with a new or reconditioned engine, they were readily snapped up on the secondhand market because of the good reputation Hansons enjoyed within the industry. With rising prices the two year old vehicles were actually sold at a profit and Robert Hanson probably got preferential treatment when it came to delivery of the next batch of replacement vehicles. The vehicles delivered from 1949 onwards tended to operate for three or four seasons before disposal. Larger Maudslay Marathon and AEC Regal III coaches were also obtained.

During 1950 the business of Hanson Travel Services Ltd was started as a booking agency for travel by land, sea and air. Private hire was encouraged with the inducement of concessions in ticket prices for parties of 25 or more for such events as the Bertram Mills circus which had its winter home at Olympia, London. It was even claimed in advertisements that German, Latvian and Russian were spoken at the friendly travel bureau – a point aimed at the many eastern European refugees who had settled in the Huddersfield district after the war.

When the coaches were already fully booked for Easter, a fire gutted the main stand at the Leeds Road home of Huddersfield Town football club, which resulted in two home games at Easter having to be played at Elland Road, Leeds. Hansons were unable to provide coaches for the Saturday match but they succeeded in hiring coaches from other operators for Easter Tuesday. Bad weather also eased the situation on the Tuesday as fewer coaches than anticipated were required for half day trips.

Some unwelcome publicity resulted when the manager of Hanson's Buses, Frank Brook Dyson, appeared before the Borough Court on 27 September 1950. He pleaded not guilty to a charge of driving a motor car in a manner dangerous to the public but was fined £3 plus costs for driving without due care and attention. He admitted that in his position he ought to have set a good example to other drivers.

During 1950 Hansons recorded a considerable decline in the demand for pleasure travel, partly owing to increases in the cost of living and growing competition from other coach operators in the town. The coaches travelled 5,980 more miles than in the previous year yet earned £6,650 less revenue. As a result the size of the coach fleet was reduced from 40 to 27 for the 1951 season. A major attraction for that year was the Festival of Britain exhibition which opened at the South Bank, London in May. This featured among other things a (successful) Dome of Discovery and a Telekinema; over 90,000 visitors a day were attracted at Whitsuntide. How many came from Huddersfield is unknown but Hansons advertised their private hire coaches from as early as January; they did not, however, operate any public excursions. Many rail excursions in this period were cancelled owing to a coal shortage. Nearer home, half day trips ran in June and July to the Festival of Britain travelling exhibition staged at Woodhouse Moor, Leeds and to the Festival ship Campania docked at Hull. Also spidermen were putting the finishing touches to the 750 feet high television mast up on the moors at Holme Moss. With transmissions due to start in July, moorland evening drives to the site were very popular.

7: POSTWAR BUS SERVICE DEVELOPMENTS (1945-1956)

After the end of the war until all the men had returned from the forces, staff shortages continued to be a problem and on some mornings in 1945 there were only 12 conductors available for 19 buses. By mid 1946 further restoration of fuel supplies allowed the bus services to be operated at their prewar frequencies and from 28 July 1946 Hansons buses were to be seen alongside those of the JOC for the first time at the moorland terminus of Nont Sarah's on an extension of the Scapegoat Hill routes via Round Ings Road and Pole Moor. This was still a popular destination for many local families and on summer Saturday and Sunday afternoons buses left Huddersfield at half hourly intervals from 1.00pm until 9.00pm, travelling alternately via Paddock Head/Scar Lane and Manchester Road/Leymoor. A generous eighteen minutes layover was allowed at Nont's and the round trip of two hours required four vehicles shared between the two operators. In the winter months a two hourly service requiring one bus operated via Paddock Head/Scar Lane.

In August 1946 some journeys on the Weatherhill service were extended 0.75 miles along the full length of Weatherhill Road to its junction with Lindley Moor Road; Huddersfield JOC had objected to this but without success. As three extra minutes of running time were needed in both directions the round trip could no longer be completed in 30 minutes. To allow the service to continue to be maintained by one bus, the basic frequency was therefore reduced to 45 minutes. On Monday to Friday 12 out of the 23 trips went through to the new terminus. On Saturdays this increased to 18 and on Sundays the whole service ran to Lindley Moor Road.

Robert Hanson noted that, by the end of 1946, out of the seven periods of reckoning for the coordination agreement, Hansons had made a balancing payment to the JOC on six occasions. He pointed out that when the original agreement had been drawn up Hansons had been using a mix of 26, 29 and 32 seater buses whereas now they were using 34 and 35 seaters compared with the 32 seaters of the JOC. He argued that, as his buses were now carrying more passengers, he was entitled to a higher percentage of the total receipts. While the analysis of the statistics by Muscroft, the JOC manager, supported this view the matter remained unresolved for almost another three years.

North Western route 160 (Oldham via Delph), which had been withdrawn as a result of the war, was finally reinstated on 2 August 1947 It used its prewar stand in Market Streat, now shared with the Hansons Oldham service as well as Meltham via Helme. There was no interavailability of return tickets on the two operators' Oldham services but in later years as soon as North Western were granted a fares increase Hansons would follow suit. At some date before November 1944 the minimum fare out of Huddersfield had been reduced from 9d to 6d but by May 1949 it had risen to 8d.

Over the years Hansons became well known for their rebuilding and rebodying work. Much of this was due to the expertise of their chief engineer, Jim Holmes, and his band of workers. This practice saved a considerable amount of money and in some cases gave the fleet a more up to date image. One new engine was always kept in stock to facilitate rebuilding.

The batch of four AEC Regals bought in 1938 (110-3) and bodied by Burlingham (bus) or Plaxton (coach) were found to be very prone to leaking in bad weather and between 1947 and 1949 three of them were rebodied by Duple as dual purpose (semi-coach) vehicles. The remaining bus (110) was rebuilt by Jennings of Sandbach as a horsebox for Robert Hanson. 111-3 retained their original registrations but received new fleet numbers 244/283-4 and gave several more years service.

On 12 January 1948, at the age of only 50, company

[Above] When Hansons started to use the new Huddersfield bus stations in July 1948, some services, including Oldham and Meltham via Helme, initially used Manchester Street Bus Station to the east of Upperhead Row. There the photographer has captured rather basic Pickering bodied Albion CX13 199 (CVH 229) which had been new in June 1946. Its destination display is also rudimentary, probably owing to shortage of linen for blinds. 199 worked for Hansons only until 1950 when the complete batch was sold to Birkenshaw Mills near Birstall for use as works buses. [P.J. Cardno collection]

[Below] Hansons Duple bodied Bedford OB coach 266 (ECX 80) was new in December 1948. Here it was working as a one man operated bus on the recently introduced Blackmoorfoot via Hoylehouse route in this Manchester Street Bus Station scene captured before 17 January 1949 when the Hansons routes were transferred to their more familiar termini in Upperhead Row Bus Station on the other (west) side of Upperhead Row. [S.T. Harling collection]

secretary Ernest Thorpe Moorhouse died at his home in Luck Lane, Paddock. Joining Hansons in 1922 he became secretary and later a director of Hanson's Buses Ltd, The Queens Carriage Co. Ltd and other companies under the Hanson umbrella. There was a large attendance of friends and business representatives at the funeral service at Lawnswood, Leeds including Donald and James Hanson (Robert Hanson's son, the future Lord Hanson), Guy Levison and Harry Kemp (of Huddersfield Corporation/JOC). The bearers included three long serving drivers, J Baxter, F Brook and T Squires.

During this period the average weekly wage for a conductor was about £5 10s and the temptation to supplement this proved too much for a Milnsbridge man. On 5 April 1948 he was conducting on a duplicate bus returning from Oldham which stopped at the Coach and Horses on Standedge to pick up a man and his wife. Unknown to the conductor, the man was a retired police inspector. The fare to Huddersfield was 8d so a half crown was offered for the two of them; whilst the correct change was given, no tickets were issued nor was an entry to that effect made on the waybill. The retired policeman reported the incident but this was not an isolated case as on another occasion the same conductor had been reported for receiving four 4d fares without issuing tickets. Previously of good character and having served on the Russian convoys during the war, he was lucky to escape a prison sentence. Having already lost his job, he was fined £5 for each offence by the Huddersfield Bench.

Another conductor, this time from Golcar, was dismissed at the end of August and also made an appearance before the magistrates but for a rather different offence. He was the conductor on a bus driven by a Mr N Kelly which arrived at Golcar at 10.00pm on 28 August. Kelly parked the bus for its 10 minutes layover and walked away. The conductor, who had no driving licence and little skill either, decided to drive the bus and after about 20 yards crashed into the outhouses of 216 and 218 Town End. Both outhouses were demolished and the bus was embedded in the debris. For driving without due care and attention without either licence or insurance he was fined £5 and disqualified from holding a licence for a year.

Meanwhile from 19 July 1948 some Hansons routes had started using the new Manchester Street bus station on the east side of Upperhead Row. From 17 January 1949 all Hansons services entering the town centre (except Weatherhill/Lindley Moor Road which stayed in Byram Street) moved into the newly opened original Up-

perhead Row bus station on the west side of Upperhead Row; these arrangements replaced the street stands in Springwood Street, Macaulay Street and Market Street.

The long distance haulage side of the business was nationalised from 1 August 1948 and from that date the remaining goods vehicles moved from Savile Street, Milnsbridge (taken over on nationalisation) to a new depot at Woodlands Road off Leeds Road. At the same time the bus fleet moved to a new garage, formerly the jam factory of Wallaces (grocers), in St John's Road, Huddersfield.

On Sunday 29 August 1948 at 1.50pm a new hourly service was started from Town via Manchester Road, Hoylehouse, Chapel Hill and Upper Clough Road. to Blackmoorfoot. The running time was 22 minutes with a layover of 8 minutes so only one vehicle was required. Officially a joint service and part of the Colne Valley pool (JOC route 56) it was initially operated by a Hansons vehicle, with the JOC operating extra mileage on the Golcar routes to compensate. The single decker used was often a 29 seater Bedford OB coach operated by the driver only. At this date the JOC had no vehicles suitable for one man operation and that is probably why Hansons operated the service at first. Some Bedford OBs, including 268 and 277, were later downseated to 26 seats to make them more suitable for one man operation.

Hansons' only utility double decker (Guy Arab 183) could easily have been written off in an accident on 25 September 1948 when driver Fred Chappell of Marsh was returning from Oldham on the 11.55am service with a standing load of passengers. Near the Coach and Horses he noticed a lorry and trailer coming up the hill in the opposite direction and suddenly a coach pulled out to try to overtake. Realising that there was insufficient room for three vehicles abreast, he flashed his lights at the coach driver but to no avail so, to avoid a head on collision, Chappell drove his bus off the road. The bus finished up tilted at an acute angle precariously overhanging the rough steep gorse covered land beyond the A62 but fortunately did not overturn. Realising that they had at least been saved from serious injury by his skill, the passengers organised a collection on the spot for Mr Chappell. The driver of the oncoming coach was successfully prosecuted for dangerous driving.

The minimum protective fare out of Town over trolleybus routes was increased from 2½d to 3d on 29 July 1949.

The first postwar double deck buses were delivered in 1949 to replace the prewar Leyland Titans. These were

285-7, AEC Regent IIIs with Roe H31/25R bodies used on the Hill Top/Wilberlee and Oldham routes and later on Meltham. The only other double decker left in service was the Guy Arab 183 mentioned above which one of the authors remembers still putting in sterling performances climbing over the Pennines to and from Oldham as a duplicate. It was scrapped without replacement in 1955, doubtless due to the deterioration of inferior wartime materials.

Analysis of traffic statistics may be tedious to those doing it for a living; for the transport historian it may reveal interesting points. The following data refer to a particular week in January for the period 1945-49. They cover only the Hansons input to the joint services; the JOC obtained separate data.

Hill Top/Wilberlee

Year	Passengers	Miles run	Revenue (£-s-d)	d/mile	Av. fare
1945	6020	1370	65-7-10	11.4	2.6d
1946	7714	1470	85-13-9	14.0	2.7d
1947	8171	1551	93-12-2	14.5	2.75d
1948	8707	1552	100-14-7	15.6	2.8d
1949	8578	1572	96-14-3	14.8	2.7d

Crimble via Wellhouse

Year	Passengers	Miles run	Revenue (£-s-d)	d/mile	Av. fare
1945	8921	1204	76-6-7	15.2	2.05d
1946	9177	1216	81-9-7	16.1	2.1d
1947	8936	1307	79-3-9	14.5	2.1d
1948	9778	1300	87-6-3	16.1	2.1d
1949	10621	1430	95-13-5	16.1	2.2d

Golcar and Scapegoat Hill

Year	Passengers	Miles run	Revenue (£-s-d)	d/mile	Av. fare
1945	15779	2165	143-8-5	15.9	2.2d
1946	16408	2280	152-19-6	16.1	2.2d
1947	18479	2685	176-3-9	15.7	2.3d
1948	18883	2630	171-15-0	15.7	2.2d
1949	15739	2179	148-15-7	16.3	2.3d

It will be observed that:

(1) The number of miles operated on all routes increased after easing of wartime fuel restrictions.

(2) The number of passengers carried also increased as life returned to normal after the war and people were able to travel for pleasure again.

(3) The increased revenue was not obtained from fares increases, as would be the case in later years.

(4) The average fare paid is notably higher on the Hill Top route, probably owing to the protective fares discouraging short journeys which applied over a greater proportion of the route.

(5) The mileage operated on the Golcar route for the week in January 1949 seems to be particularly low. This

[Above] Brush bodied AEC Regal 231 (DCX 448), new in July 1947, is seen in Upperhead Row Bus Station. It was sold to the Bertram Mills circus in 1954.
[R. Marshall collection]

[Above] 1947 Burlingham bodied Albion CX13 235 (DCX 885) is about to leave Upperhead Row Bus Station for Linthwaite Church, for many years just a short working of the Meltham via Helme service but in 1924 one of the first two Hansons bus routes from Huddersfield. [P.J. Cardno collection]

[Below] Three Roe bodied AEC Regent IIIs which came to Hansons in June 1949 were the company's only new postwar double deckers. [Seven AEC rebuilds appeared in later years and some Daimler Fleetlines are believed to have been on order at the time of the sale of the buses to Huddersfield Corporation.] 285 (ECX 414) is resplendent in original condition in Upperhead Row Bus Station. [W.J. Haynes]

[Below] Hansons Albion CX13/Burlingham 236 (DCX 886), new in October 1947 and used until 1958, is about to return from Weatherhill to Byram Street. [R. Marshall]

The one man operated Blackmoorfoot route had moved into Upperhead Row Bus Station by the time it was being worked by Hansons Bedford OB/Duple coach 273 (ECX 599), new in June 1949 and withdrawn in 1954.
[R. Marshall collection]

1950 AEC Regal III/Duple bus 290 (EVH 84) had been repainted in unrelieved red by the time it was photographed about to turn from Swallow Street into Upperhead Row en route to Golcar via Greenhead Road, Paddock Head and Scar Lane. Among the last of the traditional front engined half-cab single deckers to enter service with Hansons, 290 passed to the Duke of Wellington's Regiment, Catterick at the end of January 1963 for the transporting of bandsmen and sports teams.
[P. Yeomans]

The four AEC Regal IV/Roe saloons were used on both bus and coach duties. 302 (FVH 358) has nearly completed the "round the houses" terminal loop at Lindley and is about to turn from Thomas Street back into Lidget Street before returning on the inter-suburban route to Newsome via Reinwood Road. New in February 1952, 302 was scrapped in 1965.
[S.T. Harling collection]

may have been in order to balance the mileage worked by Hansons on the new Blackmoorfoot route on which the JOC did not operate at that time. No doubt the JOC figures for the same week would have shown a corresponding increase in both miles run and passengers carried.

Statistics are available for the Blackmoorfoot route for the first two weeks of March 1949:

Passengers	Miles run	Revenue	d/mile	Av. fare
3305	960	39-1-7	9.77	2.84d
3156	960	37-13-4	9.37	2.86d

As 105 return trips were worked per week the average number of passengers per trip can be shown to be only fifteen, making the route a suitable candidate for one man operation from the beginning.

At last on 17 September 1949 it was agreed to amend the percentages in the coordination agreement. Hansons were to receive 41.515% of the total receipts backdated to 1 July 1947, which resulted in them receiving a cumulative balancing payment from the JOC of £1,030. This amended agreement was to last a further ten years.

In 1944 Robert Hanson had suggested to the JOC that it would be useful to the travelling public to link the Meltham services of each operator (via Helme and via Netherton) to form a circular service, as requested by the local authorities ten years earlier; this would also have alleviated "traffic congestion" in Meltham Market Place caused by buses turning round. Without giving reasons, the JOC could not agree. The matter resurfaced in early 1950 and this time the JOC manager put forward the following reasons for opposing the proposal:
(1) The Hansons service was operated by single deck buses whereas the JOC used double deckers (soon afterwards Hansons also began to use double deckers).
(2) No public demand for linking the services.
(3) The sphere of Hansons operations would be extended.
(4) Congestion in Meltham Market Place could be alleviated by other means.
Surprisingly the manager failed to mention the small matter of the incompatible frequencies on the two routes for most of the day.

From 27 December 1950 Hill Top journeys were extended from Royd Street (junction with Hawthorne Road) in a loop, outwards via Longlands Avenue and returning via Longlands Road.

From the early 1950s it was becoming increasingly uneconomic to run single deck buses on the Hansons routes with a crew of two. Deficits on the stage carriage side of the business for the years ending March 1949 and 1950 were reported as £6,300 and £9,363 respectively. In August 1951 fares up to 4d were increased by ¹/₂d and those above by 1d after the traffic commissioners granted only part of the requested increase. New buses suitable for one man operation were expensive but in 1952 four AEC Regal IVs with DP41F bodies by Roe (301-4) were purchased. The underfloor engines in these heavy vehicles proved very thirsty on the hilly routes and gave only about five miles to the gallon of fuel. Because of this and their semi-coach bodywork they were used as much as possible on the Blackpool service. 301-4 introduced a simplified livery of all over red (dispensing with the white relief), which was subsequently adopted for the entire Hansons bus and coach fleet. In 1954 a further three underfloor engined buses (333-5) joined the fleet; these were lighter vehicles, AEC Reliances with Roe DP41F bodies.

From 7 March 1954 the joint routes to Crimble via Scar Lane were extended from Radcliffe Road via Carr Lane and Cross Street to New Street, Slaithwaite. From 5 November 1954 the Blackmoorfoot route was modified to serve Causeway Side and Waingate.

In thick fog and icy road conditions two AEC Regals operating school specials were involved in a head on collision in West Street, Lindley on the morning of 3 March 1955. Driver William Cave of Ashenhurst was travelling towards Lindley when his bus skidded and crashed into the front of a bus being driven to the annexe of Oakes Secondary School in Crosland Road by Gordon Baxter of Golcar. It took several minutes to extricate Baxter from his crushed cab and oxyacetylene equipment was required to cut away some of the cab structure before the buses could be separated. Nine ambulances raced to the scene but fortunately only nine of the seventy children needed hospital treatment.

On 11 January 1956 Colne Valley High School, an early West Riding County Council comprehensive school at Linthwaite, opened and Hansons started to operate school buses from Bolster Moor via Golcar and Milnsbridge and from Hill Top via Slaithwaite. A twelve bay bus park was provided inside the school grounds at a cost of £3,561. In August, despite objections from Hansons, the traffic commissioners also granted a licence to Stanley Baxter and George Pennington, trading as Star Coaches of Slaithwaite, to operate school buses from Hill Top to the high school. Other buses to the school were operated by Baddeleys.

[Top] AEC Regal IV/Roe 304 (FVH 360) differs in appearance from 302 in several interesting details. It is waiting on the Weatherhill/Lindley Moor Road stand in Byram Street (between the St Peter's Street and Northumberland Street junctions) which was shared with the West Riding (formerly B & S) Blackpool express service. The bus would soon go past the depot in St John's Road and later in Birkby Road would pass very close to the Hanson family mansion, Norwood Grange.
[P.J. Cardno collection]

[Centre] Barnaby bodied Maudslay Marathon 2 coach GWU 624 had been supplied new to Scott of Mytholmroyd in 1948 but almost immediately passed to Marsh, Huddersfield based Bottomleys. After Bottomleys were taken over GWU 624 was transferred to Hansons in June 1951 and numbered 305. Here it still carries its original Barnaby body and is awaiting departure from Upperhead Row Bus Station for Meltham via Helme.
[S.T. Harling collection]

[Bottom] In 1955 Maudslay 305 (GWU 624) was rebodied with this 1949 Duple 35 seat body taken from prewar AEC Regal 284 (AVH 903). 305 was then, as here, used as a one man bus on the Blackmoorfoot route, which was technically joint with Huddersfield JOC but until 1957 in practice 100% Hansons. The route number 56 shown on the bus stop sign was allocated by the JOC; Hansons never used route numbers. 305 was dismantled in 1960. [R. Marshall]

With the shelters of Manchester Street Bus Station in the background, Albion CX13/Burlingham 235 (DCX 885) is turning from Upperhead Row into the bus station of that name to work a journey to Nont Sarah's, the Scammonden moorland inn. Hansons buses ran to Nont Sarah's only between 1946 and January 1959, when the Scapegoat Hill to Nont Sarah's section was replaced by connections on diverted JOC route 55. 235 has been repainted in unrelieved red and fitted with a shallow destination indicator box in this mid 1950s view. [Photobus]

Three Roe bodied AEC Reliances with dual purpose seating were new in June 1954. 334 (HVH 210) is parked on the Oldham stand in Upperhead Row Bus Station. It was scrapped in 1967. [Photobus]

8: BOB HANSON'S BUYING SPREE: COACHING EXPANSION (1951-1959)

Throughout the 1950s there were many developments on the coaching side of the business aimed at improving profitability. Fares were increased, competitors were acquired and excursion licence applications were regularly made for new destinations.

The name Bottomley had long been associated with coaches in Huddersfield. In 1876 Eleanor Bottomley advertised the Kirkgate Carriage Works, Huddersfield, where carriages were designed and constructed. This coachbuilding business was noted for its angular dog cart and was also inventor and patentee of the Pentagon brougham. The premises, on the south side of Kirkgate above the Rose and Crown, were demolished in 1884 but appropriately enough a new thoroughfare, Venn Street, for many years used by long distance coaches, was later opened through the site.

In 1890 a John Bottomley of Longwood Gate was known to be a taxi-cab proprietor; by 1909 he was listed as a general carrier and by 1924 John W Bot-

tomley and Son were running a business from Thornton Lodge Road. During 1928 at the latest, JW Bottomley of Thornton Lodge began operating his "Princess" coach. By August of that year he was advertising excursions in a Lancia coach (and probably two others) which could be booked at the Luck Lane (Marsh) garage or at Longleys (confectioners) in John William Street. For the 1930 August holiday week two excursions were offered daily, including the long trip to Windermere. The name of the business was changed in 1931 to JW Bottomley and Son of Providence Garage, Luck Lane, Marsh. It was purchased by Hansons in 1951 and renamed as Bottomley's Motors (1951) Limited, which was then operated as a subsidiary company until 1962.

Immediately following a visit to the Luck Lane garage on 30 September 1951 Donald Hanson, brother of head of the firm Robert Hanson, collapsed and died. Donald, who by this time was no longer an active member of the firm, had recently won many trophies with his shire gelding Grand Duke, named after the 7th Duke of Wellington's Regiment in which Donald had been a captain in the First World War.

The Bottomley livery was two tone blue and fleet numbers were not used. One interesting vehicle immediately transferred into the Hansons fleet was GWU 624, a Maudslay Marathon 2 with a C33F Barnaby body new to Scott of Mytholmroyd in 1948. It was later fitted with a Duple body from a Hansons AEC Regal and used as a one man bus. At the time of the takeover there were six vehicles in the Bottomley fleet, five of which had been owned from new. By 1955 these had been replaced. Under Hansons ownership, as might have been expected,

vehicle replacement policy followed the practice of the parent company. Eleven new coaches were purchased for the Bottomley fleet during the period 1952-61. Six vehicles were transferred unnumbered to the main Hansons fleet in January 1962. Some still wore a blue livery but all were disposed of by 1968. New coaches continued, however, to be delivered in blue with Bottomley fleetname until 1973.

The Bottomley excursion licences were for a maximum of two coaches daily, except for Easter and the July/August holiday period when this was increased to three. Probably more important was the aggregate of 12 coaches permitted for the period return holiday traffic to Blackpool, Bridlington and Scarborough with the proviso that a maximum of six coaches could operate to any one resort. All these licences passed to the parent company in 1962.

Wombwell Lane, Stairfoot was the scene of a spectacular multiple pile up in fog early on the morning of 28 February 1952. It started with a van driver stopping to clean his windows; in quick succession a Yorkshire Traction single deck bus crashed into the back of the van and coaches of Burrows of Wombwell and Wallace Arnold ploughed into the rear. A car, a motor cycle and a Yorkshire Traction double decker full of schoolchildren became involved before a Hansons coach transporting mill girls to Huddersfield approached the scene. Fortunately driver Kenneth Ramsey of Birchencliffe, not thinking of his own life, avoided the pile up only by driving his coach into a house wall. The door of the house was ripped off and many bricks were dislodged, much to the amazement of those inside, but none of the coach passengers were seriously hurt. Ramsey was later chief driving instructor for the Hanson School of Motoring.

Advance bookings for day trips during the 1952 summer holiday period were not particularly heavy except for the new longer distance excursions. During the first Engineers week the new venues of Mablethorpe and Stratford upon Avon proved popular while in the second week trippers favoured Betws y Coed and Gretna Green. In 1952 the Hansons livery was changed from red with white relief to all over red.

A much respected regular driver on the Blackpool service for over 25 years, Norman Greenwood of Fartown, collapsed and died at the wheel of his coach near Whalley at 7.30pm on 28 August 1952. His full load of passengers returning from Blackpool had a narrow escape as the coach immediately began to veer across the road; fortunately a quick thinking passenger on the front seat, Nora Bottomley of Brighouse, realised what had happened, applied the handbrake and brought the coach to a stop. The last act of the conscientious driver was to apply his feet to the clutch and brake. A relief driver was sent to the scene by car but it was midnight before the shocked passengers reached their destination. The Huddersfield Examiner published a tribute from a

Plaxton bodied Bedford SB coach 306 (FVH 21), new in August 1951, was withdrawn in 1954. Here it awaits its next duty in the parking ground by Huddersfield's bus stations. The Plaxton style of side mouldings encouraged a slightly more flamboyant interpretation of the Hansons livery. [R. Marshall collection]

310 (FVH 351) was a Duple bodied Bedford SB new in April 1952 which lasted with Hansons until 1958. Duple's side mouldings created a more restrained band of white relief. [R. Marshall]

Duple bodied AEC Regal III coach 294 (EVH 807), new in 1950, was modernised with a full front by Plaxtons and renumbered 325 in 1954. After withdrawal in 1961, the chassis metamorphosed into double deck rebuild 370 in 1962. [S.T. Harling collection]

passenger to the effect that the driver would be greatly missed for his kindness and consideration. A wreath with the simple inscription "From Grateful Passengers" was placed on the grave at Edgerton Cemetery.

In 1953 the opportunity arose to purchase the small local business of Chapman's Ivy Coaches Ltd (no connection with the firm trading as Ivy Coaches after deregulation). Ann Chapman of 73 Lowerhead Row began operating as a general carrier as early as 1909 and by 1917 George Chapman was running the business from 6 Brick Bank, Northgate, Almondbury. The trading name Ivy Coaches was adopted by Chapman in October 1932 after he had been running coaches for at least four years. A limited company was formed in October 1945 with its address at Helms Garage, Leeds Road. The town centre booking office, opened on 7 August 1945, was at the splendidly named Palace Mansions, Beast Market, the address doubtless derived from the Palace theatre around the corner in Kirkgate. Five vehicles were acquired in the Hansons takeover and the company was at first operated as a subsidiary.

Chapman had not operated any bus services but had concentrated on day excursions and private hire. An early advertisement in September 1928 invited patrons to "ride first class in the Ivy Coach saloon" to Blackpool Illuminations, departing on Wednesday, Saturday and Sunday at 1.30pm; as the coach did not set out for home until 10.00pm a promise was made to drop passengers off at the tram stop nearest to their home. For many years the Chapman's cream coaches were to be seen in St George's Square in competition with those of Hansons. One speciality was the running of theatre trips to the Sheffield Empire, where the combined cost of theatre and coach tickets was only about ten shillings. One trip no doubt popular with the men in July 1949 was to the "Folies Bergere Revue". For the ladies, Dr Crock (of Crackpots fame) was billed as "Britain's No. 1 pin up boy". Pantomime trips were of course another welcome source of revenue but every year Chapman's provided free transport to the Sheffield Empire pantomime for 130 children from the Huddersfield Corporation childrens' homes at All Saints, Almondbury and Fieldhead, Lindley. The theatre provided the matinee seats without charge. During the war the cruiser HMS Gambia had been adopted by the people of Huddersfield and after the war the crew of the Gambia collected money each year to provide a Christmas treat for children in the Corpora-

tion's care. Again the philanthropic nature of Chapman's was shown as they provided free transport to and from the chosen pantomime, often at the Dewsbury Empire.

A new company, Ivy Coaches Ltd, was formed by Hansons in August 1954 and separate advertisements continued to appear until the end of the year. This company was in turn totally absorbed by Hansons in June 1955. Shortly afterwards the former Ivy express licence to Grassington Hospital was transferred to Hansons. The Grassington coach left Huddersfield at noon every Sunday with a return fare of 7/-.

Details of the Chapman's Ivy Coaches vehicles taken over are shown in the fleet lists, including their Hansons fleet numbers allocated after the subsidiary company had been absorbed into the main fleet. By 1956 all these mostly elderly vehicles had been disposed of. Interestingly VH 9101 an AEC Regal dating from 1936 never ran for Hansons but parts of its chassis were used in the construction of double deck AEC rebuild 347 which appeared in 1956. VH 5731 an AEC Regent, had started life in 1933 as 116 in the Huddersfield JOC fleet where it had a double deck Brush body. It passed to Chapman's soon after the war where it ran for a time with the top deck removed before the new Burlingham single deck body was fitted in 1949. The only new coach purchased by Hansons for the Ivy fleet was HCX 491, a Bedford SBG with Plaxton C35F body new in January 1954 and

Hansons purchased Chapman's Ivy Coaches in 1953. This Ivy Coach insignia had been current in the early 1930s. [S.T. Harling collection]

numbered 343 after transfer to Hansons. This coach later passed to two Holmfirth operators; GW Castle acquired it in 1963 and in turn sold it to Baddeleys in 1966 where it was numbered 86.

Meanwhile the 1952/53 season had been a good one for the Fartown rugby league club, culminating in a visit to the Empire stadium for the cup final on 25 April 1953. For the many spectators wishing to make the long journey, Hansons obtained a licence for a special two day excursion to London. Departure time was either Friday midnight or 5.00am on Saturday morning with the return from London at midnight on Saturday. The team and officials, who normally travelled to away matches in a Hansons coach, had opted to travel by train. Two Hansons coaches, however, met them on their return at Wakefield Westgate station for the final stage of their journey to a triumphant civic reception at Huddersfield Town Hall, with rousing music provided by Lockwood Prize Silver Band.

Hansons coaches were again to be seen in London on 2 June 1953 for the coronation of Elizabeth II. Passengers arrived in London at about 7.00am with enough time to find a suitable position along the processional route and the return journey after an exhausting day of pageantry was overnight.

On 9 August 1953 the half-day Yorkshire Dales circular tour to Ripon and Studley Royal was uneventful until Birstall Smithies was reached on the way home. The coach, driven by George Lorimer, was in collision with a Yorkshire Woollen bus. Until four ambulances arrived, the snug at the Railway Hotel was used as a casualty station for injured 21 coach passengers.

Ivy AEC Regal coach VH 9101, driven by William

AEC Regal IV/Roe 302 (FVH 358) of 1952 carries a good load on the Huddersfield to Blackpool express service. The type of door usually found on coaches is fitted on what is essentially a bus body. [A.J. Douglas]

Part of a line up of Hansons coaches and buses in Black-pool in 1953 includes examples of the underfloor engined AEC Regal IV, AEC Regal III, Bedford OB and Bedford SB. [P.J. Cardno collection]

McAllister and taking nine ICI employees home to Oldham, was involved in a nasty accident in Manchester Road, Linthwaite at 10.00pm on 19 June 1954. In overtaking three parked cars, the driver misjudged the width of his coach and managed to hit the rear two cars. Even though he was travelling at less than 30mph, the force of the impact with the rear car set it on fire, trapping a lady inside who unfortunately died from extensive burns. After braking to a stop McAllister found that the flames had spread to the back of the coach and he had no fire extinguisher on board, as was legally required. The coach was so badly damaged that it was later stripped for spares.

On 2 December 1952 Star Coaches of Slaithwaite, an established booking agent for Schofields of Marsden, applied for licences to operate a batch of eight excursions starting from Slaithwaite. Taxi operators since 1938, they had only one coach but were prepared to buy another if the licences were granted. The proposed facilities would have allowed Slaithwaite people to have made "spur of the moment" decisions, booking on the day of the excursion when the state of the weather was known. These potential passengers had always had to book in advance with Hansons. Fearing loss of revenue, Hansons naturally opposed this application, successfully as it was rejected on 22 May 1953 and again, after an appeal, on 9 October 1953. Hansons also applied to the traffic commissioners for a series of new picking up and starting points, mainly in the Colne Valley. Eventually

in March 1954 Hansons were granted licences for these locations (Marsden, Wilberlee, Linthwaite, Slaithwaite and Outlane); coaches starting at Outlane were allowed to pick up at Bolster Moor and Golcar.

By 1953 some half cab coaches were thought to be outdated in appearance so the bulkheads of AEC Regals 243/5/6 were removed and they were rebuilt by Plaxton with full fronts (FC33F). They were renumbered 322-4 and survived in this form until 1956-9. 322/3 were destined to undergo a much more remarkable metamorphosis at a later date. The conversion to full fronts obviously had the desired effect of convincing passengers that they were riding in new vehicles for in 1954 a further batch of six 1950 AEC Regal III coaches (294-9) were similarly treated by Plaxton and renumbered 325-30. These too were to be more extensively rebuilt at a later date.

The resorts of Paignton and Torquay with their mild climates had always attracted holidaymakers from the West Riding but travel by train was expensive and there were no direct coach facilities from Huddersfield. From the early 1950s Hansons had acted as agents for Yelloway Motor Services of Rochdale and on summer Friday evenings duplicates on the Hansons Oldham bus

route connected with Yelloway coaches at Oldham. This arrangement was clearly more beneficial to Yelloway than to Hansons and in February 1954 a joint application was made by Hansons and Wallace Arnold Tours to the Yorkshire Traffic Commissioners for summer Saturday express service licences from Bradford, Leeds, Halifax and Huddersfield to Paignton. In the face of considerable opposition this application was withdrawn a month later.

On the evening of 19 June 1954 AEC Regal/Burlingham VH 9101, new in 1936 to Chapman's Ivy Coaches but by then running for the Hansons owned Ivy company, was in use as an ICI staff bus. In Manchester Road, Linthwaite it collided with some parked cars; it had to be scrapped and used for spares. [Kirklees Image Archive Ke24700]

KIA MOTOR ORA
SERVICES
MORECAMBE.

Every Saturday and Sunday, return any Friday or Saturday.

Hansons AEC Regal IV/Roe 304 (FVH 360) is on hire to West Yorkshire Road Car at Chester Street Bus Station, Bradford, in the mid 1950s. The "Morecambe" sticker in the windscreen is superfluous. The place appeared on their own destination blinds as Hansons themselves ran a Huddersfield to Morecambe express from 1954 onwards in partial replacement for the old Kia Ora route. [Photobus]

The origins of Kia Ora Motor Services, the Morecambe family transport business, date back to 1921 and for many years the proprietress was Lavinia Sutcliffe. A summer Saturday weekly service from Huddersfield to Morecambe started at Whitsuntide 1928. As traditionally many Bradford folk took their annual holidays at Morecambe it was not surprising that the route from Huddersfield ran via Brighouse, Elland and Halifax to Bradford, continuing via Shipley,

One of the coach firms competing on a small scale with Hansons in Huddersfield was Haighs Tours Ltd of Bulay Road, off Springdale Avenue, Longroyd Bridge. GCX 595, a Karrier (32A1240) coach with Churchill bodywork and seating 14, displays the Haighs name in the glass above the windscreen but was actually new in January 1953 to Hilditch Taxis, an associated business under common ownership and sharing the Bulay Road address. Sadly Karrier's manufacturing of buses in Huddersfield had been moved away from the town nearly 20 years before GCX 595 took to the road. [R.H.G. Simpson]

Bingley and Lancaster to Morecambe. The departure point in Huddersfield was the Progress Motor Station in Venn Street, where advance bookings could be made; the fare was 7/- single or 10/6d for a period return. By the early 1930s the service level was doubled, with passengers able to travel outwards on Saturdays and Sundays, returning on Friday or Saturday. Kia Ora also offered eight day tours to Scotland and the Lake District for 43/6d, using accommodation in Morecambe. Suspended for the duration of the war, the Morecambe express service resumed as soon as possible afterwards and generally operated from Easter to the end of October.

In 1954 the licence for the Morecambe-Yorkshire service was acquired jointly by Hansons and Wallace Arnold. A new company, Kia Ora (Yorkshire) Ltd, was set up jointly by the two operators but no coaches were involved. It was agreed that the Bradford traffic would be handled by Wallace Arnold, leaving the Huddersfield passengers for Hansons.

An express licence for summer weekends only to the popular holiday resort of Great Yarmouth was granted to Hansons just in time for the 1954 August holidays. Outward travel was on Friday evenings with the return journey on Saturdays. The first coach left Huddersfield at 10.30pm on Friday 30 July 1954 for a return fare of 45/-. A maximum of two weekly coaches was permitted, increasing to five for the main Huddersfield holiday

AEC Reliance/Roe 335 (HVH 211), new in June 1954, is operating the Hansons Blackpool express, picking up at the stand in what was then Springwood Street, Huddersfield. Springwood Street was later bisected by Castlegate (the new ring road) and to avoid confusion this (north eastern) section was renamed Henry Street. From 1974 it has formed part of the entrance to the present bus station but buses entering the station travel in the opposite direction to HVH 211. After withdrawal in 1967, 335 was used by the Hanson School of Motoring as a driver training bus.
[P.J. Cardno collection]

Seen near Wembley, Bedford SB/Plaxton FVH 627 was new to Bottomleys in 1952. One of a pair, the first vehicles bought for the recently purchased subsidiary coaching company, it wore the earlier two-tone blue livery. Bottomleys of course now followed the Hansons vehicle purchasing policy but no fleet numbers were allocated.
[P.J. Cardno collection]

weeks. The following year (1955) the licence was modified to allow passengers to board at Wakefield and also intermediate bookings were permitted to King's Lynn, Swaffham, Norwich and Caister. Up to ten coaches could be used for the Engineers' weeks.

Further improvements followed in 1956 with the introduction of an extra journey leaving Huddersfield on the Saturday evening, together with a corresponding Sunday return. Additional pick up points were established at Mirfield and Dewsbury and duplicates on either journey were allowed to run non stop between Norwich and Great Yarmouth. On the original Friday/Saturday service a maximum of 94 journeys in each direction was permitted between May and September.

On summer Fridays and Saturdays in 1955 it was planned to convey holidaymakers from various West Riding towns to Heathrow Airport. Here they would have boarded aircraft chartered by and for the exclusive use of Hanson Travel Service to fly to Jersey. As a result of widespread opposition the scheme never got off the ground.

On Sunday 17 April 1955 the first British Coach Rally took place at Clacton with a road run starting at Aldwych in London. Hansons did not enter a coach for this 560 miles round trip but the firm of WH & F Schofield of Marsden (later taken over by Hansons) entered a Sentinel SLC6 coach with Burlingham C41C body painted in a smart red and ivory livery (OWU 771). The coach, driven by 27 year old Tony Schofield, did not win an award.

A railway strike at Whitsuntide 1955 brought unexpected business to Hansons. On the Tuesday, of the 60 coach loads of passengers returning from Blackpool, four loads consisted of passengers who had travelled outwards by train. No intending passengers were turned away and coaches were hired from various Lancashire operators.

In January 1956 Hansons made a modified application for an express licence to operate to Torquay during July and August. The outward journey was to be on Friday night with the return on Saturday, at a return fare of £3, and the route proposed was via Holmfirth, Ashbourne, Stratford-on-Avon, Bath, Wells and Glastonbury which was both scenic and avoided the more congested roads. At this time no less than ten coach firms from Yorkshire were applying for similar licences to the Devon resorts. The major objectors were British Railways and Yelloway and the traffic court hearing at Leeds lasted for 12 days. The two major issues were the question of road versus

Two AEC Reliance coaches with surprisingly modern looking centre entrance Plaxton bodywork are seen on excursion duties. The first coach was 338 (JCX 755) and had been new in March 1955. After withdrawal in 1963 it re-emerged in 1964 as Roe bodied bus BCX 487B but was scrapped three years later after being burnt out on the Oldham route. [S.T. Harling collection]

rail and, on the roads, which of the coach firms had the greater entitlement to the traffic. When the previous (1954) applications had been refused, the traffic commissioners had attached great importance to the undertakings given by Brirish Railways to improve their services from Yorkshire to Devon but no such improvements had been made. For a ten hour journey four passengers were squashed into three seats, reservations were not always honoured and it was still impossible to reserve seats at all for the homeward journey. Railway loading figures were challenged as inaccurate and there was no evidence to refute this. Mr J Evans, representing Hansons, claimed that the farcical rail facilities were unlikely to be improved without the impact of further road competition. The wrangling was, however, not yet over and it was to be 1957 before this service was able to start.

In April 1956 a new programme of "pleasant Sunday evening drives covering beauty spots and picturesque routes" was advertised with fares from 3/9d to 5/3d. The Ladybower Circular travelled outwards via Woodhead, Glossop and Snake Pass returning through "Baddeleys" country via Wharncliffe Cragg, Deepcar and Langsett. The Cunning Corner and Derby Bar drive certainly made the most of the local moorland scenery, taking in Barkisland, Rishworth and Saddleworth Moors before returning via Isle of Skye. A Tadcaster tour passed through Collingham and Boston Spa before following the river Wharfe to Thorpe Arch and Tadcaster and returning via Bramham Park. Another moorland circular again through "Baddeleys" country covered about 45 miles, passing through Ingbirchworth, Flouch, Thurlstone Moor and Dunford Bridge. The final tour in this series featured

South Yorkshire or "Yorkshire Traction" country en route to Wentworth. A visit to a suitable country hostelry would of course have been an integral part of each tour, guaranteed to put the passengers in a good mood before the hat was passed round. For the three weeks that the bulbs were at their best, special Saturday and Sunday tours were run in May to Spalding. Having paid 16/6d and departing at 7.30am, participants were treated to a scenic tour of south Lincolnshire before embarking on a 40 mile ride around the actual bulb fields.

No doubt much to the relief of management and after a hearing lasting twelve days in the Leeds traffic court, on 28 December 1956 Hansons were finally granted a licence for the operation of a summer Torquay express service from Huddersfield. They were permitted to run a maximum of five coaches for the Engineers and Textiles Workers holiday fortnights only. The outward journeys would start on Friday evenings with corresponding return on the Saturday. The return fare was only £3 compared with the £4 12s charged on the train.

In December 1956 as a result of the Suez crisis, the Minister of Fuel and Power ordered fuel consumption by express services, excursions and private hire work to be cut by 50% (to 8 April 1957). A plan to permit 75% of normal mileage after this date seems to have been shelved as the situation had eased sufficiently to end the rationing.

To give passengers a wider choice of excursion destinations for 1957 fifteen new licences

were obtained. The new tours were introduced three at a time on Sundays, starting on 12 May. The first tour combined the serenity of the Regency house at Rudding Park with commercialised Knaresborough. The second tour was to York, Buttercrambe Woods near the Derwent and the old world village of Stamford Bridge, recommended for its boating facilities. The trio was completed by an evening drive through the rural East Riding followed by a stop for refreshments at Sherburn in Elmet. Longer tours rather than trips to seaside resorts were also becoming more popular and surprisingly most were advertised under the Bottomley name. These featured Snowdonia & Caernarvon, the Wye Valley and Sandringham & Hunstanton; in the pre-motorway era they were certainly marathon excursions. Hansons introduced a Yorkshire Wolds and Flamborough Head tour in their own name covering 170 miles of scenery, outwards via Pocklington and Burton Agnes and returning via Rudston, to view the large standing stone, and Sledmere, site of the famous Wagoners' Memorial. Another new venture was to the Peak District during the gliding season, with passengers allowed access to the flying fields at Bradwell and Hucklow.

From Easter 1958 the railways intensified their competition for a share in the excursion traffic by the introduction of Day-Line Diesel tickets. Priced at 15/-, they were valid on steam and diesel trains and gave unlimited

Hansons centre entrance AEC Reliance/Plaxton coach 344 (KCX 124) displays the destination "Morecambe" in Manchester Street outside the parking ground described by Huddersfield Corporation as their coach station. It was used by all Hansons excursions and all their express services except Blackpool. 344 was new in August 1955 and became Roe bodied rebuild ECX 886C in 1965. [Photobus]

Another small coaching neighbour of Hansons in Huddersfield was Dentons Tours Ltd of Manchester Road, Longroyd Bridge. Dentons acquired FCT 260, an AEC Regal IV with Burlingham centre entrance body, from Blankley of Colsterworth, Lincolnshire, in July 1956. It is pictured here at Wembley and was still in the fleet in 1964. In that year Dentons had four full size coaches, all Commers except for FCT 260. [R.H.G. Simpson]

travel to and in three areas: (1) Harrogate, Ripon, York and Doncaster; (2) Hull, Hornsea and Withernsea; (3) Hull, Bridlington, Scarborough and York. At the same time Hansons offered three new destinations, two in Cheshire and one in Nottinghamshire. Chester Zoo was noted for the fact that the animals were kept in enclosures refecting as near to natural conditions as possible; as a further inducement, reduced admission tickets to the zoo were offered. Hazelwood Castle, also near Chester, was described as an interesting old mansion with its own private Catholic chapel dating from 1286. Reduced admission to the house was offered. The third venue was Thoresby Hall in the heart of Sherwood Forest. Here visitors had the opportunity of seeing for the

first time an internationally famous collection of walking sticks.

An innovative attempt was also made to win excursion business from Darby and Joan clubs and other senior citizens by including a free salad tea as part of a highly competitive fare on certain trips. These, priced at 10/- or under, left Huddersfield at 2.00pm on Tuesdays and Thursdays (the quieter days of the week). The first ran to Aysgarth and Wensleydale, followed a week later by the Dukeries and Sherwood Forest. The success of this venture seems to have prompted Hansons to apply to the traffic commissioners in the following year to carry pensioners at two thirds of the adult fare on selected mid-week excursions (reduced private hire rates had appar-

ently been available for pensioners for some years). The benefits of this were expected to be twofold; it would have allowed coaches to run when otherwise they would have been standing idle and also the pensioners would have enjoyed an outing which otherwise they might not have been able to afford.

In July 1958 Kenneth Smith, trading as Kenmargra [=Kenneth/Margaret/Graham], applied to the traffic commissioners for four excursion licences from Linthwaite. Smith owned two coaches and was prepared to hire additional ones as required. Strong objections were raised by Leonard Hutchinson (the Hansons traffic manager) and Ernest Ramsden (the Bottomley manager) and also by John Steel of Baddeleys. Fortunately for Hansons this threat to their Colne Valley traffic did not materialise as the application was refused.

From April 1957 Huddersfield Corporation had been threatening to make very large increases to the charges levied on users of the Upperhead Row and Manchester Street bus and coach stations. Bus departures charges were to be increased from 2d to 3½d and coach departures from 1/- to 6/-. Naturally there was considerable opposition, with Hansons accurately describing the "coach station" as only a glorified car park with no amenities for the travelling public. Hansons excursions and most of their express services used this station, with the exception of the Blackpool route which continued to pick up in Springwood Street. A Ministry of Transport inquiry took place and the decision in December 1958 went against the proposed charges. The Corporation were advised to look elsewhere to increase their revenue, possibly by franchising trading outlets.

9: REBUILD AND REBODY: THE LAST YEARS OF THE BUSES (1956-1969)

In December 1956 international politics once again caused cuts to be made in bus services. As a result of the Suez crisis the Minister of Fuel and Power required a 5% reduction in the use of diesel oil to be made by all bus operators. The "joint" service to Blackmoorfoot was withdrawn from 15 December but a petition signed by 200 Linthwaite residents for its reinstatement had some effect. Following discussions between Hansons and the traffic commissioners from 21 December a restricted Monday to Friday peak hour service was provided (four return journeys in both morning and evening peaks).

Other cuts on the joint Colne Valley Services were implemented from 27 December and they remained

Hansons had longstanding contracts, goods and passenger, with ICI. 1957 Bedford SBG/Plaxton coach 348 (MCX 386) was photographed at an event at their Leeds Road, Huddersfield works in 1964; it was withdrawn in the following year. Lord Hanson attempted to buy ICI in 1991. [S.T. Harling collection]

Hansons AEC Regent/Roe 347 was the earliest of the 1956-66 rebuilds, first appearing in this form in July 1956. Originally registered KVH 899 - but quickly changed to 889 – 347 was reconstituted from parts of two prewar AEC Regal single deckers married to a new Roe body. In this Upperhead Row Bus Station picture, 347 appears to have been rushed out of the workshops to serve Hill Top (Slaithwaite) passengers minus part of the fleetname on a repaired panel. [Photobus]

North Western Albion Aberdonian/Weymann 718A (LDB 718) enjoys a brief layover at Upperhead Row Bus Station before returning to Oldham via Delph on route 160. The A suffix signified a one man bus; these 1957 lightweight Albions were North Western's first postwar buses bought with one man operation in mind and spent much of their lives at the company's Oldham depot, together with some one man Leyland Tiger Cubs. In the 1930s North Western had sometimes used 20 seat Dennis saloons on the Huddersfield route and was the first large company operator to run one man buses in Huddersfield after the war. [P. Yeomans]

largely in force until 1 April 1957. The Slaithwaite via Wellhouse routes were cut back to the junction of Radcliffe Road and Carr Lane (the terminus until 1954) except during the off peak when they were extended from there to Hill Top, replacing the Hill Top/Wilberlee route, which was operated only in the peak periods. However, the withdrawal of 25 out of the daily 38 journeys through the centre of Slaithwaite caused such an outcry that a limited off peak service on the Hill Top route was resumed from 11 March and the corresponding diversion of the Slaithwaite via Wellhouse routes ceased. The weekend extensions from Scapegoat Hill to Nont Sarah's were also suspended. As far as services operated solely by Hansons were concerned, it is thought that no major cuts were implemented.

Under the Hydrocarbon Oil Duties Act fuel prices were increased from 1 January 1957 by $1/4^1/2$d per gallon. On the joint routes this resulted in all 3d and 5d fares being increased by 1d. On Hansons' own routes most fares were increased by $^1/2$d. In the budget of 23 April the extra fuel tax was removed and fares reverted to their former levels.

Since the financial provisions of the coordination agreement had been amended in 1949 in Hansons' favour the JOC had operated 34 seater buses and had been required to make a balancing payment to Hansons in each of the reckoning periods. Robert Hanson refused to revert to the original percentages and by the end of May

1957 the net total of balancing payments received by Hansons from the start of the scheme had reached £7,340 (under the original terms the total net payment would have been a mere £2,391). Not surprisingly at a meeting in September 1957 it was agreed that in future each party would keep their own receipts while still adhering to the original mileage proportions (Hansons 41.515%,

JOC 58.485%). From 14 October 1957 the operational arrangements for the Blackmoorfoot route were altered. Thereafter it was worked by the JOC as well as Hansons, being run entirely by each operator in turn for a 4 or 5 months period; whichever operator was not working on this route would undertake certain duties on the Hill Top/Wilberlee services in exchange.

During the period 1956-58 three "new" double deckers appeared; whether by design or coincidence is not known but they were soon required to operate the hitherto single deck joint Golcar services. All three incorporated the running units of vehicles dating from 1938 or 1948 and then rebuilt in 1949 or 1953. New H37/28R bodies were supplied by Roe and the buses were given both new registrations and new fleet numbers 347/9/50.

It was only by allocating new chassis numbers that Hansons persuaded the Huddersfield licensing authorities to give these buses new registrations. The sequence of chassis numbers started at 6666, a Hansons telephone number (6666 was actually the horsebox mentioned earlier which had been constructed from AEC Regal 110). 347 in its early days was a regular performer on the Hill Top/Wilberlee route where it recorded a very high mileage. Towards the end of its life it was sometimes used on the Saturday only "Linthwaite Church flyer". Timings were very tight as only 30 minutes were allowed for the round trip in order to provide a 15 minute frequency on the Meltham route as far as Linthwaite Church.

From 13 April 1958 the Golcar Circular was rerouted between Milnsbridge and Leymoor Road via Dale Street, Royd Street, Greenway and Sycamore Avenue; the new route served recent housing developments and avoided the "low mill" in Grove Street so double deckers could be used for the first time. The Scapegoat Hill via Leymoor route continued to serve Grove Street with single deckers and was later referred to as Scapegoat Hill "via Parkwood" although there was no route change. From 2 November 1958 the Blackmoorfoot service was rerouted to serve Yews Hill Road and Park Road West, instead of running direct along Manchester Road.

A package of economies was then introduced on the Golcar area joint services from 4 January 1959. All journeys on the Golcar Circular ran on the full circle (or "figure of eight", to be precise), with double deckers running half hourly in each direction. The Scapegoat Hill via Parkwood service was rerouted via Royd Street, Wood Street, Botham Hall Road and Benn Lane but still passed under the "low mill" in Grove Street so was still restricted to single deckers. Double deckers did, however, start to appear on the other Scapegoat Hill routes and also on the Slaithwaite services. The Golcar/Scapegoat Hill via Britannia Road route was reduced to peaks only

Pristine AEC Regent/Roe rebuild 349 (MVH 837) is about to turn left from Upperhead Row onto that bus station's Oldham stand. 349 entered service in December 1957, using running units from a 1948 single decker, AEC Regal DVH 312. [Photobus]

[Right] 1938 AEC Regal 283 (AVH 902) with 1949 Duple body had been repainted in unrelieved red and was being used as a bus (to Linthwaite Church) in this Upperhead Row Bus Station view dating from shortly before its withdrawal in 1960. Huddersfield JOC exposed radiator AEC Regent V/Roe 187 was bound for Halifax. [P.J. Cardno collection]

[Above] From April 1958 a route alteration between Milnsbridge and Leymoor permitted the use of double deckers on all the joint Golcar services. In Upperhead Row Bus Station Hansons 1949 AEC Regent III/Roe 286 (ECX 415) repainted in unrelieved red overtakes Huddersfield JOC Daimler CVG6/Willowbrook 94 (EVH 904), which had been exhibited at the 1950 Earls Court Commercial Motor Show. [P. Yeomans]

but as a replacement alternate journeys (every 2 hours) on Slaithwaite via Paddock and Scar Lane were diverted via Britannia Road. Finally the weekend extensions from Scapegoat Hill to Nont Sarah's were abandoned. With increasing car ownership and a greater variety of leisure activities available, fewer people were content to enjoy themselves walking over the moors and taking refreshments at the Moorland cafe.

In late February 1959 Hansons made it known through their agent, Harold Muscroft (the former JOC manager), that they were willing to sell the stage carriage (bus) side of the business. Revenue for the first ten months of 1958 had been £72,389 or 24.54d per mile. Of the bus fleet at this date 19 were single deckers (Albion CX13 235/49/50; AEC Regal III 282/3/8-93; AEC Regal IV 301-4; Maudslay Marathon 305; AEC Reliance 333-5) and six were double deckers (AEC Regent III 285-7; AEC/Hanson Regent rebuild 347/9/50); more than half the fleet was over nine years old. The municipal operator inspected a sample of these vehicles but found that the standard of maintenance was below that of their own; their estimated value of the Hansons bus fleet was £22,000. While it was known that Huddersfield JOC were keen to acquire the Hansons routes so that operational economies could be made, no deal resulted. The Corporation's then partner in the Joint Omnibus Committee, the British Transport Commission, had been prohibited by the 1953 Transport Act from acquiring private companies so the Corporation would have had to buy the Hansons buses separately; as it was, the parties could not reach agreement on the sale price.

Hansons had gained experience of one man operation with Bedford OBs, AEC Regal IVs 301-4 and Reliances 333-5 and in March 1955 305 (GWU 624), a Maudslay Marathon of 1948 vintage acquired from the Bottomleys coaching subsidiary had been fitted with the Duple DP35F body from AEC Regal 284 for use as a one man bus on the Blackmoorfoot route. As a result it was decided to fit new Roe bodies to three 1949/50 Regals (282/8/91) to make them suitable for one man operation. The buses emerged in 1960 with new registrations and fleet numbers 358-60; they also had somewhat ungainly full fronts. Nicknamed "tanks" or "trams", they must have proved very uncomfortable for the drivers, who had to twist through over 90 degrees in their cabs when issuing tickets; the doors were of course behind the front axle.

When (in its rebuilt form) less than two years old and valued at £3,000, 360 was to make the newspaper

In the early sixties the AEC Regal rebuilds with fully fronted Roe bodywork were used on a remarkably wide variety of duties. 359 (NCX 481), rebuilt from 1950 Regal EVH 82 in 1960, carries a heavy load at the Hansons Blackpool stand in the part of Springwood Street, Huddersfield since renamed Henry Street and by the entrance to the present bus station. [Photobus]

[Below] Three AEC Regal/Roe rebuilds of 1960/1, 360 (SCX 543) and 362/3 (TVH 498/9) are seen together in Morecambe with one of their drivers soon after re-entering service. [S.T. Harling collection]

[Right] AEC Regal/Roe 363 (TVH 499), rebuilt in 1961, passes Golcar churchyard shortly before reaching the Town End "terminus" of the Golcar Circulars, by this time mostly double deck operated. 363 would have travelled outward via Paddock and Scar Lane and would return to Huddersfield via Leymoor and Manchester Road. [D.F. Parker]

headlines. After refuelling late on the evening of Friday 3 November 1961, it was parked outside the St John's Road depot in the usual way by the night cleaning staff in order to leave more room inside the depot for manoeuvring other buses. With a full fuel tank it had a range of some 500 miles and soon afterwards it was stolen by Leonard Quinn of Marsden. Spotted in Congleton, the bus continued to Leamington Spa and eventually, on the Saturday evening, it was stopped in Manchester by the police, having covered around 300 miles. Quinn, who had been discharged from the RAF, admitted driving while disqualified and without insurance. He received a six months prison sentence but this was insufficient to deter him from taking another bus soon after his release.

Some old buses gained a new lease of life as driving school vehicles for the Hanson School of Motoring, a commercial venture set up in 1962 but used to train drivers for Hansons as well. 249 (DVH 821), one of the 1948 Albion CX13s with a crash gearbox was used on these duties at first. The chief instructor was KJ Ramsey and he was able to pass two lady drivers in June 1962, Misses Turner and Brook - BB 45927/37. These duties were later undertaken by AEC Regal III 293 (EVH 87) from 1964 and AEC Reliance 335 (HVH 211) from 1967.

Acts of vandalism started to be a problem on late night buses during 1962, particularly on the Golcar route. Seats were slashed and notices warning that offenders would be prosecuted had no effect.

The postwar AEC Regent III double deckers 285-7 lasted until the early sixties; 286 was dismantled for spares but the running units of 285/7 were reincarnated in the form of "new" 368/75 in 1962/63. They had new forward entrance (Roe H37/28F) bodies with platform doors. Similar 361/70 had their origins in coaches of 1950 which had been modernised (with new fleet numbers) in 1954. For three or four years in the mid 1960s the fleet contained a maximum complement of 7 double deckers. Following the successful operation of the three one man AEC Regal single deckers (358-60), during 1961-63 five of the 1950 Regal chassis (296/9/8/2/7) were fitted with similar new Roe FB39F bodies. These received new registrations and fleet numbers 362-3/9/76-7 (327/30/29/-/28). The bracketed numbers had been allotted following the 1954 removal of the bulkheads and incorporation of full fronts.

Towards the end of 1962 the commanding officer of the First Battalion of The Duke of Wellington's Regiment (Territorial Army), Lt. Colonel ABM Kavanagh, decided that their current regimental bus needed to be re-

placed and contacted Hansons to see whether they had a suitable vehicle for transporting the bandsmen and sports teams. Managing director Albert Hirst suggested Regal 290 (EVH 84) which was still in service. Given a fresh coat of paint and emblazoned with the regimental name, the bus was duly handed over at the end of January 1963 to the lt. colonel before its journey north to Catterick.

AEC Regent rebuild double decker 350 left Upperhead Row bus station on the 1.00pm departure to Meltham on 7 February 1963 driven by P Norcliffe. Recent snowfalls had made driving a nightmare on the bleak Pennine roads between Blackmoorfoot and Meltham but fortunately the bus was empty when it hit a patch of black ice near Helme and went into a back wheel skid; it then struck a wall and fell over onto its side. The regular driver, Glynn Sykes, who was waiting in the bus station for its return to start the late shift at 2.00pm, was one of the first to realise that all was not well. After the accident chief engineer Jim Holmes went out to survey the

On a snowy 7 February 1963 AEC Regent/Roe 1958 rebuild 350 (NVH 399) was working the 1.00pm Huddersfield to Meltham journey when the (fortunately) empty bus overturned into this field near Helme.
[Kirklees Image Archive Ke27836]

The first forward entrance double decker for Hansons was AEC Regent/Roe rebuild 361 (TVH 497). Constructed using running units from 1950 AEC Regal coach EVH 805, 361 entered service in March 1961 just before Huddersfield JOC's first forward entrance double deckers, two brand new and longer AEC Regent Vs. Seen here in the bus station picking up for Oldham, in October 1969 361 passed to Huddersfield Corporation and later to Thornes of Bubwith near Selby.
[Photobus]

Returning from Oldham to Huddersfield, 1962 Roe bodied AEC Regent rebuild 368 (VVH 348) passes typical Pennine moorland on the A62 Standedge crossing, in those pre-M62 days a busy road indeed and much frequented by heavily loaded goods vehicles.
[S.T. Harling collection]

damage and prepare the bus for its recovery by Oswald Tillotson of Bradford; the bus was lifted onto its wheels before being dragged backwards onto the road. The recovery caused considerable damage itself but the bus was repaired and entered service again.

In August 1963 one of the front entrance AEC Regent rebuild double deckers was in trouble outside the David Browns factory at Meltham Mills. Driver Norman Barrett and conductress Ada Bundy were sitting inside the bus waiting for shift workers when flames were seen coming from the engine compartment. Fire appliances from Meltham and Slaithwaite who were quickly on the scene confined the damage to the nearside of the bus under the bonnet.

Another driver had a narrow escape on the Meltham route in August 1965 when very heavy rain had washed away part of the road foundations at Cop Hill, Helme. A double decker had just been overtaken by a lorry when the weight of the latter caused the road to collapse and part of the lorry fell off the road into a field. Had this happened to the bus, it might well have toppled over. Buses were diverted from the normal route until the road was repaired.

During 1964-66 running units from the 1955-56 series of AEC Reliance coaches 336-8/344/*/45-6 were rebuilt as one man buses. These underfloor engined vehicles were more suitable than the Regals as the entrance door was to the front of the axle, allowing passengers to board

Hansons AEC Reliance 382 (BCX 485B) was a rebuilt former coach which had been rebodied by Roe in 1964. Having just left Upperhead Row bus station, it was captured in Swallow Street, Huddersfield working on the Britannia Road variant of the Slaithwaite via Wellhouse routes (every two hours, from 1959). [Omnibus Society/K. Glazier]

[Below] Some Hansons bus passengers were treated to a taste of modernity of a kind in 1967/8 when three brand new 36 feet long Willowbrook bodied AEC Reliances entered service. All buses on the Hill Top/Wilberlee services, including 405 (LCX 34E), new in March 1967, had to carry a conductor to supervise the reversal necessary at Crimble Corner before the ascent of Crimble Bank. 405 became Huddersfield Corporation 1 in October 1969 and West Yorkshire PTE 4001 in April 1974. [S.T. Harling collection]

In April 1963 the last double decker to enter service with Hansons did so in the shape of AEC Regent/Roe 375 (XVH 133), rebuilt from 1949 Regent III 287 (ECX 416). [Omnibus Society/K. Glazier]

directly facing the driver. One of the coaches converted (KVH 363) had previously been painted in Bottomley livery and had not carried a Hansons fleet number. New registrations and fleet numbers (382-4/9-91/6) were allocated.

From 15 May 1966 the bus terminus in Oldham was moved from Greaves Street to the new Clegg Street bus station, a combined bus station and depot for North Western, whose 160 route was of course also rerouted into it.

In 1967 the first 36 feet long buses and the first new buses since 1954, two AEC Reliances (405/6), were purchased; it will be noted that their Willowbrook (B53F) bodies seated more than the first prewar double deckers. These would probably have been the last new buses to enter service but for two serious fires later in the year. On 21 September driver Tony Harris of Marsden was returning from Oldham with an afternoon service when his clutch failed on Manchester Road, Standedge. On slowing down, he was overtaken by a lorry whose driver shouted to him that his bus was on fire. Smoke filled the saloon and the eight passengers were safely escorted from the vehicle. Underneath the bus was a mass of flames and the passengers stood well clear in case the fuel tank exploded. Firemen from Marsden and Slaithwaite attended the blaze.

Driver Harris must have thought he was jinxed when three weeks later on 9 October on the same route his vehicle again caught fire. This time the bus was the "three year old" Reliance rebuild 384 working the 9.55pm return journey from Oldham. On the ascent beyond Uppermill towards the Horse and Jockey the engine began to splutter and he told his six passengers that they were not going to make it up the hill. When the bus finally ground to a halt in pouring rain, Harris noticed smoke coming up through the floorboards and flames licking along the chassis. The passengers hurriedly left the bus and one lost his luggage in the process; the driver could not even retrieve his takings. In vain Harris tackled the fire with an extinguisher but the blaze quickly got out of control with an exploding tyre blowing out some of the side panels. Eventually a passing van driver drove to the pub to summon the fire brigade; although three appliances from Ashton and Mossley attended, the bus was burnt out and subsequently written off. A Ministry of Transport expert was called in to investigate the cause of the fire, which in all probability was due to an electrical fault. Doubt must certainly have been cast on the standards of maintenance at Hansons. Undeterred, driver Harris was

at the wheel of the late shift bus to Oldham on the following day. Another AEC Reliance/Willowbrook B53F (412) was obtained as a replacement in 1968.

The Oldham service was also suffering from a severe decline in passenger numbers and from 12 April 1968 five Monday to Friday round trips were withdrawn. This left only three round trips from Huddersfield at 6.55am, 2.55pm and 4.55pm, although a more attractive timetable continued to be offered at weekends (every 2 hours).

North Western were still running their 160 via Delph, although its Sunday service had been withdrawn two years earlier. This poorly patronised route had been one man operated since about 1958 and would be withdrawn altogether without replacement after 31 December 1970.

For several years the railway stations between Huddersfield and Manchester Victoria had been under threat of closure as British Railways wanted to withdraw the stopping trains. After various hearings and inquiries at which petitions were presented, it was finally agreed that the stations at Saddleworth, Diggle, Slaithwaite, Golcar and Longwood & Milnsbridge would close, providing certain additional bus services were instituted. One of these was a new (subsidised) Monday to Saturday journey at 6.30am from Oldham to Huddersfield to be operated by Hansons from 7 October 1968.

By 1967 economics dictated that even the Golcar services (Hansons journeys only), conductor operated with double deckers during the daytime, were one man operated during evenings and on Sundays. The Scapegoat Hill routes also saw a mixture of conductor and one man operation. All the other services were one man except for Meltham and Hill Top/Wilberlee which were still entirely conductor operated, mostly using double deckers. Conductors were required to supervise reversing at Crimble Corner on Hill Top/Wilberlee while the timings on the Meltham route were too tight to allow one man operation without a new timetable. Hansons single decks could still be seen carrying conductors on various routes in the last years when a double decker was not available. Towards the end, with six double deckers, perhaps not in the best of health or bloom of youth, it was inevitable that single decks had to be substituted from time to time.

An argument about fares which got out of hand was the last straw for a driver of a Golcar bound bus on the evening of 28 February 1968. A middle aged woman boarded the bus in Scar Lane and asked for a ticket to Parkwood Road. The driver correctly asked for 9d but the woman was adamant that the fare should only have been 7d, despite being shown the faretable. An off duty

conductress who happened to be a passenger on the bus agreed with the driver that the fare was indeed 9d but to no avail. The woman continued shouting and in the end the frustrated driver could take no more; he left his seat, put a chock under the front wheel and walked away! The other passengers then got off the bus, with one of them closing the driver operated front door. Some walked home while others waited for the next (JOC) bus. On the following morning the driver, who was still very upset by the incident, was interviewed by Albert Hirst in the Hansons offices.

Driver Hedley Roebuck was assaulted at the Lindley Moor Road terminus by an irate male passenger as he was completing his waybill after his last journey of the day from Town. The passenger was fined a mere £5 on 5 August 1968 after admitting striking the driver across his face and breaking his spectacles. The unsavoury incident was said to have resulted from a disagreement over his change.

Hansons buses did not visit Lindley Moor Road for much longer as from 16 January 1969 the route was shortened to terminate in a loop via Yew Tree Road, Lindley Avenue, Ainley Road and Weatherhill Road. This eliminated the reversal necessary at Lindley Moor Road on this one man route; an elderly passenger had recently been run over and killed by a bus there.

From 8 May 1969 a number of journeys, including the entire evening and Sunday service, were withdrawn on the joint Blackmoorfoot route as an economy measure. This had been delayed when Colne Valley UDC had pointed out that it would cause hardship to pensioners living in the old people's bungalows at Field Head, Linthwaite. Hansons were asked to consider diverting some Meltham buses to serve this part of Linthwaite but by this stage the company had no future as a bus operator.

Despite the many problems facing the bus industry in general the Hansons stage carriage (local bus) side of the business was still profitable; before depreciation the profits for the financial years 1967 and 1968 were £12,645 and £15,216 respectively. On the joint Colne Valley Services nearly a quarter of a million miles were run annually, with a further half a million miles on the independently operated Lindley-Newsome, Weatherhill, Meltham and Oldham routes; revenue was approximately 37d per mile. 17 one man single deck buses and six double deckers, used mainly on the Golcar, Meltham and Hill Top/Wilberlee routes, were in use but all bar three single deckers were rebuilds of earlier stock and

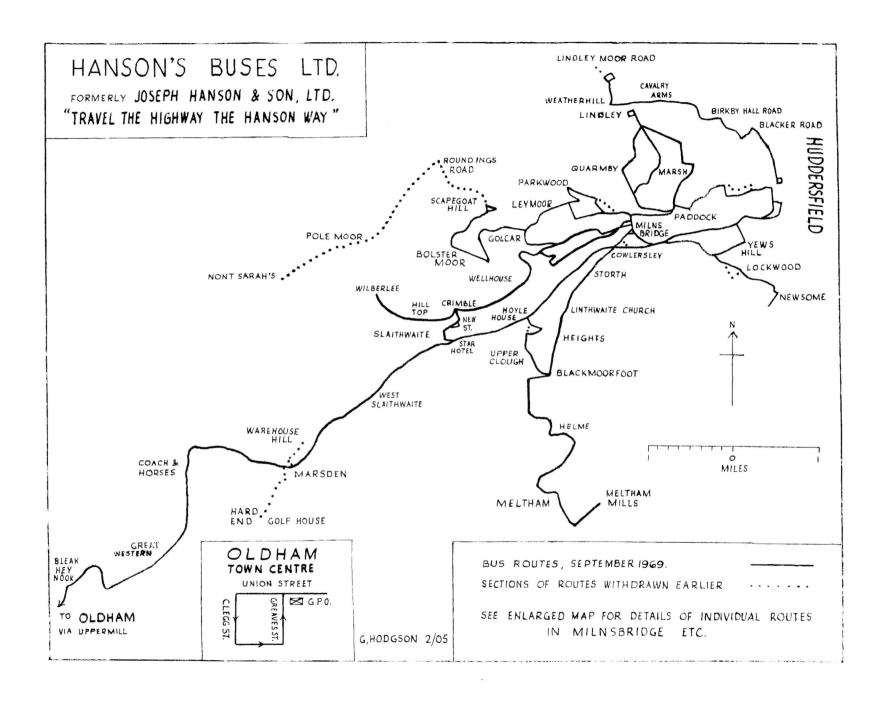

HANSON'S BUSES LTD.
FORMERLY JOSEPH HANSON & SON, LTD.
"TRAVEL THE HIGHWAY THE HANSON WAY"

HUDDERSFIELD

LINDLEY MOOR ROAD
WEATHERHILL
CAVALRY ARMS
LINDLEY
BIRKBY HALL ROAD
BLACKER ROAD
QUARMBY
MARSH
PARKWOOD
LEYMOOR
PADDOCK
ROUNDINGS ROAD
SCAPEGOAT HILL
MILNS BRIDGE
GOLCAR
POLE MOOR
YEWS HILL
COWLERSLEY
LOCKWOOD
BOLSTER MOOR
WELLHOUSE
STORTH
NONT SARAH'S
NEWSOME
WILBERLEE
CRIMBLE
HILL TOP
HOYLE HOUSE
LINTHWAITE CHURCH
NEW ST.
SLAITHWAITE
HEIGHTS
STAR HOTEL
UPPER CLOUGH
BLACKMOORFOOT
N
WEST SLAITHWAITE
HELME
WAREHOUSE HILL
MILES
COACH & HORSES
MARSDEN
MELTHAM MILLS
HARD END
GOLF HOUSE
MELTHAM
GREAT WESTERN
BLEAK HEY NOOK

OLDHAM
TOWN CENTRE
UNION STREET
CLEGG ST.
GREAVES ST.
G.P.O.

TO OLDHAM
VIA UPPERMILL

G. HODGSON 2/05

BUS ROUTES, SEPTEMBER 1969. ——————
SECTIONS OF ROUTES WITHDRAWN EARLIER ·······

SEE ENLARGED MAP FOR DETAILS OF INDIVIDUAL ROUTES
IN MILNSBRIDGE ETC.

46

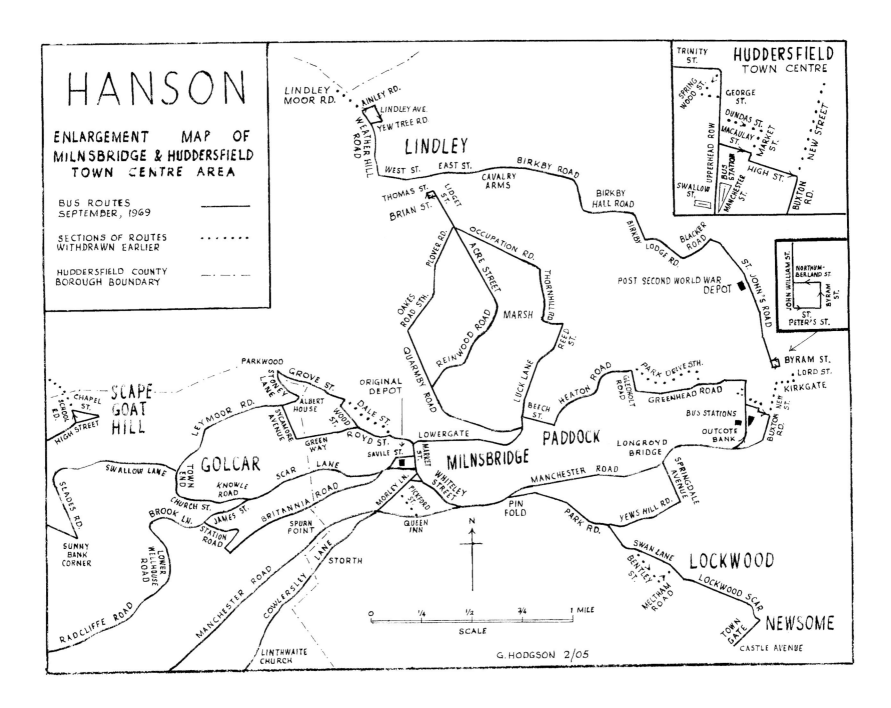

HANSON

ENLARGEMENT MAP OF MILNSBRIDGE & HUDDERSFIELD TOWN CENTRE AREA

BUS ROUTES SEPTEMBER, 1969 ————

SECTIONS OF ROUTES WITHDRAWN EARLIER · · · · · ·

HUDDERSFIELD COUNTY BOROUGH BOUNDARY - - - - -

HUDDERSFIELD TOWN CENTRE

TRINITY ST.
SPRING WOOD ST.
GEORGE ST.
UPPERHEAD ROW
DUNDAS ST.
MACAULAY ST.
BUS STATION
MANCHESTER ST.
MARKET ST.
HIGH ST.
NEW STREET
BUXTON RD.
SWALLOW ST.

JOHN WILLIAM ST.
NORTHUMBERLAND ST.
ST. PETER'S ST.
BYRAM ST.

LINDLEY MOOR RD.
AINLEY RD.
LINDLEY AVE.
YEW TREE RD.
WEATHER HILL ROAD

LINDLEY

WEST ST.
EAST ST.
BIRKBY ROAD
CAVALRY ARMS
THOMAS ST.
LIDGET ST.
BRIAN ST.
PLOVER RD.
OCCUPATION RD.
ACRE STREET
THORNHILL RD.
BIRKBY HALL ROAD
BIRKBY
LODGE RD.
BLACKER ROAD
ST. JOHN'S ROAD
POST SECOND WORLD WAR DEPOT

BYRAM ST.
LORD ST.
KIRKGATE

OAKES ROAD STH.
REINWOOD ROAD
MARSH
REED ST.
LUCK LANE

QUARMBY ROAD

PARKWOOD
GROVE ST.
STONEY LANE
ORIGINAL DEPOT
SYCAMORE AVENUE
ALBERT HOUSE
WOOD ST.
DALE ST.
GREEN WAY
ROYD ST.
LOWERGATE
SAVILE ST.
LEYMOOR RD.
TOWN END
KNOWLE ROAD
SCAR LANE
MARKET ST.
MILNSBRIDGE
WHITELEY STREET
PADDOCK
PARK DRIVE STH.
GLEDHOLT ROAD
GREENHEAD ROAD
BUS STATIONS
OUTCOTE BANK
BUXTON RD.
NEW ST.
LONGROYD BRIDGE
HEATON ROAD
BEECH ST.

SCAPE GOAT HILL
CHAPEL ST.
SCHOOL RD.
HIGH STREET

GOLCAR
SWALLOW LANE
CHURCH ST.
BROOK LN.
JAMES ST.
STATION ROAD
BRITANNIA ROAD
SPURN POINT

SLADES RD.
SUNNY BANK CORNER
LOWER WELLHOUSE ROAD
RADCLIFFE ROAD
MANCHESTER ROAD
COWLERSLEY LANE
LINTHWAITE CHURCH

MORLEY LN.
PICKFORD ST.
QUEEN INN
STORTH
PIN FOLD

N

MANCHESTER ROAD
PARK RD.
YEWS HILL RD.
SPRINGDALE AVENUE

SWAN LANE
BENTLEY ST.
MELTHAM ROAD
LOCKWOOD
LOCKWOOD SCAR
TOWN GATE
NEWSOME
CASTLE AVENUE

0   ¼   ½   ¾   1 MILE
SCALE

G. HODGSON 2/05

47

On 16 May 1969 AEC Regent/Roe rebuilds 368 (VVH 348) and 370 (VVH 350) were nearing the end of their long and complex careers with Hansons. Upperhead Row Bus Station itself, demolished two years later, looked out of place when contrasted with the new town centre buildings in the background. The Linthwaite Church journeys were unadvertised short workings on the Meltham via Helme route. [H.J. Black]

the fleet was in reality considerably older than a casual glance at registration letters would have suggested. In this period some vehicles were shabby looking internally and externally while some appeared underpowered and worn out after long service on tortuous and hilly routes with indifferent road surfaces. There was a staff of 63, including 31 drivers, 15 conductors, 4 inspectors and a traffic superintendent.

In November 1968 Huddersfield Corporation Passenger Transport Department renewed their interest in purchasing the Hansons stage carriage side following the passage of the 1968 Transport Act. This gave specific powers to local authorities already operating buses to acquire other undertakings whose vehicles operated in the same area. The Corporation were planning to acquire the state's 50% share in the JOC; the takeover of the Hansons routes as well would give them an opportunity to redraw the route map of the town's buses. A detailed examination of the Hansons bus fleet was carried out by the Corporation's engineering staff who arrived at a valuation of £50,219. Eventually the two parties agreed on the figure of £74,000 for the combined value of the fleet and the goodwill of the business.

In advance of the takeover the Hanson family made their official farewell to employees who worked on the bus side at the St John's Road depot on 21 September 1969. The company chairman, Robert Hanson, paid

tribute to the work done by the employees in the past and wished them luck in the future. His son and vice-chairman, James Hanson (later Lord Hanson) explained that the present climate did not favour small private bus companies and that they had reluctantly decided that it was best to sell out to the Corporation. A poignant touch of nostalgia was provided by the presence of two men who had driven the earliest buses to Golcar and Linthwaite way back in 1924. Frank Brook (aged 83) and Tommy Squires (aged 78) had each given 43 loyal years of service to the company. Mr Brook even remembered driving a steam wagon fitted with seats to Blackpool during the First World War when petrol was scarce. Once the daily Blackpool service had started, he had completed the return trip about 300 times each year.

Presentations were made to two long serving employees who were retiring at the end of the month. Miss Ada Bundy of Crosland Moor had been a conductress for 30 years and Mr JT Johnson, an inspector, had been with the company for 35 years. Most of the other staff working with the buses transferred to Huddersfield Corporation.

Local transport enthusiasts were busy recording the

North Western used to complain that their Huddersfield to Oldham buses often ran almost empty but 1968 Bristol RESL/Marshall 302 (KJA 302G) looks comparatively well patronised as it passes the bad weather warning sign – still there today - at Scouthead on the A62 between Delph and Waterhead. The reappearance of North Western Bristol saloons in Huddersfield was brief as the route was abandoned after 31 December 1970. This bus passed to the Crosville company in the subsequent division of North Western. [Photobus]

last departures on each route on the final day of bus operation, Tuesday 30 September, until the very last bus (36 feet long AEC Reliance 405) entered the St John's Road depot shortly after 11.50pm. Most of the vehicles are shown in the following table.

Route	Huddersfield		Last bus
	Dep.	Arr.	
Wilberlee	5.20	6.12	Regal rebuild 369
Hill Top	6.35	7.27	Reliance 406
Oldham	4.55	6.53	Reliance 405
Scapegoat Hill	10.03	10.57	Reliance rebuild 396
Golcar Circular	11.18	11.50	Reliance 405
"Lindley Moor Road"	10.15	10.48	Regal rebuild 359
Meltham	10.30	11.29	Regent rebuild 375
Lindley-Newsome	dep. Lindley 10.30; arr. Newsome 10.57 – Reliance rebuild 390		
Newsome-Lindley	dep. Newsome 10.30; arr. Lindley 10.57 – Reliance rebuild 391		

From 1 October 1969 Hanson's Buses Ltd was a coach operator only.

To commemorate the end of nearly 45 years of local bus operation the "oldest" bus in the fleet, AEC Regent rebuild double decker 349, had been suitably decorated by Hansons employees. On the previous Thursday evening nearly 60 present and past employees had used the bus, driven by Mr Shelmerdine, for a last sentimental journey over most of the Hansons routes. The party departed from St George's Square and travelled to Lindley via Birkby, passing the Hanson family residence on the way (double deckers had of course never been used in service on this route). The Lindley-Newsome via Reinwood Road route was followed as far as Milnsbridge where a diversion was made via Leymoor to Golcar and Scapegoat Hill. The tour continued via Wellhouse and Crimble to Slaithwaite, from where the Oldham route was followed as far as Marsden. A JOC route had to be used towards Meltham before the bus regained the Hansons route via Helme and Linthwaite Church to Town.

The passing of the Hansons bus services stimulated correspondence to the Huddersfield Examiner "Letter Bag". One writer said that the takeover of a small family business was just a sad sign of the times. There had, he said, always been a special relationship between the Hansons crews and their passengers, probably on account of their long service and also because they tended to stick to the same route. He fondly remembered Hansons as pioneers in the days when engines and tyres were not as good as they had become; yet they somehow managed to get through to their destinations even in the worst weather. Recalling his courting days, he said that

From 1959 the standard Hansons coach was the Ford Thames Trader with (usually) Plaxton bodywork. 355 (RVH 336), seen here in the London area, was of the second batch and new in March 1960. Withdrawn in 1967, 355 was later used by the Reliance Gear Company of St Helen's Gate, Almondbury.
[S.T. Harling collection]

Thames Trader/Plaxton PCX 131 was new to the Bottomleys subsidiary in April 1959. The entire Bottomleys fleet passed into the ownership of the main Hansons company in January 1962 but the vehicles retained Bottomleys two-tone blue livery and fleetname and remained unnumbered. PCX 131 is seen at Wembley; it was withdrawn in 1966.
[R.H.G. Simpson]

New in March 1960 to Bottomleys, RVH 377 retained its Bottomleys identity on transfer of the fleet to Hansons in 1962. This two-tone blue livery was more cheerful than the smart but perhaps somewhat sombre unrelieved dark blue adopted later. RVH 377 awaits its next duty, a visit to Bridlington, in the familiar Huddersfield bus and coach parking ground.
[Photobus]

several young men regularly used to catch the last bus from Crimble to Golcar; at the departure time the crew would look round to see if any of the regulars were missing and, if so, they would wait a minute or two for their breathless arrival.

10: COACHING WITH FORDS INTO THE MOTORWAY ERA (1959-1974)

In advertising, the rival firm of Baddeleys was always more innovative and regularly made a point of specifying which excursions their newest coaches would operate. From April 1959 Hansons also used this ploy to attract additional custom, starting with the first Ford Thames Trader (570E) coaches in the fleet. [Bedfords and AECs had been favoured earlier and the choice of these chassis for coaches, as well as the Thames Trader, was influenced by the supplying of goods vehicles from the same manufacturers to the associated Hanson Haulage business.] 353/4 were built to what were described as the "new maximum dimensions of 30 feet long and 8 feet wide" (actually legalised nearly a decade earlier!) with Plaxton C41F bodies and advertised as observation touring coaches. The ventilation and air conditioning system was said to be designed to provide ideal touring conditions whatever the weather. Wide windows gave all round vision and the dunlopillo seats were fitted with ivory coloured headrests which would be cleaned after each trip. Their first public appearance was on Sunday 19 April for the "ever popular" spring tour of the Derbyshire Dales while a week later they were used on the tour of the Spalding bulb fields.

Knowing that intending excursion passengers were often deterred from booking by the threat of bad weather, Hansons now stressed in advertisements that great care was taken in selecting destinations with ample covered attractions and accommodation. It was emphasised that the maximum possible time during tours was to be spent actually riding on the coach – a point which might have discouraged some from booking.

Two drivers made the news during 1959. After Robert Hanson's son James had married Geraldine Kaelin of New York, he introduced his wife to Hansons employees at the St John's Road depot on 2 May and on their behalf long serving driver Tommy Squires presented the couple with a silver salver. Tommy, of Luck Lane, Paddock had driven coaches for over 40 years without an accident and had never failed to get his passengers back home safely. On one occasion when he was bound for Redcar Races,

his engine had failed and his passengers had to continue their journey on another vehicle. The engine fault was rectified and Tommy was able to drive on to Redcar in time to collect his passengers after the last race. His worst journey was returning from Hull when a fuel pump fault developed; in second gear the 70 mile journey took almost five hours. Tommy had been the regular driver of the Fartown team coach for 16 years and the Huddersfield Town coach for eight years; in that time he saw most of the away games but hardly any of the home games. The longest stretch of driving he managed in a single day was during the war when he had to get a party of soldiers to Melton Mowbray for 6.00am. Back in Huddersfield at midday, owing to the shortage of drivers he had to set off again for Blackpool. At the age of 67 he was still driving to Blackpool daily during the holiday season. As for his own holidays - he went to Blackpool on the Hansons coach.

A former Bottomley driver, Harold Dyson of Cowlersley, drove on a 2,000 miles round trip to Besancon in France, which was twinned with Huddersfield. Corporation officials and their friends went on a 17 day tour through France, Switzerland and Italy. A framed photograph of Castle Hill inscribed with suitable greetings was presented to the Mayor of Besancon on behalf of the Twinning Committee. For the driver the tour brought back memories of his wartime service with the King's Own Scottish Borderers in France as this was his first peacetime venture to the continent.

"Popular coastal economy excursions" was the branding used from July 1960 to advertise a range of half day trips to the usual Lancashire and Yorkshire coastal resorts. Allowing four hours at the resort and arriving back at 10.00pm, these trips were possibly aimed at shop workers who traditionally did not work on Wednesday afternoons. Probably not coincidentally, Baddeleys started running similar trips at the same time. Also new this year were "inland waterway cruises" (by canal boat) for which Hansons provided connecting road transport. Parts of the M6 were now open and passengers were given a foretaste of motorway travel on an Ingleton and New Preston tour. Rivals Baddeleys were rather more ambitious and offered a Coventry tour using the M1 at Newport Pagnell.

Two new directors were appointed in December 1960. Albert Hirst of Crosland Moor, who had started as a clerk in 1932 and had been secretary of Hanson's Buses since 1948, became the new managing director.

In April 1961 Geoffrey Davey stands in front of his Thames Trader/Plaxton opposite the Hansons St John's Road depot with the trophies won at the first National Coach Rally at Blackpool. The coach had just entered service in the previous month and was 366 (TVH 244). [Kirklees Image Archive Ke13453]

Guy Levison of Bradley, who had joined Hansons from Baddeleys and had become traffic manager in 1942, was promoted to managing director of Hanson Haulage.

Fares on express services were increased by 8.5% in January 1961. The previous increase on these services had taken place in 1954.

Thick fog was the cause of nightmare journeys for two Hansons drivers early in 1961 and both involved the Huddersfield Town football team. After an away match at Plymouth, the team travelled back as far as Doncaster by train where they were due to be picked up by coach at 12.50am. Owing to the thick blanket of fog which delayed the coach, they sought refuge in the only all night cafe in Doncaster until it arrived. After visibility had improved somewhat they finally set off on the last leg of their journey, arriving in St George's Square after 4.00am. A few weeks later the return journey from Norwich took eight hours and, where fog was thickest, the players had to take turns at walking in front of the coach to guide the driver.

The old established family transport business of WH

Schofield letterhead dated 1901

Schofield letterhead c1920

& F Schofield of Premier Garage, Marsden was taken over by Hansons in February 1961. Over a hundred years earlier an Albert Schofield had invested in a horse and cart and set up a one man carriers business in Marsden. In the early 1920s his son or grandson Albert Schofield purchased his first charabanc, patriotically named "The Victory" as was the custom in that period. Often driven by George Dodson, trips were undertaken to the usual coastal resorts. In the next decade Albert formed a partnership with his sons and expanded to own garages and a car hire business as well as operating coaches and small buses. One of the authors remembers a Pleasureways holiday tour to Brighton in the mid 1950s for which a Schofield half cab coach was used. After the takeover two of their Sentinel coaches (OWU 772/3) with Burlingham C41C bodies were licensed to Hanson Haulage Ltd before transfer to Hanson's Buses. Jack Whitwam, formerly manager of the old Queen's Carriage Co. Ltd (also previously acquired by Hansons) took over as manager at the Marsden depot.

[Above] The parking ground off Manchester Street, Huddersfield looks a little more than usual like a coach station in this picture of newish 1961 Thames Trader/Plaxton 365 (TVH 243), ready to operate the summer express service to Torquay started in 1957. Advertised outside the Hansons kiosk are excursions "tonight" to: Knaresborough (5/3d); Ilkley and Bolton Abbey (5/3d); and a mystery tour costing 3/9d. [Photobus]

[Right] Inside St John's Road depot Hansons managing director Albert Hirst congratulates Geoffrey Davey on his return with trophies from the 2nd National Coach Rally at Blackpool in April 1962. His Thames Trader/Plaxton 371 (VVH 189) had only just entered service earlier in the month. Note the livery variation; the 371-4 batch of coaches was delivered with a reintroduced white band (white relief had been discontinued in the early 1950s in favour of unrelieved red). The white band on 371-4 did not meet with approval so was not perpetuated. [Kirklees Image Archive Ke16957]

The licences of Ben Smith of Central Garage, Marsden, a subsidiary company of Schofield, were transferred to Hansons in April 1961, allowing further consolidation in the Colne Valley. Ben Smith was licensed to operate an aggregate of six vehicles on daily excursions and was also licensed for period return holiday traffic from both the Star Hotel, Slaithwaite and Central Garage, Marsden; the range of destinations included Cleveleys, Colwyn Bay, Rhyl and Llandudno. Hansons soon moved out of Premier Garage and centralised their coaching activities in Marsden at Central Garage.

Easter 1961 saw the first National Coach Rally held at Blackpool and Hansons gained two prestigious awards. Geoffrey Davey was Champion Driver and was awarded the Ford Motor Company Trophy. Ford Thames Trader 570E coach 366 with Plaxton body was awarded the Thames Challenge Trophy for the outstanding performance in the road test and the concours d'elegance. Naturally Hansons made the most of this and subsequent advertisements made reference to the "National Coach Rally trophy winners". The public was informed that the fleet of these Ford "observation" coaches was being considerably increased for the 1961 season. In fact, including vehicles already delivered in 1959 and 1960, there were nine in Hansons livery and a further five in the Bottomley fleet. In response to a Baddeleys boast that their coaches were for people who were particular about the vehicle in which they travelled, Hansons claimed that their "observation" coaches contained "every known refinement for passenger comfort and safety".

Even by Huddersfield standards the weather was atrocious over Easter 1961 and particularly so on the Tuesday when snow caused the cancellation of almost the entire excursion programme. Two destinations reached were Belle Vue and Ripon; one of the authors recalls booking for Ripon and Fountains Abbey but because of the state of the roads Fountains could not be visited. Anyone not wishing to travel was offered a credit note and many accepted the offer. Coach drivers were redeployed in bringing back holidaymakers from west coast resorts earlier than expected. Coaches from Morecambe had to be diverted via Preston instead of following the normal route through Settle and Skipton.

Historic York was always a popular destination but in June 1961 there was the added attraction of the royal wedding between the Duke of Kent and Miss Katherine Worsley at York Minster. Prior to the wedding itself coach loads went just to view the floral decorations.

By this period most of the coaches were kept at the

W.H. & F. Schofield of Marsden had a batch of unusual Sentinel SLC6 coaches with Burlingham Seagull centre entrance bodies. OWU 773, new in early 1955, is seen on a journey to Morecambe. After the Schofields' coach and road haulage businesses were taken over by Hansons, OWU 773 was licensed to Hanson Haulage before joining the main Hansons fleet in April 1963.
[R.F. Mack]

Plaxton's rival Duple won the bodywork contracts for new Hansons coaches for 1963 and 1964. Thames Trader 380 (XVH 136), new in early 1963 with Duple Firefly bodywork, is competing at the 1963 Blackpool Coach Rally.
[P.J. Cardno collection]

[Top left] The 1966 Hansons intake of coaches looked much more modern. Ford R192/ Plaxton 41 seater 398 (GVH 413D) arrived in March and is participating in the 1966 Blackpool Coach Rally shortly afterwards. [S.T. Harling collection]

[Above] Hansons usually sent a new coach or two to the Blackpool rally and 1967 was no exception. Ford R226/Duple 52 seater 401 (KVH 244E) and shorter sister R192/Duple 45 seater 403 (KVH 246E) were both new in March 1967. [S.T. Harling collection]

[Left] 1964's Thames Traders also had Duple bodies. 385 (BCX 488B) arrived in March 1964 and was on excursion duties on 23 April 1967. 385 was withdrawn after the 1970 summer season.
[S.T. Harling collection]

Leeds Road (Woodlands Road) depot of Hanson Haulage. There was not enough space at St John's Road where the buses were garaged.

In July 1961 British Railways offered combined rail and road tours from Huddersfield. It is doubtful whether this posed a serious threat to Hansons as the destinations were much the same as those of the coach companies and passengers had the inconvenience of changing their mode of travel on both outward and return journeys. The only possible advantage was the provision of toilets on the trains.

Irrespective of the competition, business was particularly good during the main Huddersfield holiday weeks with the longer excursions continuing to gain in popularity. On some days over 1000 passengers were taken to over 20 destinations and coaches were hired from firms in Barnsley and Halifax. A sunny morning could be guaranteed to generate last minute bookings for afternoon tours, of which Richmond topped the popularity stakes.

Traditionally the illuminations at Blackpool had always been a money spinner for Hansons with many local people either going for the day or for a short break. The 29th annual display in 1961 was switched on by Violet Carson, who became famous playing the character of Ena Sharples in "Coronation Street". The £400,000 display over six miles of promenade was expected to attract three million people to the resort. For the transport enthusiast "Tramnik 1" made its debut on the promenade; this was an old Blackpool tram transformed into a rocket to give passengers the thrill of space travel. An added attraction for some was the first match between the newly formed Blackpool Borough rugby league club and Fartown. The excursion on 23 September offered either six hours of sightseeing or the opportunity to watch the match followed by a full length tour of the lights before returning at 7.30pm.

Following the coldest Christmas in Huddersfield for 71 years, the main water supply was frozen at the St John's Road depot. On 27 December 1961 the main pipe was

The final batch of Thames Traders arrived in 1965 and had Plaxton bodies. 394 (ECX 112C) was photographed outside the Empire Cinema in John William Street, Huddersfield on 16 September 1970; Viaduct Street is on the left. 394 and the two other remaining Traders were all withdrawn in the following year. [H.J Black]

Hansons 419 (TVH 419H) was a 45 seat Ford R192/Plaxton new in March 1970. After the sale of the business to West Yorkshire PTE it became Metro Hanson 75. [S.T. Harling collection]

found to be fractured, all vehicle washing had to cease and water had to be brought in for the canteen. Despite the weather good business was reported on the Blackpool service as well as to the greyhound races and to Preston for Huddersfield Town's away match.

Entry number 13 (out of a total of 45) was certainly not unlucky for driver Geoffrey Davey at the the second National Coach Rally, held at Blackpool in April 1962. At the wheel of Ford Thames 371 with destination indicators set at "Hanson" and "Huddersfield", he was the proud winner of four prestigious cups; he was personally rewarded with a cash prize and a tankard. On returning to his depot he was congratulated by Albert Hirst on behalf of Hansons and photographed in front of the vehicle with the trophies. Unusually Ford Thames coaches 371-4 new in 1962 were painted in the old livery of red with a white band but this style was not perpetuated.

Rival coach operator Baddeleys again demonstrated more enterprise than Hansons with the introduction of nine new excursions including London Airport, which proved to be an exceptionally popular destination. A vigorous Baddeleys advertising campaign throughout the summer of 1962 brought no immediate response from Hansons. The Bottomley name continued in use for private hire advertisements for its loyalty value but all public excursions appeared under the Hansons name from this time.

Much business, however, resulted from the fact that Fartown rugby league team had enjoyed a good cup run and reached the final at Wembley on Saturday 12 May 1962. Not all spectators travelled by coach; British Railways laid on five special trains with seats for 2,500 and, for the more affluent, Thomas Cook offered an inclusive £4-2s package of train ticket for the Friday evening and breakfast in London, followed by a sightseeing tour and lunch. All the Huddersfield coach operators charged £2 and departed at 6.00am on the Saturday morning. Knowing that there would be competition from minibus operators who touted for custom in pubs and clubs, Baddeleys had wanted to reduce the fare to 28/- but their request was turned down by the traffic commissioners.

While Hansons normally provided the Fartown team coach, for this occasion the club elected to travel to London by train. Despite losing the match to Wakefield Trinity, the team and officials arrived for a civic reception at the Town Hall in a convoy of Hansons coaches. The leading coach had its sun roof open but sadly there was no cup to display.

In November 1962 Hansons pleaded not guilty to a licence offence; it was claimed by the traffic commissioners that they had "used a motorbus as an express carriage otherwise than under a road service licence". A Linthwaite lady organised bingo trips to Mirfield and hired a coach from Hansons for £3-2s-6d. She collected 2/6d from each passenger and eventually paid the money to Hansons. According to Gilbert Fox, manager of the Private Hire Department, on one occasion an unknown man had boarded the coach in Mirfield for just the single journey and was charged 1/3d by the organiser. As the driver had refused the money, Hansons denied the charge.

Traditionally pantomime trips provided much needed work for the private hire side of the business during the winter months. In January 1963, however, Billy Smart's Circus at Leeds proved more of an attraction than the pantomimes. On the evening of 5 January Huddersfield ICI Social Club chartered 19 coaches to take 1,000 children and their supervisors to the circus. On the return journey one of the coaches collided with a van, blocking Gelderd Road at Gildersome for half an hour, but fortunately nobody on the coach was injured.

For the 1963 National Coach Rally, Duple bodied Ford Thames 380 was in the hands of RS Redfern of Crosland Moor who had been with the firm for 12 years. Even the high standards of the previous years were surpassed, with five out of a possible seven trophies won. In the driver of the year competition, Redfern himself came a creditable third.

For the wedding of Princess Margaret of Kent and Angus Ogilvy at Westminster Abbey on 16 April 1963, Hansons coaches departed from Huddersfield at 12.05am to guarantee an early arrival in London. New destinations for the summer season besides London were Beau-

For many years North Western express coach services from Manchester (and some nearby towns) to Scarborough via Bridlington and Filey used to pick up at Marsden (former tram terminus), Slaithwaite (Star Hotel) and Linthwaite (Bargate). Booking agents were the same as for the Tyne Tees Mersey "Limited Stop" and included Schofields (later Hansons) at Marsden. 256 (KJA 256F) was a Leyland Leopard with Duple Commander bodywork new in 1968. [Photobus] maris, Coventry, Flamingo Park and Hadrian's Wall.

The first excursion to Coventry took place on 4 May with time allowed for visiting the modern cathedral and the new shopping precinct. Whitsuntide tours ran to Beaumaris and Flamingo Park zoo. As a result of the successful application for new excursion licences, Hansons coaches were soon to be seen in London on a regular basis. Much advertising heralded the London tour, which was to operate each Saturday from 20 July. For 35/- a very long day out was on offer, with departure from Huddersfield at 6.30am and the return from Euston Road at 5.30pm. Baddeleys, who already ran an excursion to London Airport, responded with a new tour to Tower Bridge from the same date. The more leisurely and certainly more scenic tour to Hadrian's Wall and the Northumberland Borders was offered first on 14 July as part of the Holiday Week programme.

In 1962 the legal maximum dimensions for single deck coaches and buses had been increased to 36 feet in length and 8 feet $2^1/2$ inches in width, which allowed bodies to be built seating up to 53 passengers in comfort. Rival operator Baddeleys introduced new coaches to these dimensions in 1963/64 and their advertisements for a new group of excursions using the M1 and M6 motorways made the most of these coaches with headings such as "Motor coach travel - a look at things to come". This brought no response from Hansons and it was to be 1966 before longer higher capacity coaches appeared in the Hansons fleet.

For two weeks in August each year starting in 1964 the giant radio telescope at Jodrell Bank in Cheshire was open to the public. Anticipating the attraction of the world's largest steerable radio telescope, Hansons were quick to obtain a special excursion licence. A new tour for Easter 1965 was to Blenheim Palace in Oxfordshire, birthplace and final resting place of Sir Winston Churchill.

On the evening of Friday 1 April 1966 Ford R192 398 left Huddersfield to travel to Wigan in readiness for the first stage of the annual Blackpool coach rally. The weather was atrocious, with many transpennine roads blocked by snow, and by Saturday morning the whereabouts of the coach was not known. Unlike the 7.45pm limited stop bus from Leeds to Liverpool (a Lancashire United Transport vehicle, which was stranded overnight at the top of Standedge cutting) the driver finally made it to his destination and as usual secured several prestigious trophies for Hansons.

1967 was known in some quarters as the year of the

Ford R226/Duple 53 seater 427 (FVH 427L) entered service in March 1973 and is seen here soon afterwards. In 1974 427 was renumbered 83 in the Metro Hanson fleet owned by West Yorkshire PTE. Working for Bingleys in 1978 it played a tragic role in the short history of the PTE's coaching subsidiaries when it had to be scrapped after suffering a fatal collision on the edge of Wakefield while on a private hire for the Police Federation. [S.T. Harling collection]

breathalyser. Baddeleys responded with advertisements encouraging partygoers to hire a 12 seater minicoach to avoid risking their own licences. Hansons did not respond. Two new long distance excursions were introduced for the August holidays, one to Slimbridge Wildfowl Park and the new Severn Bridge and the other to Milton Manor House and Park (between Abingdon and Didcot).

Much good publicity was generated by the opening of the first branch travel office in Brighouse on 14 August 1968. The opening ceremony was performed by the mayor, Councillor W Holdsworth, who was presented by Robert Hanson with a ticket for the Tor Line service from Immingham to Amsterdam. The official party then travelled by coach for lunch at the Marmaville Club in Mirfield. Six weeks later publicity of a different kind was obtained when a coach skidded on the granite setts at the bottom of Gledholt Bank and crashed into Shaw's general store. Mrs Shaw got the shock of her life when

she opened the door to her sitting room over the shop only to find that the outside wall had collapsed. A relief coach was summoned to take the party from Paddock cricket club on their outing.

The investiture of the Prince of Wales took place at Caernarvon Castle on 1 July 1969. Hansons, in keeping with many coach operators, ran special excursions over a three day period starting on the day before the actual ceremony. A 7.00am start was made from Huddersfield with passengers being picked up along the Colne Valley as far as Marsden.

Hansons coaches were to be seen speeding along the new M62 motorway following the opening of certain sections early in 1970. To allow the public to sample the scenic section of the motorway five new cheap excursions were introduced:
Brown Cow Bridge and Booth Wood via Ripponden
M62 and Scammonden Dam via Littleborough
Pennine Motorway via Milnrow and Clifton Wood

Hanson Coach Services

COACH RALLY WINNERS
1961-62-63-64-65-66

August Excursions 1967

* BOOKED TO PLAN

SUNDAY, 20th AUGUST

8-00 a.m.	*Keswick & Lakes	17/6
8-00 a.m.	*Llandudno	20/-
8-00 a.m.	*Rhyl	18/3
8-30 a.m.	Blackpool (ret. 6 p.m.)	13/3
9-00 a.m.	*Scarborough	16/-
9-00 a.m.	*Bridlington	16/-
9-00 a.m.	*Filey	16/-
10-00 a.m.	*Gelia Valley	12/9
10-30 a.m.	*Morecambe Illuminations (ret. 10 p.m.)	16/-
12 noon	*New Brighton (ret. 7 p.m.)	12/6
1-00 p.m.	*Southport (ret. 7 p.m.)	11/-
1-30 p.m.	*Buxton and Matlock	11/9
2-00 p.m.	*Byland Abbey & Thirsk	11/-
2-00 p.m.	*Belle Vue	7/-
6-00 p.m.	*Grassington Tr.	6/3
6-00 p.m.	*Boroughbridge Tour	6/3
6-00 p.m.	Evening Drive	4/3

MONDAY, 21st AUGUST

7-30 a.m.	Beaumaris on the Isle of Anglesey	21/6
7-30 a.m.	*Skegness	20/-
8-00 a.m.	*Lincolnshire Circular	14/-
8-30 a.m.	*Scarborough	16/-
8-30 a.m.	*Bridlington	16/-
8-30 a.m.	*Filey	16/-
8-30 a.m.	*Morecambe	16/-
8-30 a.m.	*Southport	13/3
8-30 a.m.	Blackpool (ret. 6 p.m.)	13/3
8-30 a.m.	*Chester Zoo	12/9
10-00 a.m.	*Alton Towers	15/-
12 noon	*Scarborough (ret. 7 p.m.)	12/9
12-30 p.m.	Pontefract Races	5/-
2-00 p.m.	*Belle Vue	7/-
2-00 p.m.	*Knaresborough via Harrogate	8/6
6-30 p.m.	Leeds G'hounds	4/3

TUESDAY, 22nd AUGUST

7-00 a.m.	*London (5½ hrs. stay)	36/6
7-00 a.m.	*Sandringham & Hunstanton	24/9

7-30 a.m.	*Whitley Bay	22/9
7-30 a.m.	*Stratford - on - Avon	21/9
8-00 a.m.	*Llandudno	20/-
8-00 a.m.	*Rhyl	18/3
8-00 a.m.	*Whitby and Goathland Mrs.	18/9
8-30 a.m.	*Scarborough	16/-
8-30 a.m.	*Bridlington	16/-
8-30 a.m.	*Filey	16/-
8-30 a.m.	*Morecambe	16/-
8-30 a.m.	*Southport	13/3
8-30 a.m.	Blackpool (ret. 6 p.m.)	13/3
10-00 a.m.	*Trentham Gdns.	14/3
11-30 a.m.	York Races	8/6
12 noon	*New Brighton	12/6
1-30 p.m.	*Tatton Park	11/-
2-00 p.m.	*Yorkshire Dales	10/-
2-00 p.m.	*Buxton	10/-
2-00 p.m.	*Belle Vue	7/-

WEDNESDAY, 23rd AUG.

7-00 a.m.	*Wild Fowl Trust, Slimbridge and New Severn Bridge	32/6
7-00 a.m.	*Cambridge (University City)	24/3
7-30 a.m.	*Welsh Mountains & Coast Tour	21/6
7-30 a.m.	*Hadrian's Wall & Northumberland Border Tour	21/6
7-30 a.m.	*Marsden Grotto and Rock	21/-
8-00 a.m.	*Windermere and Morecambe	21/-
8-00 a.m.	*Llandudno	20/-
8-30 a.m.	*Rhyl	18/3
8-30 a.m.	*Scarborough	16/-
8-30 a.m.	*Bridlington	16/-
8-30 a.m.	*Filey	16/-
8-30 a.m.	*Morecambe	16/-
8-30 a.m.	*Southport Flower Show (return 7 p.m.)	13/3
8-30 a.m.	Blackpool (ret. 6 p.m.)	13/3
10-00 a.m.	*Flamingo Park	13/3
11-30 a.m.	York Races	8/6
12 noon	*Bridlington	12/9
1-30 p.m.	*Chatsworth Hse.	8/6
1-30 p.m.	*Richmond and North Yorkshire Tour	13/3

2-00 p.m.	*Dukeries	12/9
2-00 p.m.	*Ingleton	11/-
2-00 p.m.	*Belle Vue	7/-
6-30 p.m.	Bradford G'hds.	3/6

THURSDAY, 24th AUGUST

7-00 a.m.	*London (5½ hrs. stay)	36/6
7-30 a.m.	*Penrith, Ullswater & Windermere	21/6
7-30 a.m.	*Coventry	18/6
8-00 a.m.	*Whitby	18/9
8-30 a.m.	*Scarborough	16/-
8-30 a.m.	*Bridlington	16/-
8-30 a.m.	*Filey	16/-
8-30 a.m.	*Morecambe	16/-
8-30 a.m.	*Southport Flower Show (return 7 p.m.)	13/3
8-30 a.m.	Blackpool (ret. 6 p.m.)	13/3
8-30 a.m.	*Gelia Valley Tr.	12/9
10-00 a.m.	*Gelia Valley Tr.	12/9
11-30 a.m.	York Races	8/6
12 noon	*New Brighton	12/6
1-00 p.m.	*Southport (ret. 7 p.m.)	11/-
1-30 p.m.	*York, Harrogate and Knaresborough	11/-
2-00 p.m.	*Ripon	9/6
2-00 p.m.	*Thornton Dale	11/9
2-00 p.m.	*Belle Vue	7/-

FRIDAY, 25th AUGUST

8-30 a.m.	*Scarborough	16/-
8-30 a.m.	*Bridlington	16/-
8-30 a.m.	*Filey	16/-
8-30 a.m.	*Southport Flower Show (return 7 p.m.)	13/3
8-30 a.m.	Blackpool (ret. 6 p.m.)	13/3
8-30 a.m.	*Chester Zoo	12/9
2-00 p.m.	*Belle Vue	7/-
2-00 p.m.	Hollingw'th Lake	4/3

SATURDAY, 26th AUGUST

12-30 p.m.	Pontefract Races	5/-
6-00 p.m.	Evening Drive	4/3
6-30 p.m.	Bradford G'hds.	3/6
6-30 p.m.	Leeds G'hounds	4/3

SUNDAY, 27th AUGUST

8-30 a.m.	Blackpool (ret. 6 p.m.)	13/3
9-00 a.m.	*Scarborough	16/-
9-00 a.m.	*Bridlington	16/-
9-00 a.m.	*Filey	16/-
9-00 a.m.	*Southport	13/3
10-30 a.m.	*Morecambe Illuminations (ret. 10 p.m.)	16/-
12 noon	*Scarborough	12/9
1-00 p.m.	*Blackpool	11/-
1-30 p.m.	*Chester Zoo	11/-
2-00 p.m.	*Aysgarth and Wensleydale	11/-
2-00 p.m.	*Buxton	10/-
6-00 p.m.	*Monk Fryston and Selby	6/3
6-00 p.m.	*Harewood Cir.	6/3

MONDAY, 28th AUGUST

8-30 a.m.	*Scarborough	16/-
8-30 a.m.	*Bridlington	16/-
8-30 a.m.	*Filey	16/-
8-30 a.m.	Blackpool (ret. 6 p.m.)	13/3
10-30 a.m.	*Morecambe Illuminations (ret. 10 p.m.)	16/-
11-30 a.m.	Ripon Races	9/6
12 noon	*New Brighton (ret. 7 p.m.)	12/6
1-30 p.m.	*Tatton Park	11/-
2-00 p.m.	*Yorkshire Dales	10/-
2-00 p.m.	*Belle Vue	7/-
6-30 p.m.	Leeds G'hounds	4/3

TUESDAY, 29th AUGUST

8-30 a.m.	*Scarborough	16/-
8-30 a.m.	*Bridlington	16/-
8-30 a.m.	*Filey	16/-
8-30 a.m.	Blackpool (ret. 6 p.m.)	13/3
11-30 a.m.	Ripon Races	9/6
2-00 p.m.	*Airedale and Wharfedale	8/6
2-00 p.m.	*York	8/6

WEDNESDAY, 30th AUG.

8-30 a.m.	*Scarborough	16/-
8-30 a.m.	*Bridlington	16/-
8-30 a.m.	*Filey	16/-
8-30 a.m.	Blackpool (ret. 6 p.m.)	13/3
10-00 a.m.	Beverley Races	12/9
10-30 a.m.	*Morecambe Illuminations (ret. 10 p.m.)	16/-
1-00 p.m.	*Southport (ret. 7 p.m.)	11/-
1-30 p.m.	*Chatsworth Hse.	8/6
2-00 p.m.	*Thornton Dale	11/9
2-00 p.m.	*Belle Vue	7/-

THURSDAY, 31st AUGUST

8-30 a.m.	*Scarborough	16/-
8-30 a.m.	*Bridlington	16/-
8-30 a.m.	*Filey	16/-
8-30 a.m.	Blackpool (ret. 6 p.m.)	13/3
10-00 a.m.	Beverley Races	12/9
2-00 p.m.	*Ripon (Market Day)	9/6
2-00 p.m.	*Historic York	8/6

Book at our Travel Bureau

35 John William Street
HUDDERSFIELD   **Tel. 26666**
OR LOCAL BOOKING AGENTS

Express Travel by HANSON COACH SERVICE

NORFOLK BROADS

SERVING
NORWICH
WROXHAM
HORNING
POTTER HEIGHAM
&c.

JUNE to SEPTEMBER
INCLUSIVE

CELEBRATE
90 YEARS
of Passenger
Travel with

HANSON

MYSTERY DESTINATION
WEEKENDS
IN 2008

Sets off from Huddersfield at 10.30 am
Saturday Morning to a Secret
Destination where you will have an
Evening Meal and stay the night.
Returning Sunday after Breakfasting,
via an entirely Different Route.

£59 per person
Includes one night's Bed & Breakfast
And Evening Meal
Single Rooms Available no supplement

interchanges
Booth Wood and M62 via Ainley Top interchange
Scammonden Dam and Luddenden Valley via Mount Tabor

These licences were for all year round operation, in contrast to the usual seasonal restriction (March to October). This was a portent as on 17 July 1970 all excursion licences hitherto valid for a seasonal period became valid for all year operation. Just in time for the illuminations traffic, an alternative route via the M62 was granted for the Blackpool express service (duplicates presumably) and excursions, joining at Outlane.

An ICI contract required three coaches to transport workers from the Barnsley district to Huddersfield. Towards the end of September 1970 Yorkshire Traction bus crews decided to take industrial action in support of a pay claim. On 2 October two car loads of 'flying pickets' pulled up immediately behind and in front of one of the coaches at Kexbrough Hill near Darton. Some of the pickets engaged the Hansons driver in conversation while others let down one of the tyres. A relief coach was despatched from Huddersfield to collect the stranded workers.

Following the disposal of the bus operations in 1969, licence applications were made in the name of Hanson Coach Service Ltd, an existing company reformed, from July 1971 onwards.

At the end of the 1971/72 season Huddersfield Town football club were relegated from the first to the second division. In order to continue running excursions to the away matches, Hansons had to apply for a new group of licences to include Bristol, Cardiff, Carlisle, Luton, Oxford and Swindon. Worse was to follow and in 1973 Town were relegated at the end of the season to the third division. A further group of licences to grounds at Aldershot, Bournemouth, Brighton, Chesterfield, Grimsby, Hereford, Plymouth, Walsall and Wrexham was duly obtained.

The final licence to be obtained by Hansons as a family owned business - in March 1974 - was for a Monday to Friday private charter service to ICI Hexagon House at Blackley, Manchester. The route was via the M62 from Outlane as far as Junction 20 and Heaton Park. On 8 March 1974 the last new coaches ordered by the Hanson family business entered service as 432/3 (PCX 932/3M), Plaxton bodied Ford R114s.

AEC/Hanson Regent/Roe rebuild 370 (VVH 350) is parked in Upperhead Row Bus Station on 12 June 1969. The Meltham via Milnsbridge, Linthwaite, Blackmoorfoot and Helme route, operated entirely by Hansons, was an arduous one, featuring narrow lanes, awkward bends and particularly steep and lengthy hills. Latterly it ran half hourly with 65 seater double deck rebuilds. There were also extensions to Meltham Mills for David Browns shift changes and short workings as far as Linthwaite Church. [H.J. Black]

AEC Regent rebuild 370 (VVH 350) leaves Upperhead Row Bus Station on 5 August 1968. Hansons buses never carried external advertising. 370 was rebuilt in 1962 from the running units of a single decker, 1950 AEC Regal III coach 325 (EVH 807). [H.J. Black]

A slow climb up Slaithwaite Gate is bringing AEC/Hanson Regal rebuild 369 (VVH 349) into Scapegoat Hill. Previously the bus would have passed through a wintry Bolster Moor which can scarcely be seen in the background. After withdrawal by Huddersfield Corporation, this vehicle was later used by an operator in Wyke, Bradford. [Photobus]

The Lidget Street, Lindley terminus of the cross-suburban routes to Newsome via Paddock Head, Milnsbridge and Lockwood Bar is the location of AEC/Hanson Reliance rebuild 391 (ECX 889C) on 9 July 1969. Although rebuilt only in 1965, it was subsequently disposed of by Huddersfield Corporation in 1972. [H.J. Black]

Four coaches new in April 1968 included Ford R192/Plaxton 409 (NVH 372F). This 45 seater is parked in St John's Road on 8 September 1971. The next picture – in the Metro Hanson section - shows this vehicle after the sale to the PTE in May 1974. [H.J. Black]

11: METRO HANSON, METROCOACH, ABBEYWAYS HANSON AND HANSON EUROPA (1974 onwards)

On 1 May 1974 Hansons became the first coach operator to be acquired by the very recently established West Yorkshire Passenger Transport Executive, which has always used the name Metro. A price tag of £250,000 was rumoured but this was neither confirmed nor denied by Christopher Harding, managing director of the Hanson Transport Group. It had been agreed with the PTE that the sum would not be disclosed. The public was assured that from their point of view there would be no changes as the same coaches would be driven by the same drivers and even the Hanson name would be retained. The PTE had been keen to acquire a coach company, as was then the fashion; they had even briefly considered making an offer for Leeds based Wallace Arnold.

The fleet at this date comprised 23 full size and mostly Plaxton bodied Ford coaches (408-11/3-29/32/3) and two Ford Transit minicoaches (430/1). In the PTE fleet numbering scheme, the Transits were in theory allocated 36/7 but 430 became 88 and 431 was only used as a service vehicle (in Bradford); the other coaches were renumbered 65-87 in the same order as their former Hansons numbers. The use of the Bottomley livery and name, still in evidence on a handful of coaches, was discontinued; Ford 85 was the last to run in the blue livery. Most of

For a short period not long after the takeover, West Yorkshire PTE painted some older Hansons coaches in this buttermilk and green livery. Metro Hanson Ford/Plaxton 66 (NVH 372F) is parked opposite the depot in St John's Road on 20 June 1975. Compare this picture with that of Hansons 409 at the same location – this is the same coach. [H.J. Black]

Never mind the man on the Clapham omnibus, here we see Metro Hanson's Clapham coach, Ford/Plaxton 82 (BCX 426K) parked in the North Yorkshire village of that name on 15 April 1977. The vehicle had been new as Hansons 426 in March 1972. [H.J. Black]

Mercedes L406D/Deansgate 13-seater 30 (YUA 530J) was new to Leeds City Transport in 1970 when it was exhibited at the motor show at Earl's Court. 30 was operated by the PTE's Metro Hanson business from August to October 1975 and is pictured here on 26 August in St John's Road opposite the Hansons depot. It was later exported to Sri Lanka. [H.J. Black]

West Yorkshire PTE Bristol LHS/ECW 38 (JUG 354N) with "dual purpose" high backed seating was new in July 1975 when it was allocated to Hansons along with two others. Parked here in St John's Road, Huddersfield on 11 August, in November it was transferred to Leeds, where such buses were used on city centre routes. 38 was afterwards operated by Merseyside PTE and City of Nottingham Transport. [H.J. Black]

The first of the Plaxton bodied Volvo B58-B56 coaches obtained by West Yorkshire PTE and licensed to Hanson Coach Service Ltd were new in August 1975. 1508 (LUB 508P) is seen in Freiburg, Germany during a visit to the Black Forest. This coach was later operated by various small Scottish independents, including a then obscure Perth firm called Stagecoach. [V. Nutton]

the coaches were gradually repainted into a new Hanson buttermilk and dark red livery with "Metro Hanson" as the fleetname; the PTE's "WY" logo was also displayed. Late in 1975 a new insignia began to appear on the boot consisting of a large rectangle divided into two halves. The first half bore the word 'Metro' in white on a red background while the word 'Hanson' in red on a white background appeared in the second half. There was some movement of vehicles between Metro Hanson and the Calderdale and Leeds districts of the PTE, which resulted in coaches (and Bristol LHS midibuses with dual purpose seating) in buttermilk and verona green, the standard PTE colours, running from St John's Road depot. Also some older Metro Hanson coaches were painted in PTE buttermilk and green on the basis that they were "second rank" vehicles as for a period red was used only on front rank stock. It was only in March 1976 that Ford 84, the last coach in traditional Hansons livery, was repainted buttermilk and red.

On 1 December 1974 the new Huddersfield bus station in Upperhead Row had been brought into use. Metro Hanson opened a travel office and their excursions and express services initially used bays 17 and 18 but were later transferred to 1 to 6, the draughty unenclosed bays at the Westgate end of the station.

By May 1976 the 12 oldest Fords had been replaced by nine Volvo B58 (1506-14) and five Ford R1114 (1515-9) coaches, all with Plaxton bodywork. At this stage Metro Hanson were running the following express services:
Huddersfield-Blackpool, daily May to October; also over Christmas and Easter
Huddersfield-Bridlington, Saturday during Huddersfield Holidays only
Marsh (Luck Lane)-Huddersfield-Scarborough, Saturday during Huddersfield Holidays only
Huddersfield-Llandudno, Saturday during Huddersfield Holidays only
Huddersfield-Torquay, Friday out/Saturday return July and August
Huddersfield-Morecambe, Saturday Spring Bank Holiday to September; also Easter
Huddersfield-Great Yarmouth, Friday out/Saturday return June to September
These routes were also operated in 1977, basically unchanged except that the Marsh-Bus Station section of the Scarborough service was no longer advertised.

On 27 January 1977 as an economy measure the Metro Hanson fleet was transferred to the former Hud-dersfield Corporation depot at Longroyd Bridge. At this stage the rolling stock consisted of 16 Fords (77-87, 1515-9), 9 Volvos (1506-14) and 2 Leyland Leopards (99/100). The PTE sold the St John's Road depot, which had recently been allocated garage code 4C (the former Corporation Leeds Road depot was 4A and Longroyd Bridge was 4B), but retained the ex-Bottomley Luck Lane premises.

It soon became clear that all was not well financially and the PTE placed their three coaching subsidiaries (Metro Hanson, Baddeleys, acquired in March 1976, and Bingleys of Kinsley, near Hemsworth, acquired in April 1977) under common management to ensure better utilisation of resources. In December 1977 an overall red livery, first seen on Volvo 1507, reappeared with the 'Hanson' fleetname over the front wheel arches and 'MetroCoach' resplendent in the middle of both sides.

Volvo 1506 was entered in the 1978 Blackpool Coach Rally (April 1-2), bringing back memories of happier times when the independent firm had regularly won trophies at this prestigious event. From 24 March to the end of October 1978 a combined "Hanson's and Baddeley Metrocoach" excursions programme from Huddersfield and district was advertised. A wider range of picking up points was available and agencies of both companies could take bookings for all the excursions. There was also a combined booking office in Huddersfield Bus Station. Summer express services, now operated under the MetroCoach identity, were to some extent rationalised. The former Hansons Morecambe route was withdrawn with facilities provided by a diverted Bingleys service but the Metro Hanson Yarmouth service gained a stop at Upton to replace Bingleys. Metro Hanson also ran Holiday Saturday services from Meltham via Marsden to Blackpool, Filey and Morecambe.

The rationalisation of the coaching subsidiaries' activities led to a reduction in the size of the Metro Hanson fleet. By April 1978 the Leopards and most of the Fords had been sold or transferred elsewhere within the PTE and by May only 15 coaches were left: Volvo B58 1506-14 and Ford R1114 87/1515-9, with 87 the only survivor from the independent company.

Unfortunately the financial results for the year ending March 1978 turned out to be much worse than expected and the PTE management ordered a review of the loss making operations of the Hanson and Baddeleys subsidiaries. With catastrophic timing on 15 May 1978 Ford coach 83 (FVH 427L), new to the independent Hansons as 427 but actually operating for the PTE's Calderdale District, was involved in a fatal collision at Newton Hill roundabout on the outskirts of Wakefield as a result of brakes failure. The coach was on a private hire for the Police Federation and five police officers were killed and 24 injured. Public confidence in all the MetroCoach subsidiaries was soon at a low ebb and it later became clear that some of their employees had little confidence in the PTE management's handling of the coaching side. An invoice later came to light which showed that the coach involved in the crash was one of four which had been sold to Bingleys on 4 April for £37,850. A PTE spokesman said, however, that the coach was still owned by Metro Hanson at the time but was being operated by Bingleys who had in turn loaned it to Metro Calderdale. The PTE were criticised for failing to keep adequate maintenance records, as a result of which the brakes defect had not been dealt with.

The financial problems of Metro Hanson and Baddeleys were alleged to have arisen in part because the PTE had insisted on employing only full time drivers on the coaches. It was said that major policy decisions were taken by senior PTE management who had little experience of the coaching business and did not consult anyone who had.

The report reviewing the PTE's coaching subsidiaries appeared in October 1978 and contained a statement that Metro Hanson, together with Baddeleys and Bingleys, had lost more than £400,000 since the PTE takeovers. The three companies survived a traffic commissioners' disciplinary hearing but it was soon clear that the PTE wished to dispose of the Metro Hanson and Baddeleys businesses, in accordance with the political philosophy of the Conservative controlled Passenger Transport Authority who regarded coach operation as a private sector business.

Christopher Harding of Hanson Haulage pointed out that Hanson Coach Service had been a profitable operation before the PTE takeover. He stressed that Hansons had not offered the business for sale in 1974; the approach had come from the PTE. Moreover the PTE had made a payment for the goodwill of the business, which suggested that it was making a reasonable return for the capital employed running it. He added that the PTE operation had become a political football and that he had no desire to be in the arena.

Richard Faulkner, prospective Labour parliamentary candidate for Huddersfield West, claimed that inadequate financial discipline had been the cause of the vast loss since the takeover. Raymond Lax, Conservative chairman of West Yorkshire Passenger Transport Authority accused Mr Faulkner of not knowing all the facts. While refusing to admit to any maladministration, he did regret that the Hanson Travel Agency business had not been bought along with the coach business; as it was, a vital bank of expertise had been lost.

An employee who had worked for Hansons before and after the 1974 takeover blamed both the PTE and the unions for the bleak outlook. He pointed out that Hansons had previously bought only four new coaches each year whereas the PTE had immediately ordered 14 new Volvo coaches, each costing approximately £5,000 more than a comparable British vehicle. [As we have seen, only nine of these were actually delivered to Metro Hanson.] He also claimed that the new managers seemed obsessed with the idea that they would eventually wipe all competing firms off the coaching map with their streamlined operation.

Just before noon on 1 March 1979 Metro Hanson staff positioned a number of coaches to seal off the entrance and exit of Huddersfield bus station for one hour as a protest about the impending sale. A telegram was sent to William Rodgers, the transport minister, calling for his intervention.

A buyer had, however, been found for Hansons and in a separate move all the Volvos quickly passed to a dealer in early March, being temporarily replaced by two Leyland Leopards from Bingleys and a Ford from Baddeleys. On 1 April 1979 the share capital of Hanson Coach Service Ltd was sold to Geoffrey Wainwright of Halifax, who was also involved with the Abbeyways coach firm. Abbeyways were already part of the coaching scene in Huddersfield because of an earlier connection with the long established Haighs Tours, which had ceased trading in 1974. The remaining six Ford coaches (87, 1515-9) were garaged at the former Bottomley premises in Luck Lane, Marsh which the PTE passed to Wainwright at the same time. The company concentrated on traditional work such as excursions to Blackpool.

On 1 October 1979 David Peace, a former traffic manager of Hansons, acquired three of the Fords (1516/8/9) together with the Luck Lane, Marsh premises from Wainwright. He set up a new company, Tovinco Ltd, and traded as Hanson Europa, mostly using the traditional red livery. Interestingly from 14 July 1987 Hanson Europa ran a minibus service under contract to West Yorkshire PTE. Route 277 (Netherton-Horbury-Ossett) was operated on Tuesday and Friday only and there were five return journeys during off peak shopping periods. West Riding ran Monday to Friday peak hour journeys on 277 and after 24 June 1988 took over the Hanson Europa share as well so this Hanson bus service was shortlived. Peace later closed the business down and the Tovinco company was dissolved on 17 October 1995.

Meanwhile in November 1979 Steven Ives had bought the goodwill of Abbeyways together with a controlling interest in Hanson Coach Service Ltd. He also set up and

MNW 518P was one of five Ford R1114/Plaxton 51 seater coaches (1515-19) new to Metro Hanson in May 1976 and sold by the PTE with the Hanson concern to Wainwright of Abbeyways in April 1979. Three of these Fords quickly passed to former Hansons manager David Peace's new Tovinco company. Tovinco traded as Hanson Europa and MNW 518P carried its fleet number 3 at Huddersfield Bus Station on 25 July 1980. [H.J. Black]

TGD 999R AEC Reliance 6U32R with Caetano Lisboa II coachwork, photographed on the 9th July 1982 at Scratchwood Services on the M1 Motorway
[Omnibus Society/P. Sparrow]

A brand new coach for Hanson Europa in August 1981 was 11 (OCX 670X), a Ford R1114/Duple 53 seater. 11 upholds the traditional Hansons style in Huddersfield Bus Station on 23 March 1982. [H.J. Black]

63

Ford R1114/Caetano 53 seater NHD 838W wears a more contemporary livery. New in June 1981, this Hanson Europa coach stands in the old Bottomleys parking ground at Marsh, Huddersfield on 29 November 1982. [H.J. Black]

Also at the Marsh parking ground – on 24 November 1987 – is Hanson Europa 27 (D175 XCP), a Toyota/Caetano 19 seater new in March 1987. A Pride of the Road fleetname was also displayed, indicating at this stage an association with that company, which ran local bus services in Huddersfield from the former Hansons depot in St John's Road for a period soon after deregulation. [H.J. Black]

Hanson Europa 29 (KCX 826S) was a Duple bodied Ford R1114. On 2 March 1988 it was parked in Luck Lane, Marsh by the junction with Jim Lane and the former Bottomleys garage. KCX 826S was not, however, this coach's original registration. It had been new in April 1978 to Smith of Wigan as WED 974S; re-registration in November 1987 to a Huddersfield mark was doubtless intended to give the impression of a genuine Hanson coach. Far from it – KCX 826S with Hanson livery, fleet number and fleetname and working from Luck Lane garage actually belonged to then associated company Pride of the Road. [H.J. Black]

acquired several other companies and his business became known as the Traject Group. He traded extensively as Abbeyways-Ivesway but he also continued to use the Hanson name (but not the livery). In 1984 the Hanson Coach Service Ltd subsidiary owned, appropriately enough, four AEC Reliances – in Abbeyways Ivesway orange and white livery. By 1988 the Ivesway part of the name had been dropped. Probably by December 1989 most Traject Group vehicles (such as Scania coaches and a MetroRider mini) carried an "Abbeyways Hanson" fleetname on Abbeyways livery and this is still the trading name of the Abbeyways booking office at Huddersfield bus station.

After deregulation of local bus services for a time Abbeyways ran an assortment of routes, commercial and tendered, in the Halifax and Huddersfield areas. From 28 February 1988 they operated service 398 (Huddersfield Bus Station-Lepton-Houses Hill), replacing Yorkshire Traction, and this seems to have been the route that survived for the longest period. Of particular interest is the final timetable leaflet (9 September 1995) in which the operator was shown not as Abbeyways but as "Hansons Coach Service" at the Abbeyways Halifax address. The service was withdrawn shortly afterwards so this leaflet would seem to be the very last Hansons bus timetable.

[Above] Three months after Wainwright of Abbeyways had acquired Hanson Coach Service from the PTE, Hanson 1 (LJX 700T), a 35 seater Ford R1014/Plaxton brand new in June, was seen in Huddersfield Bus Station on 5 July 1979. This particular Hanson image was shortlived as soon afterwards Wainwright sold part of his business to Ives (Traject) and some of his vehicles to Marsh based Hanson Europa. [H.J. Black]

[Right] Not many AEC buses or coaches were running in Huddersfield by 16 May 1988 when Abbeyways 1980 AEC Reliance/Plaxton FCX 576W was entering the bus station on service 398 (Huddersfield-Lepton-Houses Hill). The Traject Group was a late buyer of Reliances and the destination display is typical of that of many coaches used on bus services soon after the 1986 deregulation. [H.J. Black]

The Hanson company was dissolved on 27 February 1996. Hanson and Abbeyways are now trading names of Abbeyways-Hanson Coach Services Ltd. Some Abbeyways-Hanson coaches have been painted in all over deep red with Hanson fleetname; this development had presumably been a possibility since the demise of the Hanson Europa company.

The St Johns Road depot had been disposed of separately by the PTE but has since been used as a bus depot by Pride of the Road, who introduced commercial services in Huddersfield some years after deregulation, and later by Paul's Travel/Easirider (Singh). The latter has even run bus routes to Golcar and Marsden.

On long term contract hire from Hyndburn Transport to Abbeyways was JND 997N, a Leyland Leopard/Duple new in 1975 to Greater Manchester PTE (SELNEC Travel). The coach is leaving Huddersfield Bus Station for Marsden on 22 June 1988. [H.J. Black]

Hyndburn Transport of Accrington 43 (EHG 43S), a Leyland Leopard/East Lancs new in 1977, was on long term loan to Abbeyways Hanson when seen entering Huddersfield Bus Station on 5 September 1988 on route 398 (Houses Hill). [H.J. Black]

Latterly various minibuses were used on Abbeyways Hanson route 398 to Lepton/Houses Hill. MCW Metrorider G685 KNW waits in Huddersfield Bus Station on 12 March 1990. The bus station was undergoing major alterations, hence the temporarily primitive appearance of the bays on the right. [H.J. Black]

Abbeyways bought Mercedes 609D/Reeve Burgess 25 seater minicoach F794 UVH new in November 1988. It is pictured entering Huddersfield Bus Station on 19 January 1989 and was one of several minis passed to Yorkshire Rider later in the year (21 June) when Abbeyways abandoned commercial bus operation. [H.J. Black]

One of the smallest vehicles used by Abbeyways Hanson on the 398 to Houses Hill was 15 seater F69 SPA built in 1988. This Mercedes 407D/Reeve Burgess minicoach had been acquired from Bicknell of Godalming, Surrey during 1989. It was about to be reversed off the stand in Huddersfield Bus station on 25 July 1990. [H.J. Black]

Abbeyways Hanson Scania K93CRB/Van Hool 55 seater G802 FJX was new in January 1990 and is entering Huddersfield Bus Station on 7 October 1994. The Blue Bus Leyland Leopard/Alexander on the right, PRA 114R new to Trent, was operating a competitive service to Marsden over a route run by Hansons in the 1930s.
[H.J. Black]

Mercedes 0404/Hispano Y741 DDA was new in July of 2001 to Austin of Earlston in the Scottish Borders. It was later acquired by Abbeyways Hanson and painted in the reintroduced red Hanson livery complete with fleetnames. The lettering in front of the emergency door towards the rear reads "In a Different Class"; this also appears as a slogan on recent Hanson excursion leaflets.
[S.T. Harling collection]

APPENDIX 1: TICKETING

Hansons used punch tickets printed by the Bell Punch Company. Early issues had J Hanson and Son Ltd as the title whereas after 15 April 1935 the title became Hanson's Buses Ltd. As routes increased in length, higher value tickets were required. Most tickets were 2.5 inches x 1.25 inches, with two exceptions, the 3d and exchange tickets, which measured 3.125 inches x 1.25 inches. For the Meltham route the maximum single fare was originally 6d and the minimum the $^1/_2$d half fare. The minimum fare from Town was $2^1/_2$d so the 1d ticket was only issued outside the borough, for example, for the journey between Linthwaite Church and Heights. A $4^1/_2$d ticket was required for the fare between Pinfold and Helme and a $5^1/_2$d ticket for the fare between Town and Will's o'Nat's Road. Workmen's returns at one and a half times the single fare were issued for journeys ending before 9.00am; these tickets had a large red W overprint and were different in colour from the single tickets. The colours of the single tickets were as follows: $^1/_2$d green; 1d white; $1^1/_2$d orange; 2d light blue; $2^1/_2$d purple; 3d pink; $3^1/_2$d lilac; 4d green; $4^1/_2$d brown; 5d cerise; $5^1/_2$d white; 6d yellow; 7d beige.

For the longer Oldham route higher value tickets were required. Minimum fares of 6d (or 9d) and 7d applied for many years out of Huddersfield and Oldham respectively The through single fare was 1/6d so tickets in penny increments between 8d and 1/6d were required besides the lower values already mentioned. The colours of a few higher value singles are known: 9d pale brown; 1/- magenta; 1/1d pink with a vertical central blue stripe; 1/6d stone.

Workmen's returns on this route were issued only on the first bus of the day at the rate of only one and a quarter times the single fare, presumably as this was the rate charged by the North Western company on routes out of Oldham for many years. Ordinary returns up to 2/6d were also used on this route. Few return tickets seem to have survived, probably because on the return journey they were retained by the conductor, who then issued an exchange ticket. The colours of those known are: $2^1/_2$d orange; 4d purple and 7d deep salmon.

As already mentioned Hansons tickets were of the shorter type, probably on grounds of cost, with the exception of the 3d single and the exchange ticket. The routes varied considerably in length, as did the number of stage letters required. Golcar used stages A to H whereas Oldham required stages A to T, Huddersfield being stage A. The variations in the stage letter ranges actually printed on the different values of tickets may seem puzzling but some examples will clarify the situation. While it was desirable to use the same tickets for all routes, if they had been printed with the full range of stages, A to S (out) and T to B (in), all would have been of the greater length. As, however, minimum fares were in operation at both ends of the Oldham route, only the intermediate stages were actually required on low value tickets. For example, 1d tickets were only issued on outward journeys between Marsden (H) and Horse and Jockey (M) and on the inward journey between Ambrose (M) and Warrington Terrace (I). To cater for half fares the inward stage (O) Uppermill was also needed. Therefore, so that the ticket was also suitable for the short routes, the full range of printed stages was A to N (out) and O to B (in). Even so, correct punching was impossible from Meltham (Q) and, later, Meltham Mills (R).

The 3d ticket, for use on the Oldham route as either an adult single or a child's half 6d fare, required outward stages A to P (Greenfield) and inward S to D (Jovil); all half fares from Jovil, Pickford Street or Thornton Lodge to Huddersfield were 3d so stages C and B in this direction were superfluous. The sixteen fare letters made the extra length necessary.

The higher the fare, the smaller was the range of stages which was actually required. For a 7d fare on the Oldham route, stages A to M (Horse and Jockey) were required outwards with T to I (Warrington Terrace) inwards; in fact, to keep the printing symmetrical, stages T to H were printed. For a 1/1d fare outward stages A to G (Olive Branch) were required along with inward stages T to O (Uppermill) but for symmetry T to M was actually printed. Two different $5^1/_2$d tickets exist with stages (A to M and T to H) and (A to I and T to L) respectively. It would appear that the former was an adult ticket for the Meltham route while the latter was a half fare ticket used on Oldham buses. The fare stage letters used on Hansons tickets did not appear on the publicly available faretables so remained something of a mystery as far as passengers were concerned.

The white exchange ticket with a large blue E overprint was printed with all stages (A to T) so that it could be used on all routes including Oldham – with 17 letters the longer version was again needed.

From 23 September 1939 on the joint Colne Valley Services both Hansons and Huddersfield JOC used the same tickets overprinted CVS in red or green. These had the usual JOC stage letters A to O printed down both sides. The maximum single fare was 6d to Wilberlee with a corresponding 9d workmen's return. For the minimum fares of $^1/_2$d child and 1d adult small (two and a half inches by one and a quarter inches) yellow and white tickets were used. Larger (three and four sevenths inches by one and a quarter inches) composite tickets were used for values $1^1/_2$d to 9d. With a tear off tab, these could be punched as either singles or returns. The usual Huddersfield JOC colours were used: $1^1/_2$d blue; 2d pink; $2^1/_2$d mauve; 3d green; 4d purple; $4^1/_2$d dark orange; 5d khaki; 6d rust; 8d fawn; 9d bright green. Subsequent fares increases in 1949 and 1951 led to the introduction of further composite tickets for these values: $3^1/_2$d grey; $5^1/_2$d light brown; 7d sepia; $7^1/_2$d fawn; 11d purple; 1/- mauve. There was also a small size $1^1/_2$d ticket.

From 31 March 1953 Hansons started using Setright machines. The tickets were preprinted with the slogan "Travel the highway the Hanson way". The title was Hanson's Buses Ltd, Huddersfield and the colour of the paper rolls varied (white, pink, orange or beige). Long after the demise of the Hansons buses the name lived on in Gwynedd, North Wales, as Purple Motors of Bethesda purchased surplus Setright rolls from Hansons. They were noted in use in 1980 in machines which printed the word 'Purple' but had still not been converted for decimal currency.

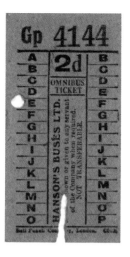
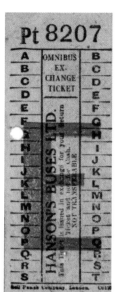
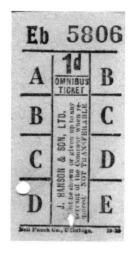
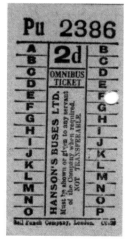
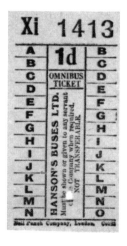

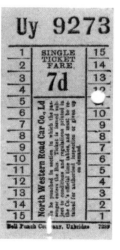

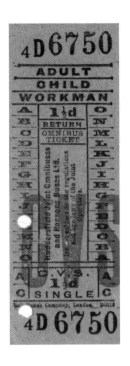

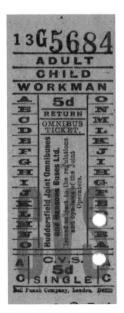

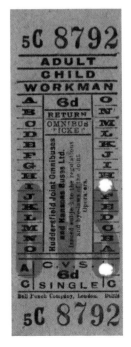

71

APPENDIX 2: FLEET LIST

The early fleet is particularly complicated. Fleet numbers were not used from the beginning and when their use started, probably in 1924, they were not used in sequence. In later years the haulage vehicles were numbered in the same series. Many vehicles were rebodied, sometimes more than once; this sometimes but not always resulted in a change of fleet number. Some of the later rebuilds gained both a new fleet number and a new registration number.

NO.	REG'N	CHASSIS	BODY	IN	OUT	NOTES
"Midget"		Leyland	Ch14	1919		
"Kitchener"		Leyland	Ch30?	1919		
-	DN 721	Leyland	Ch?	pre-1922		
-	CX 2578	Dennis	?	ditto		
-	CX 2882	Karrier WDS	?	ditto	1924	
8	CX 3133	Leyland	B30F	ditto	1929?	
?	CX 5169	Crossley	?	1922	1938	
3	MH 1281	Lancia	B19	1924	1934	
6	CX 6914	Leyland SG9	Leyland B38D	1924	1932	
9	CX 6882	Leyland A13	Leyland B26	1924	1925	
7	CX 7916	Karrier JK	B30?	1925	?	
12	CX 9925	Leyland PLSC1	Leyland B31F	1927	1936	
14	CX 9969	Leyland PLSC1	Leyland B31F	1927	1934	
18	VH 1071	Leyland PLSC1	Leyland B?R	1927	1936	
4	VH 1438	Leyland PLSC3	Massey C32	1928	1935	*1
5	VH 1463	Lancia	C20	1928	1935	
19	VH 1703	Leyland PLSC1	Leyland B31F	1928	1938	
20	WW 3672	Leyland PLSC1	B32	1929	1935	*2
21/2	VH 2066/7	Leyland TS2	Ramsden C32R	1929	1935	
23/4	VH 2215/6	Leyland LT1	Leyland B30F	1929	1941-5	*28
28	WW 7234	Leyland PLSC1	Leyland B31F	1929	1938	*3
25	VH 2728	Leyland LT1	Leyland B30F	1930	1940	Also recorded as C30F.
26/7	VH 2852/1	Leyland LT1	Leyland B30F	1930	1939-47	
30	VH 3015	Leyland TS2	Leyland B30F	1930	1942	Also recorded as C30F.
31	VH 3097	Maudslay ML6	Buckingham B30F	1930	1936	
36/7	VH 3541/2	AEC Regal	Burlingham C32R	1930	1936	
35	VH 3544	Leyland LT2	Buckingham B32F	1931	1939	
38	VH 3543	Leyland LT2	Burlingham B32F	1931	1940	
51/2	VH 4214/5	Leyland LT5	Burlingham C30F	1932	1939-47	*4
54	VH 2087	Albion LB40	C20F	1932	1936	*5
55	VH 4576	AEC Regal	Brush B32F	1932	1947	*6
59/61	VH 4873/4	AEC Regal	Brush B32F	1933	1947	*6
60	VH 4875	Leyland TD2	Leyland H24/24R	1933	1939	
62	VH 5138	Leyland TS4	Leyland B32F	1933	1945	
63	VH 5137	Leyland TD2	Leyland H24/24R	1933	1949	*7
65	VH 5335	Leyland TS6	English Electric B30F	1933	1942	Also recorded as C30R.

66	VH 5428	AEC Regal	Duple C32R	1933	1940	Also recorded as B32F.
70/1	VH 6430/1	Leyland LT5A	Burlingham B32R	1934	1947	
72/3	VH 6432/3	Leyland LT5A	Plaxton C32F	1934	1945	
76	VH 8081	Leyland TD4	Leyland H26/26R	1935	1949	*8
78-80	VH 8700-2	AEC Regal	Burlingham C32F	1936	1947-9	
87-9	ACX 366-8	AEC Regal	Burlingham C32F	1937	1947	
110-2	AVH 900-2	AEC Regal	Burlingham B35F	1938	*9	*9
113	AVH 903	AEC Regal	Plaxton C32F	1938	*10	*10
124/5	BVH 480/1	AEC Regal	Plaxton B32F	1939	1949	
151/2	CCX 446/7	Albion CX13	Burlingham B35F	1941	1950	
176/7	CCX 762/3	Bedford OWB	Duple B32F	1945	1946	
183	CCX 810	Guy Arab II 6LW	Roe L27/28R	1945	1955	
186-9	CCX 880-3	Albion CX13	Pickering B34F	1945	1950	
196-9	CVH 226-9	Albion CX13	Pickering B35F	1946	1950	
211-13	CVH 239-41	Bedford OB	Duple C29F	1946	1948	
216-9	CVH 986-9	Bedford OB	Plaxton C29F	1947	1948-9	
221/2	DCX 256/7	Bedford OB	Plaxton C29F	1947	1949	
215	DCX 301	Bedford OB	Duple C29F	1947	1949	
230-2	DCX 447-9	AEC Regal	Brush DP35F	1947	1952-3	
223/4	DCX 626/7	Bedford OB	Plaxton C29F	1947	1949	
233	DCX 628	Bedford OB	Plaxton C29F	1947	1950	
237	DCX 738	Bedford OB	SMT C29F	1947	1950	
227/8	DCX 838/83	Maudslay Marathon 3	Plaxton C32F	1947	1950	
235/6	DCX 885/6	Albion CX13	Burlingham B35F	1947	1958-60	
238	DVH 81	Bedford OB	SMT C29F	1947	1950	
239	DVH 169	Bedford OB	Duple C29F	1947	1950	
244	AVH 901	AEC Regal	Duple DP32F	*9	1952	*9
261	DCX 884	Bedford OB	Plaxton C29F	1948	1952	
240	DVH 183	Bedford OB	Duple C29F	1948	1952	
241/2	DVH 210/7	Bedford OB	Duple C29F	1948	1948-50	
229	DVH 276	Maudslay Marathon 3	Plaxton C32F	1948	1950	
243	DVH 311	AEC Regal III	Duple C35F	1948	*11	*11
245/6	DVH 312/3	AEC Regal III	Duple C35F	1948	*11	*11
247/8	DVH 409/682	Maudslay Marathon 3	Plaxton C32F	1948	1950	
262/3	DVH 434/531	Bedford OB	Duple C29F	1948	1952	
249/50	DVH 821/2	Albion CX13	Duple B35F	1948	1960-2	
264	DVH 837	Bedford OB	Duple C29F	1948	1952	
266/7	ECX 80/1	Bedford OB	Duple C29F	1948	1950-1	
265	ECX 79	Bedford OB	Plaxton C29F	1949	1951	
268-71	ECX 82/3/412/3	Bedford OB	Duple C29F	1949	1950-2	
285-7	ECX 414-6	AEC Regent III	Roe H31/25R	1949	1961-3	*12
272-4	ECX 566/99/983	Bedford OB	Duple C29F	1949	1952-4	
282	ECX 741	AEC Regal III	Duple DP35F	1949	1959	*12
283/4	AVH 902/3	AEC Regal	Duple DP35F	*9*10	1953-60	*9*10

288-93	EVH 82-7	AEC Regal III	Duple B35F	1950	1959-64	*12
275/6/9	EVH 283/719/578	Bedford OB	Duple C29F	1950	1953-4	
294-6	EVH 807/5/6	AEC Regal III	Duple C33F	1950	*13	*13
297-9	EVH 808/9/4	AEC Regal III	Duple C33F	1950	*13	*13
277/8	EVH 882/3	Bedford OB	Duple C29F	1950	1954	
280	FCX 697	Bedford SB	Duple C33F	1951	1954	
306-8	FVH 21/180/232	Bedford SB	Plaxton C33F	1951	1954	
309	FVH 274	Bedford SB	Duple C33F	1951	1954	
305	GWU 624	Maudslay Marathon 2	Barnaby C33F	1951	1960	*14
301-4	FVH 357-60	AEC Regal IV	Roe DP41F	1952	1964-5	
310/1	FVH 351/411	Bedford SB	Duple C33F	1952	1958-61	
312-5	FVH 314/402/3/12	Bedford SB	Plaxton C35F	1952	1958-60	
321	FVH 480	Bedford SB	Duple C33F	1952	1954	
322-4	DVH 311-3	AEC Regal III	Plaxton FC33F	*11	1956-9	*11
325-30	EVH 807/5/6/8/9/4	AEC Regal III	Plaxton FC33F	*13	1960-2	*13
331	HCX 213	Bedford SBG	Plaxton C35F	1954	1962	
332	HCX 214	AEC Regal IV	Plaxton C41C	1954	1963	
333-5	HVH 209-11	AEC Reliance	Roe DP41F	1954	1966-7	
336-8	JCX 753-5	AEC Reliance	Plaxton C41C	1955	1963	*12
339	VH 5731	AEC Regent	Burlingham C33F	1955	1955	*15 *16
340	JH 8067	AEC Regal	Burlingham FC35F	1955	1956	*15 *17
341	ECX 135	AEC Regal	Santus C33F	1955	1955	*15 *18
342	COV 851	AEC Regal	Burlingham C33F	1955	1955	*15 *19
343	HCX 491	Bedford SBG	Plaxton C35F	1955	1962	*15 *20
344	KCX 124	AEC Reliance	Plaxton C41C	1955	1964	*12
345/6	KVH 345/4	AEC Reliance	Plaxton C41C	1956	1964-5	*12
347	KVH 889	AEC/Hanson Regent	Roe H37/28R	1956	1966	*21
348	MCX 386	Bedford SBG	Plaxton C41F	1957	1965	
349	MVH 837	AEC/Hanson Rgnt III	Roe H37/28R	1957	1969	*21
350	NVH 399	AEC/Hanson Rgnt III	Roe H37/28R	1958	1969	*21
351	NCX 548	Bedford SB3	Plaxton C41F	1958	1965	
352	NVH 604	Bedford SB3	Plaxton C41F	1958	1965	
353/4	OVH 978/9	Ford 570E	Plaxton C41F	1959	1965-6	
355-7	RVH 336-8	Ford 570E	Plaxton C41F	1960	1966-7	
358/9	NCX 367/481	AEC/Hanson Regal	Roe FB39F	1960	1969	*21
360	SCX 543	AEC/Hanson Regal	Roe FB39F	1960	1969	*21
361	TVH 497	AEC/Hanson Rgnt III	Roe H37/28F	1961	1969	*21
362/3	TVH 498/9	AEC/Hanson Regal	Roe FB39F	1961	1969	*21
364-7	TVH 242-5	Ford 570E	Plaxton C41F	1961	1967	
368/70	VVH 348/50	AEC/Hanson Rgnt III	Roe H37/28F	1962	1969	*21
369	VVH 349	AEC/Hanson Regal	Roe FB39F	1962	1969	*21
371-4	VVH 189/91/90/2	Ford 570E	Plaxton C41F	1962	1968	
	KVH 363	AEC Reliance	Plaxton C41C	1962	1964	*22 *23
	PCX 130/1	Ford 570E	Plaxton C41F	1962	1965-6	*22 *24

	RVH 377	Ford 570E	Plaxton C41F	1962	1967	*22 *25	
	SCX 935	Ford 570E	Plaxton C41F	1962	1966	*22 *25	
	TVH 650	Ford 570E	Plaxton C41F	1962	1968	*22 *26	
375	XVH 133	AEC/Hanson Rgnt III	Roe H37/28F	1963	1969	*21	
376/7	XVH 134/5	AEC/Hanson Regal	Roe FB39F	1963	1969	*21	
378-81	XVH 137/8/6/9	Ford 570E	Duple C41F	1963	1969		
	OWU 772/3	Sentinel SLC6	Burlingham C41C	1963	1964-5	*27	
382-4	BCX 485-7B	AEC/Hanson Reliance	Roe B41F	1964	1967-9	*21	
385-8	BCX 488-91B	Ford 570E	Duple C37F	1964	1970		
389-91	ECX886/7/9C	AEC/Hanson Reliance	Roe B41F	1965	1969	*21	
392-5	ECX 110-3C	Ford 570E	Plaxton C37F	1965	1970-1		
396	GVH 411D	AEC/Hanson Reliance	Roe B41F	1966	1969	*21	
397/8	GVH 412/3D	Ford R192	Plaxton C41F	1966	1972		
399/400	GVH 414/5D	Ford R226	Plaxton C51F	1966	1972		
401/2	KVH 244/7E	Ford R226	Duple C52F	1967	1973		
403/4	KVH 246/5E	Ford R192	Duple C45F	1967	1973		
405/6	LCX 34/5E	AEC Reliance	Willowbrook B53F	1967	1969		
407	LVH 911F	Bedford J2SZ10	Plaxton C20F	1967	1972		
408-11	NVH 371-4F	Ford R192	Plaxton C45F	1968	1974		
412	OCX 312F	AEC Reliance	Willowbrook B53F	1968	1969		
413/4	RCX 713/4G	Ford R192	Plaxton C45F	1969	1974		
415/6	RCX 715/6G	Ford R226	Plaxton C52F	1969	1974		
417-20	TVH 417-20H	Ford R192	Plaxton C45F	1970	1974		
421-4	WVH 721-4J	Ford R192	Plaxton C45F	1971	1974		
425/6	BCX 425/6K	Ford R226	Plaxton C53F	1972	1974		
427	FVH 427L	Ford R226	Duple C53F	1973	1974		
428/9	FVH 428/9L	Ford R192	Duple C45F	1973	1974		
430	GVH 287L	Ford Transit	Ford C12F	1973	1974		
431	NVH 467M	Ford Transit	Ford C12F	1973	1974		
432/3	PCX 932/3M	Ford R1114	Plaxton C53F	1974	1974		

Buses 349/50/8-63/8-70/5-7/82/3/9-91/6/405/6/12 were sold to Huddersfield Corporation on 1 October 1969. Huddersfield fleet numbers (in full) were: 349/350/58/59/60/361/62/63/368/69/370/375/76/77/82/83/89/90/91/96/1/2/3 respectively.

Coaches 408-11/3-33 were sold to West Yorkshire PTE on 1 May 1974. PTE fleet numbers initially allocated were: 65-85/36/37/86/87 respectively.

Notes:
*1   4 was later renumbered 40.
*2   20 was new to Bower (Blue and White) of Holmbridge in 1927.
*3   28 was new to Sykes (Calder) of Bailiff Bridge in 1928.
*4   51/2 were renumbered 121/120 in 1939.
*5   54 was new to Percy Gee of Huddersfield in 1929.
*6   Rebodied Burlingham B35F in 1941.
*7   Rebodied Burlingham L27/26R in 1946

*8   Rebodied Massey L27/24R in 1946

*9   110 withdrawn 1950. 111/2 were rebodied Duple DP32F and DP35F in 1947/9 and renumbered 244/83.

*10 113 was rebodied Duple DP35F in 1949 and renumbered 284. It was subsequently rebuilt, rebodied, renumbered 347 and reregistered.

*11 243/5/6 were rebuilt to FC33F in 1953 and renumbered 322-4. Some subsequently rebuilt, rebodied, renumbered and reregistered (see summary table in Appendix 3).

*12 Some or all rebuilt, rebodied, renumbered and reregistered (see summary table in Appendix 3).

*13 294-9 were rebuilt to FC33F in 1954 and renumbered 325-30. All were subsequently rebuilt, rebodied, renumbered and reregistered (see summary table in Appendix 3).

*14 New in 1948 to Bottomley; rebodied in 1955 with Duple DP35F body from 284.

*15 Acquired from subsidiary company Ivy Coaches in 1955.

*16 339 was new in 1933 to Huddersfield JOC as a double decker bus (116)

*17 340 was new in 1934.

*18 341 was new in 1948.

*19 342 was new in 1937.

*20 343 was purchased for the subsidiary by Hansons in 1954.

*21 These vehicles were rebuilt from earlier stock. See summary table (Appendix 3) for details.

*22 Acquired from the Bottomley subsidiary company in 1962 and not allocated a fleet number.

*23 KVH 363 was new in 1956. Note *12 (see above) also applies.

*24 PCX 130/1 were new in 1959.

*25 RVH 377 and SCX 935 were new in 1960.

*26 TVH 650 was new in 1961.

*27 New in 1955 to Schofield, Marsden. Acquired from Schofield or ("772") Ben Smith in 1962 but licensed to Hanson Haulage until 1963. Fleet numbers were not allocated.

*28 Also recorded as Buckingham body.

After the sale of the bus fleet in October 1969, the Hanson School of Motoring 1954 AEC Reliance/Roe 335 (HVH 211) was retained until 1971. Used as a driver trainer since 1967, 335 stands in St John's Road opposite the depot on 10 June 1970. [H.J. Black]

A 20 seater Plaxton bodied Bedford J2SZ10 was obtained in August 1967. Diminutive coach 407 (LVH 911F) is passing through John William Street, Huddersfield on an ICI contract on 17 September 1970. [H.J. Black]

APPENDIX 3: SUMMARY OF 1947-66 REBUILDING PROGRAMME

Orig. no.	Year new	Next no.	Year rebuilt	Final no.	Year later rebuilt
111	1938	244	1947		
112	1938	283	1947		
113	1938	284	1949	347	1956
243	1948	322	1953	350	1958
245	1948	323	1953	349	1957
246	1948	324	1953		
282	1949	358	1960		
285	1949	368	1962		
287	1949	375	1963		
288	1950	359	1960		
291	1950	360	1960		
292	1950	376	1963		
294	1950	325	1954	370	1962
295	1950	326	1954	361	1961
296	1950	327	1954	362	1961
297	1950	328	1954	377	1963
298	1950	329	1954	369	1962
299	1950	330	1954	363	1961
336	1955	382	1964		
337	1955	383	1964		
338	1955	384	1964		
344	1955	389	1965		
*	1956	390	1965		
345	1956	391	1965		
346	1956	396	1966		

[* = Bottomley KVH 363]

The front engined Roe bodied AEC/Hanson single deck rebuilds were nicknamed "tanks" or "trams". 377 (XVH 135), rebuilt from 1950 AEC Regal III 328 in 1963, ran for Huddersfield Corporation for only a few months after the 1969 takeover. It was very awkward for the driver to collect fares. Soon after the rebuilding, it stands in the Manchester Street parking ground.
[Omnibus Society/K.Glazier]

APPENDIX 4: TYPICAL HANSONS BUS DESTINATION BLIND (1960s)

DEPOT
PRIVATE
SPECIAL
EXCURSION
MILNSBRIDGE
BLACKPOOL
MORECAMBE
HUDDERSFIELD
MELTHAM MILLS VIA MILNSBRIDGE HELME
MELTHAM VIA MILNSBRIDGE HELME
HUDDERSFIELD VIA HELME MILNSBRIDGE
HEIGHTS VIA MILNSBRIDGE
LINTHWAITE CHURCH VIA MILNSBRIDGE
OLDHAM VIA UPPERMILL
HUDDERSFIELD VIA UPPERMILL
NEWSOME VIA REINWOOD ROAD
NEWSOME VIA QUARMBY
NEWSOME VIA LUCK LANE
LINDLEY VIA REINWOOD ROAD
LINDLEY VIA QUARMBY
LINDLEY VIA LUCK LANE
LINDLEY MOOR ROAD VIA BLACKER ROAD
WEATHERHILL VIA BLACKER ROAD
HUDDERSFIELD VIA BLACKER ROAD
SCAPEGOAT HILL VIA MANCHESTER ROAD LEYMOOR
SCAPEGOAT HILL VIA MANCHESTER ROAD BRITANNIA ROAD
SCAPEGOAT HILL VIA PADDOCK HEAD SCAR LANE
HUDDERSFIELD VIA LEYMOOR MANCHESTER ROAD
HUDDERSFIELD VIA SCAR LANE PADDOCK HEAD
BLACKMOORFOOT VIA HOYLEHOUSE
HUDDERSFIELD VIA HOYLEHOUSE
GOLCAR VIA MANCHESTER ROAD LEYMOOR
GOLCAR VIA PADDOCK HEAD SCAR LANE
SLAITHWAITE VIA PADDOCK HEAD SCAR LANE
SLAITHWAITE VIA MANCHESTER ROAD SCAR LANE
HUDDERSFIELD VIA SCAR LANE MANCHESTER ROAD
HUDDERSFIELD VIA BRITANNIA ROAD PADDOCK HEAD
WILBERLEE VIA HOYLEHOUSE SLAITHWAITE
HILL TOP VIA HOYLEHOUSE SLAITHWAITE
HUDDERSFIELD VIA SLAITHWAITE HOYLEHOUSE

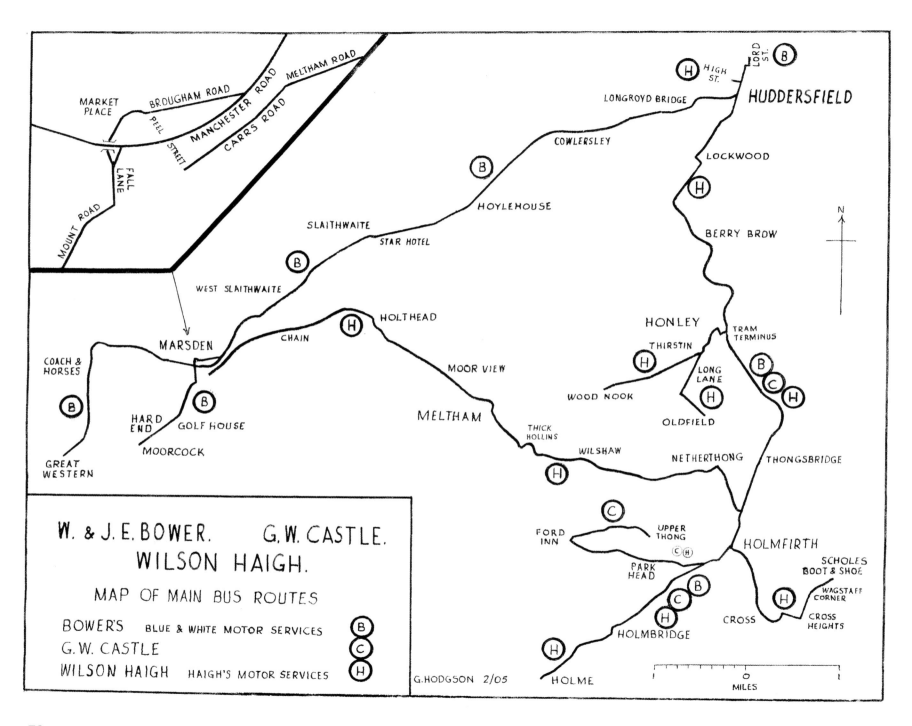

MARKET PLACE

BROUGHAM ROAD
MELTHAM ROAD
MANCHESTER ROAD
CARRS ROAD
PEEL STREET
FALL LANE
MOUNT ROAD

HUDDERSFIELD

H HIGH ST.
LORD ST.
B

LONGROYD BRIDGE

LOCKWOOD
H

COWLERSLEY

BERRY BROW

B

HOYLEHOUSE

SLAITHWAITE
STAR HOTEL

WEST SLAITHWAITE
B

HOLTHEAD
H

HONLEY

TRAM TERMINUS

THIRSTIN
H

LONG LANE
B
C
H

MARSDEN
CHAIN

MOOR VIEW

WOOD NOOK

COACH & HORSES

HARD END
GOLF HOUSE
B

MOORCOCK

MELTHAM

THICK HOLLINS

OLDFIELD
H

B

GREAT WESTERN

WILSHAW

NETHERTHONG

THONGSBRIDGE

H

C

FORD INN

UPPER THONG

PARK HEAD

C H

HOLMFIRTH

SCHOLES BOOT & SHOE

WAGSTAFF CORNER

H

W. & J. E. BOWER.   G. W. CASTLE.
WILSON HAIGH.

MAP OF MAIN BUS ROUTES

BOWER'S   BLUE & WHITE MOTOR SERVICES   B
G. W. CASTLE   C
WILSON HAIGH   HAIGH'S MOTOR SERVICES   H

B
C
H
HOLMBRIDGE

CROSS

CROSS HEIGHTS

H

HOLME

G. HODGSON 2/05

N

MILES
1   0   1

PART 2
HOLME & COLNE VALLEY RURAL BUSES.

1: WILSON HAIGH AND HAIGH'S MOTOR SERVICES (H.M.S.)

1.1: CABS, CHARABANCS AND OMNIBUSES

By the 1920s the Haigh family had been in the transport industry in the Holme Valley for over 50 years, acting mainly as local carriers. Wilson Haigh's grandfather was a pioneer in the conveyance of passengers as well as goods and operated a waggonette or horsebus between Holmfirth and Huddersfield. By 1907 the Haighs had a livery stables and carriers' business in Station Road, Holmfirth. They also ran horsedrawn cabs, which were later replaced by up to eight petrol driven taxi-cabs. When petrol omnibuses appeared, suspecting that their taxi-cab business would be adversely affected, the Haigh family ventured into the bus business.

Their garage was at Ribbleden Mills in Dunford Road, Holmfirth. Haigh's were the main dealers in the Holme Valley for Morris cars and Garner commercial vehicles and sub-agents for Wolseley cars and Bradbury motor cycles. They were also the most important petrol dealers in the area, advertising Shell No.1 at $1/2^1/2$d per gallon. Wilson Haigh advertised his willingness to meet clients at the Olympia motor shows to demonstrate the virtues of Morris cars.

By August 1919 the Haighs were advertising charabanc excursions from Holmfirth. A trip on Sunday 24 August to Buxton and Castleton was possibly the first; the 15/- fare included dinner (lunch) at the Peak Hotel. On the following Saturday passengers were conveyed by chara to Harden Moss sheepdog trials.

The Haighs were not the first in the field for running charabanc excursions in the Holme Valley. Fred H Beaumont of Honley had started day excursions in May 1919 and by June was offering a five day Scottish tour using first class hotels at an inclusive price of 8 guineas. Further competition was soon provided by Kilner and Brook of Honley Bridge Garage, Herbert Booth of New Mill and Joe Middleton of Midlothian Garage, Holmfirth.

On 24 January 1920 Walter Haigh, Wilson Haigh's father, was summoned by Holmfirth Police Court for having an inadequate licence for a motor taxi. He was fined £5 with the alternative of being sent to prison for one month. Haigh's colourful reply was "It's nowt but

Bolshevism. I will go down. That's telling you straight." Doubtless he soon thought better of this and paid the fine.

On 10 July 1920 the Haighs announced the arrival of a brand new 50 horsepower, 30 seat Karrier charabanc named "Pratty Flowers" [CX 3820 ?]. They boasted that with experienced drivers this was the best passenger Karrier on the road. The programme of excursions for the summer, mostly with this vehicle, is shown; the fares, where known, were certainly not cheap.

Sunday 1 August: Buxton-Castleton-Sheffield, fare 12/6d (dinner 4/6d, if ordered)
Monday 2 August: Ripon Races, fare 14/-
Sunday 8 August: Bretton-Wortley Park-Langsett, fare 7/- (starting from Holmbridge)
Saturday 14 August: Woodhead and Stalybridge, fare 5/-
Sunday 15 August: Woodhead-Stalybridge-Nont Sarah's
Sunday 22 August: Round the moors from Holmbridge
Thursday 26 August: Penistone Show
Sunday 5 September: Dukeries
Sunday 5 September: Nont Sarah's (2.00pm from Holmbridge), fare 5/- [not same vehicle]

On Saturday 21 August 1920 the chara had operated the first period return service for holidaymakers to Blackpool. Passengers could be picked up at Holmfirth and Honley and the return journey from Talbot Mews, Blackpool was one week later on 28 August. Passengers' luggage was conveyed separately by lorry. On Saturdays during the season Haigh ran to football matches in Huddersfield at Fartown and Leeds Road. The charabanc left Holmbridge at 1.30pm (for a 3.00pm kick off) and the return fare was 3/- (or 2/6d from Holmfirth).

The following summer (1921) from the beginning of July a period return service was again offered to Blackpool on Saturdays, using a new 14 seat "de luxe" charabanc [CX 3963?], provided a minimum of six advance bookings had been received. For August Bank Holiday Monday 1921 Haigh advertised a separate excursion for each of his three charabancs and fares and departure times were now clearly stated:

7.30am, Ripon Races, fare 12/6d
8.30am, Dukeries via Mansfield and Doncaster, fare 14/-
12.00 noon, Harrogate and Knaresborough via Wetherby, Fare 9/-

Advance notice was also given of two three day tours to North Wales. More charabanc operators in the Holme Valley starting to advertise their excursions at this time included John Littlewood of Newtown Garage, Honley and Heeley Brothers of New Mill while George Willie

Castle was about to follow suit.

It was during the latter part of 1921 that Haigh began to operate what might almost be described as early attempts at running buses to serve popular local events or places. On 6 August he operated an hourly service from Holmfirth to Meltham Show and similarly on 25 August he operated hourly to Penistone Show. On Tuesday evenings during at least the last three months of the year he ran at 7.30pm to New Mill and at 8.30pm to Hade Edge from his garage for a 6d fare. He also ran to Hade Edge at 9.00pm on Saturdays.

A new venture on 8 July 1922 (and repeated in subsequent years) was the provision of a half-hourly service to Holme for the Motor Trials. This was a hill climbing contest arranged by the Bradford and Huddersfield automobile clubs which attracted over a hundred motorists and a larger number of spectators. Penistone Show provided lucrative business and from 1923 a half-hourly service was operated on show days.

On Whit Sunday 1924 Haigh advertised a service to New Mill running "every few minutes" for a 3d fare to take people to the 16th annual Music Festival. So popular was this event that other bus operators doubled their services from Honley (Huddersfield Corporation), Barnsley (Barnsley & District Traction) and Wakefield (West Riding). Donations were made out of the proceeds to the Nurses' Fund, Holme Valley Memorial Hospital and Huddersfield Royal Infirmary.

Haigh's first actual bus service began on Saturday 17 April 1926 according to the Holmfirth Express newspaper. It ran from the bottom of Victoria Street, Holmfirth to Meltham via Netherthong, Wilshaw and the Golf Links. The journey took 25 minutes and the bus had a five minute layover at Meltham outside the Swan Inn. On Monday to Friday buses departed from Holmfirth at 1.00pm, 3.00pm, 5.00pm, 6.00pm, 7.00pm, 8.00pm and 10.00pm; a morning service at 9.00am and 10.00am operated only on Tuesdays. An hourly frequency was run on Saturdays from 12.00 noon and on Sundays a two hourly frequency operated from 2.00pm. All departures from Meltham were 30 minutes later. Only one bus was required to provide the basic service and Garner WU 7176 was initially licensed for a six month period. The fare table was:

Holmfirth
2 Netherthong
4 2 Wilshaw
6 4 2 Golf Links
6 6 4 2 Meltham

'BUS SERVICE. TIME TABLE.

Holmfirth to Meltham

(BOTTOM OF VICTORIA STREET TO SWAN INN)

Commencing THIS DAY (Saturday) April 17th, 1926.

WEEK DAYS.

Depart.				Arrive.	Depart.				Arrive.
Holmfirth	Netherthong	Wilshaw	Golf Links	Meltham	Meltham	Golf Links	Wilshaw	Netherthong	Holmfirth
1 0	1 7	1 15	1 20	1 25	1 30	1 37	1 45	1 50	1 55
3 0	3 7	3 15	3 20	3 25	3 30	3 37	3 45	3 50	3 55
5 0	5 7	5 15	5 20	5 25	5 30	5 37	5 45	5 50	5 55
6 0	6 7	6 15	6 20	6 25	6 30	6 37	6 45	6 50	6 55
7 0*	7 7	7 15	7 20	7 25	7 30	7 37	7 45	7 50	7 55
8 0	8 7	8 15	8 20	8 25	8 30	8 37	8 45	8 50	8 55
10 0	10 7	10 15	10 20	10 25	10 30	10 37	10 45	10 50	10 55

Morning Service—TUESDAYS ONLY.

9 0	9 7	9 15	9 20	9 25	9 30	9 37	9 45	9 50	9 55
10 0	10 7	10 15	10 20	10 25	10 30	10 37	10 45	10 50	10 55

SUNDAYS ONLY.

2 0	2 7	2 15	2 20	2 25	2 30	2 37	2 45	2 50	2 55
4 0	4 7	4 15	4 20	4 25	4 30	4 37	4 45	4 50	4 55
6 0	6 7	6 15	6 20	6 25	6 30	6 37	6 45	6 50	6 55
8 0	8 7	8 15	8 20	8 25	8 30	8 37	8 45	8 50	8 55
10 0	10 7	10 15	10 20	10 25	10 30	10 37	10 45	10 50	10 55

SATURDAYS ONLY.

Every Hour : starting from Holmfirth at 12 noon.

Last 'Bus leaves Holmfirth 11·0 p.m.   Last 'Bus leaves Meltham 11·30 p.m.

FARES: 2d. per stage ; 6d. through.

This Time Table is subject to alteration to suit the needs of the Public.

HAIGH'S GARAGE, HOLM...

Although Beardsell Bros had already been granted a licence for a Jackson Bridge-Holmfirth-Netherthong route, it is thought that this potentially competitive service was never operated.

By April 1926 Haigh was advertising Easter excursions under the banner of "Pratty Flowers Tours". A 14 seat charabanc was running to Southport while a closed bus was going to both Castleton and Belle Vue (the Manchester amusement park).

In early June two Haigh charabancs inspected by the Holmfirth UDC hackney carriage inspector, Arthur Wakefield of Lydgate, were found to be defective. These were CX 3820, a Karrier with brakes and steering in a worn and loose condition, and WY 7199, a Fiat with the steering in a bad condition. A third charabanc in the fleet at this time was CX 3963 and driver's licences were held by Haigh himself, Charles Lofthouse and Alfred Swallow. Mr Wakefield was paid 5/- per vehicle inspection; he was responsible for inspecting all the vehicles which plied for hire within the Holmfirth UDC area with the exception of buses owned by Huddersfield Corporation, Barnsley & District Traction and West Riding Automobile of Wakefield.

From 3 July 1926 the Holmfirth-Meltham bus service was extended from Meltham to Marsden via Holthead

and Chain Road with two buses needed for the basic service. Holmfirth was enjoying a heatwave at the time and a Holmfirth Express reporter soon found that an ideal way of keeping cool was to take an evening bus ride to Marsden. He thought that the variety of scenery on the route would be difficult to equal in other areas of the country which would have cost £1 or more to visit compared with the 2/- return charged by Haigh for this "capital" ride. He also appreciated the amenities at the park near the Marsden terminus. The through fare was soon reduced from 1/- to 10d.

As mentioned earlier the 20 seater Garner, operated by a driver without a conductor, was used on the Marsden route. According to Wylbert Kemp, the regular driver sometimes failed to turn up so Wilson Haigh would call in at the barber's shop in Victoria Square, Holmfirth and ask Mr Kemp senior if he would spare his son, Wylbert, for an hour or so to drive the bus. Wylbert recalled the following anecdote. While crossing the Chain he noticed a woman dragging a child across the fields from a farm, waving to halt the bus. After he had stamped on the brake, the bus stopped and mother and son climbed on board. Tickets were punched but the youngster cried out "Mother, Mother, I want to do a job" [go to the toilet]. Mother promptly gave him such a cuff that sent him reeling up the gangway before shouting "Damn thee! You're just like your father, always wanting something just as we are setting off". Wylbert Kemp was to become a skilled playwright; although the history of the Holme Valley was featured in some of his one act plays, Wilson Haigh's buses had no part.

A shortlived Holmfirth-New Mill bus service, used mainly by mill workers, started on 6 July 1926. The Holmfirth UDC licence granted on 12 July was for journeys before 9.00am only as after this time "adequate" services were already provided over this road by Barnsley & District (Barnsley-Holmfirth) and West Riding (Wakefield-Holmfirth). It was also convenient for Wilson Haigh to run at this time of day as his Marsden route did not start before 9.00am. The service was suspended from 7 August while the mills were idle with the intention of starting again after 16 August. This was not to be and the route was officially withdrawn from 13 September owing to lack of patronage.

Haigh's fleet was also increasing because of the flourishing local excursion trade. On Sunday 11 July 1926 afternoon trips were run to Cawthorne and Boardhill. Three evening trips were operated (Glossop, Stocksbridge and Delph) so at least five vehicles were now in

stock allowing for the Marsden bus service. Later in the month a daily service ran to the Great Yorkshire Show at Harrogate; advertisements boasted of the ride on giant pneumatic tyres - the only charabancs in the district so equipped.

In November 1926 Haigh proposed a new route between Holmfirth and Huddersfield using minor roads between Holmfirth and Honley to avoid direct competition with Huddersfield Corporation's service along the main road. It would have served Muslin Hall, Deanhouse Hospital, Woodlands and the Mytholmbridge area but Holmfirth UDC refused a licence on the grounds that some of the proposed roads were unsuitable for a bus service. Huddersfield Watch Committee also refused to license their end of the route.

Not to be deterred, Haigh started a truncated version of the service on 14 December 1926 between Honley (Bradshaw Gate) and Huddersfield via Moorbottom Road, Honley village, Berry Brow and Lockwood. The route soon became known as Long Lane, as buses turned round in Bradshaw Road by reversing at the junction with Long Lane. The Corporation's Honley tram service terminated at Honley Bridge, not penetrating the main part of the village to the west of Woodhead Road and no doubt they could not have justified introducing their own motorbus service which would have taken passengers from the trams. The railway station was even more inconveniently sited - almost a mile away from the village. Initially the Haigh service was licensed for a trial period of six months by Honley UDC. The buses had of course to run on the return ticket system within Huddersfield; only passengers already in possession of a return ticket were supposed to be carried. An hourly service was provided by one bus in the morning and in the afternoon the frequency was doubled. Wilson Haigh was proved correct in anticipating a demand for this service as he was soon carrying nearly 6000 passengers per week.

Mr JA Littlewood of Newtown Garage, Honley had proposed a service at the same time from Deanhouse to Huddersfield but was refused a licence by Honley UDC on the advice of the Highways Committee. In June 1927 Haigh was summonsed for carrying passengers from Huddersfield to Honley for a 4d fare when they were not in possession of a return ticket. His drivers were also instructed to keep to the nearside of the narrow roads in Honley. The buses now ran every half hour with a journey time of 25 minutes but were so overcrowded on Tuesdays and Saturdays that a 20 minute frequency was introduced from October 1927.

Meanwhile in January 1927 Wilson Haigh was licensed by Holmfirth UDC for four 20 seater buses, one 28 seater charabanc and two 6 seater taxi-cabs. By May 1927 the timetable of the Holmfirth-Marsden route had been improved to hourly from 11.00am. After leaving Holmfirth, buses passed Netherthong in 7 minutes, Wilshaw in 15 minutes, Golf Links in 17 minutes, Meltham in 25 minutes and arrived at the Liberal Club in Marsden after 50 minutes. Haigh wanted to divert some buses at Thick Hollins to run via Meltham Mills but his licence application was refused by Meltham UDC in September 1927.

During the 1927 season competition for the excursion trade was again keen. JE Bower of Hinchliffe Mill claimed that his 26 seater "super saloon" coach was the finest in the district while Leonard Baddeley of Huddersfield said his saloon bus was the only one of its kind in Yorkshire. It boasted pneumatic tyres all round, a sliding roof and drop windows. Not to be outdone, Haigh advertised 20 and 26 seat saloon safety coaches, the 26 seater allegedly the smartest and most comfortable coach in the North of England!

In February 1928 Haigh applied to Linthwaite UDC for a licence for a service from Marsden to Huddersfield, which would have been in direct competition with the similar service started a year earlier by Walter Bower of Hinchliffe Mill. Haigh never appeared on that corridor; had he done so, there would have been the possibility of through running from Huddersfield via Marsden to Holmfirth.

The Haigh fleet expanded again during 1928 with the acquisition of Leyland Lion and Lioness Pullman coaches. During the August holiday weeks up to seven different destinations were offered daily besides the regular Blackpool trip. It is interesting to note the Blackpool fares: 8/- by charabanc but a premium 10/- fare for the saloon coach. Further interest was shown in stage carriage work when Haigh offered to operate the Holmfirth-Penistone service in the event of Baddeleys having their licence withdrawn.

1.2: A THORN IN HUDDERSFIELD'S SIDE

During autumn 1928 the inhabitants of the moorland village of Holme, who had to walk over a mile to Holmbridge bus terminus, drew up a petition requesting a bus service to their village. Holme council duly presented this to Huddersfield Corporation but the Tramways Manager's reply was that the Corporation could not

grant the requested extension. The Corporation had in fact considered operating to Holme during the summer months only but such a service would have been for Huddersfield people visiting the moors rather than catering for the travel needs of Holme residents. Huddersfield Corporation considered the steep Holme Bank section of Woodhead Road with its hazardous drops alongside altogether too dangerous a route for the winter months when this main road was often covered with ice and snow.

On 10 November 1928, however, Wilson Haigh wrote to the clerk of Holme council, pointing out that with a fleet of ten buses (as well as the coaches) and with a staff of mechanics to maintain them he was in a position to start operating a service from Holme to Huddersfield (direct via the main Woodhead Road) immediately. Haigh proposed twelve trips from Holme daily, starting at 6.50am with a frequency of 90 minutes. The through fare was to be 9d, with workman returns on the first two buses at one and a half times the single rate. Holme, Holmfirth and Honley councils welcomed the offer and licensed the service, which commenced on Saturday 24 November. It was not licensed within Huddersfield County Borough, hence Haigh's press announcement: "We shall appreciate your patronage of this service but passengers must book return if they intend to board our bus in the Borough of Huddersfield for their return journey." The round trip, including a five minute layover at each terminus, took 90 minutes so just one vehicle was needed.

The Chief Constable of Huddersfield (Captain Moore) was quick off the mark to prosecute Wilson Haigh for his pains. The charges were of leaving deposits of oil on High Street and of allowing the blue and white buses to stand on High Street for longer than was necessary to drop off and pick up passengers. Haigh was ably defended by his solicitor, Mr Steele, who pointed out that Corporation buses also spilled oil and waited in High Street. After a few moments' deliberation, the magistrates dismissed the case. The Holme route was an immediate success and carried over 16,000 passengers per month with about half of them originating on the section between Holme and Holmbridge. Revenue averaged 9.5d per mile while the Corporation admitted to reduced revenue of 3.2d per mile on their Holmbridge route.

The next new service to start, on Saturday 15 December 1928, was from Cross via Dunford Road (Underbank), Holmfirth and Woodhead Road to Huddersfield. This operated hourly from 6.20am and, as the round

HAIGH'S MOTOR SERVICES.

RIDE H.M.S. HOLMFIRTH.

NEW BUS SERVICES

EASE, SILENCE AND RELIABILITY

Holme to Huddersfield.

THIS SERVICE IS NOW IN OPERATION.

HOLME. dep.	H'FIRTH. dep.	HUDD'D. dep.	H'FIRTH. dep.	HOLME arr.
			w6-27	w6-45
w6-45	w7-7	w7-30	w7-57	w8-15
w8-20	w8-37	w9-0	w9-27	w9-45
9-50	10-7	10-30	10-57	11-15
11-20	11-37	12-0 noon	12-27	12-45
12-50	1-7	1-30	1-57	2-15
2-20	2-37	3-0	3-27	3-45
3-50	4-7	4-30	4-57	5-15
5-20	5-37	6-0	6-27	6-45
6-50	7-7	7-30	7-57	8-15
8-20	8-37	9-0	9-27	9-45
9-50	10-7	10-35	10-57	11-15
11-15	11-30 Garage.			

w Workman Buses.

PLEASE NOTE.—On *Saturdays* and *Sundays* after 11-37 the times leaving Holmfirth will be 2 mins. EARLIER—1-5, 2-35, and so on.

SUNDAY—First bus Holme 12-50, and ordinary Saturday Service.

FARES :—

Holme to Huddersfield	9d.	1/6 return.
Holmbridge to Huddersfield	7d.	1/2 return.
Holmfirth to Huddersfield	5d.	10d. return.
Thongsbridge to Huddersfield	4d.	8d. return.

WORKMEN'S FARES—Fare and Half.

Cross (Underbank) to Huddersfield.

THIS SERVICE WILL COMMENCE THIS DAY (Saturday), DECEMBER 15th. at 12-20.

EXPRESS BUS—

CROSS. dep.	H'FIRTH. dep.	HUDD'D. dep.	H'FIRTH. dep.	CROSS. arr.
w6-20	w6-27	w6-50	w7-10	w7-17
w7-20	w7-27	w7-50	w8-10	w8-17
w8-20	w8-27	w8-50	w9-10	w9-17
9-20	9-27	9-50	10-10	10-17
10-20	10-27	10-50	11-10	11-17
11-20	11-17	11-50	12-10	12-17
12-20	12-27	12-45	1-5	1-12
1-15	1-22	1-43	2-5	2-10
2-15	2-22	2-43	3-5	3-10
3-15	3-22	3-43	4-5	4-10
and every hour until 10-15	and every hour until 10-22	and every hour until 10-43	and every hour until 11-5	and every hour until 11-10
Sats. only 11-15	Sats. only 11-22	Sats. only 11-43	Sats. only 12-5	Sats. only 12-10

w Workman Buses.

PLEASE NOTE.—These are Express Services from Holmfirth, and are what the Holmfirth Public have been clamouring for; you must board this Bus in Holmfirth by the Martin's (L. & Y. Bank), Victoria Square.

SUNDAYS—Saturday Service, commencing Cross 1-15, and every hour till 10-15 p.m.

FARES :—

Cross to Huddersfield	6d.	1/- return.
Cross to Holmfirth	1½d.	
Underbank to Holmfirth	1d.	
Holmfirth to Huddersfield	5d.	10d. return

WORKMEN'S FARES—Fare and Half.

Cross Roads (Park Head) to Huddersfield.

THIS SERVICE WILL COMMENCE SHORTLY.

EXPRESS BUS—

CROSS ROADS, PARK H'D. dep.	H'FIRTH. dep.	HUDD'D. dep.	H'FIRTH. dep.	CROSS ROADS, PARK H'D. arr.
w5-57	w6-5	w6-25	w6-45	w6-50
w6-55	w7-0	w7-25	w7-45	w7-50
w7-55	w8-0	w8-25	w8-45	w8-50
w8-55	w9-0	w9-25	w9-45	w9-50
9-55	10-0	10-25	10-45	10-50
10-55	11-0	11-25	12-45	11-50
11-55	12-0	12-20	12-40	12-45
12-45	12-52	1-14	1-35	1-40
1-45	1-52	2-14	2-35	2-40
2-45	2-52	3-14	3-35	3-40
and every hour until 10-45	and every hour until 10-52	and every hour until 11-14	and every hour until 11-35	and every hour until 11-40

w Workmen Buses.

on Sats. after 10-55 Buses leave 5 mins. sooner	on Sats. after 11-0 Buses leave 5 mins. earlier	on Sats. after 11-25 Buses leave	on Sats. after 12-45 Buses leave	on Sats after 11-50 Buses arr.
12-50	11-55	12-17	12-37	12-42
and every hour till 10-50	12-55	1-17	1-37	1-42
	and every hour till 10-55	and every hour till 11-17	and every hour till 11-37	and every hour till 11-42

SUNDAYS—Saturday Service, commencing from Cross Roads, Park Head, 1-50 p.m.

FARES :—

Cross Roads to Huddersfield	6d.	1/- return.
Cross Roads to Holmfirth	1½d.	
Park Head to Holmfirth	1d.	
Holmfirth to Huddersfield	5d.	10d. return

WORKMEN'S FARES—Fare and Half.

No Waiting or Annoying Stops on the Two Express Services.

These Services are Fully Sanctioned by the Holmfirth and Holme Urban District Councils.

You can board these Buses for anywhere Single Fare, but if you intend to return from Huddersfield you must book RETURN.   These Tickets you can use at any time.

WE HOPE YOU WILL APPRECIATE THESE SERVICES.

HOME FIRST -- HOLMFIRTH!

CUT THIS OUT FOR REFERENCE.

---

trip took one hour, again one bus was needed for the basic service. The introductory timetable is of interest as Haigh claimed that to satisfy demands from the Holmfirth public this service would operate "express" from Victoria Square to Huddersfield, stopping only at Thongsbridge and Honley [Bridge]. Huddersfield Watch Committee did not sanction the service and claimed that it was "express" in name only as the speed limit was still 12mph. The running times are not clear from the timetable as only departure times and not arrival times are given for Huddersfield.

The "express" feature may well have been a gimmick on Haigh's part to attract passengers from the Corporation buses on the main road. In any case, over 15,000 passengers were soon travelling monthly on the Cross bus with, according to Haigh's waybills, 60% of the traffic originating on the section between Cross and Holmfirth.

Haigh's traffic notice for the 1928 Christmas holiday is of interest. Like Huddersfield Corporation he did not operate on Christmas Day when a skeleton service was provided by Beardsells between Holmbridge and Huddersfield. On Boxing Day Haigh advertised a 20 minute service from Oldfield to Huddersfield so the Long Lane route appears to have been already extended to the hamlet of Oldfield, although the extension via Bradshaw Road and Cross Lane to a terminus at the junction with Oldfield Road was not actually licensed by Honley UDC until 7 January 1929. The normal Long Lane frequency was half hourly until 9.00am, then hourly until 1.00pm and every 20 minutes for the rest of the day. Not all these journeys were extended to Oldfield.

Early January 1929 saw the start of the second "express" service, this time from Parkhead (Cross Roads) hourly via Greenfield Road and Holmfirth to Huddersfield. The round trip took 55 minutes and again one bus provided the basic service. This route was soon carrying 11,500 passengers monthly. The timetable carried the message that there was no waiting or annoying stops on the two express services which were both fully sanctioned by the relevant UDCs. As usual, single fares could be booked to any point from the Holme Valley but a return ticket, valid for use at any time, had to be bought by passengers intending to return from Huddersfield.

The recently established Holme Valley Joint Licensing Committee were very supportive towards Haigh, particularly in relation to the refusal of Huddersfield Corporation to allow him to pick up passengers without return tickets within the borough. They were also concerned

Wilson Haigh's Leyland Tiger TS1 12 (WW 8274) was new in January 1929 with Fielding & Bottomley 30 seat body-work. It is parked on the stone setts just off Woodhead Road at the terminus in the centre of Holme village.
[P.J. Cardno collection]

single tickets in advance from the H.M.S. office and from conductors, outside Huddersfield, for 5d for the journey from Huddersfield to Holmfirth.

Another initiative of Haigh was the issuing of free travel passes to eighteen blind people. He also allowed women to travel to the labour exchange at Holmfirth at the workmen's fare on production of their insurance cards.

To reduce the risk of prosecution when passengers boarded his buses in Huddersfield without return tickets, Wilson Haigh relied on the services of his uncle Albert, a retired grocer living at 45 Newsome Road. At certain times of day, Albert would sell what appeared to be return tickets to anybody in the High Street queue not in possession of a valid return ticket. These were presumably sold at the price for a single journey and were pre-punched in such a way as to be immediately recognised by the conductor; once the bus was outside the borough, they were exchanged for normal tickets. The Corporation frequently complained about this procedure, which

about safety aspects, insisting on periodic inspection of Haigh's ten buses and the carriage of fire extinguishers. Anti-skid chains had to be available for winter use when the roads were covered with ice and snow. The committee were also critical of any deviations from the published timetable and overcrowding incidents.

After again being refused licences for his services by Huddersfield Corporation, Haigh, with the backing of both the Holme Valley Joint Licensing Committee and West Riding County Council, lodged an appeal with the Ministry of Transport. The result was an inquiry conducted at Huddersfield Town Hall on Wednesday 13 March 1929 by Mr CB Rammage.

Mr Haigh's appeal was conducted by Mr RI Steele who in his introduction said that his client's application was to supply services which Huddersfield Corporation themselves had declined to provide, for the benefit of those people living in the higher districts on both sides of the Holme Valley. Mr Haigh had, he said, adapted his business to meet the needs of these people and invested over £11,000 in providing the necessary vehicles. He also provided regular employment for 35 men.

Alderman Canby, chairman of Huddersfield Tramways Committee, explained that the Corporation had been the first to seek running powers to Holmbridge, in 1920. Baddeleys, he said, had tried operating on the route but did not find it very profitable and had eventually sold out to the Corporation, agreeing not to operate again for five years. Having spent a considerable amount of money in obtaining running powers (and paying off Baddeleys), the Corporation expected to be the sole operator on the

corridor.

Several witnesses complained of the inadequacy of the Corporation service and explained how they benefitted from Haigh's services. It was stated that Haigh had endeavoured at all times to maintain an efficient and regular service and had spared neither time, trouble nor expense in meeting the comfort and convenience of the public. Only recently on one foggy December day his buses had remained on the road when the Corporation vehicles had returned to their garage.

In general Mr Haigh based his appeal on the following grounds. He merely asked for the same privileges as those enjoyed by the Corporation. They could already ply for hire both within and outside the borough boundary and he wanted to be able to do likewise. On the other hand his services differed from those provided by the Corporation in two ways. Firstly the services other than Holme and Oldfield were express and therefore aimed at removing congestion rather than causing it. Secondly he ran to localities not served by the Corporation where the gradients were particularly steep and very trying for old people.

After the conclusion of the inquiry Mr Rammage visited each route in turn. Unfortunately the result announced in June went against Haigh.

Haigh's buses were now carrying about half a million passengers annually, much to the dismay of the Corporation. Contract tickets were introduced in June 1929 for travel between Holmfirth and Huddersfield for 4/6d weekly. The sales slogan was "Ride in comfort on any bus as often as you like". It also became possible to buy

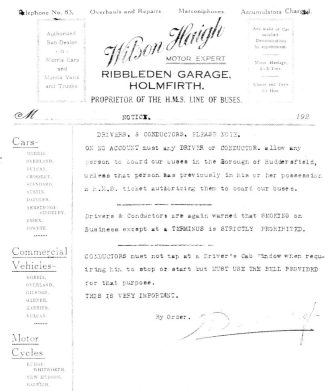

contravened Section 276 of the Huddersfield Improvement Act. On one occasion when a prosecution followed, Albert was fined 10/- and Wilson Haigh 40/-. In court, however, it was suggested that the Corporation were infringing the terms of their licence by running 12 buses an hour to Holmbridge when it suited them instead of the permitted six. Uncle Albert was not easily deterred and he continued selling tickets despite further prosecutions until the matter came to a head in March 1931 when, on threat of an injunction, a written undertaking was given to abandon the practice.

1929 also saw innovations on the coaching side. A seven day touring holiday to Devon and the Wye Valley was advertised for the inclusive price of eight guineas. A 24 seater de-luxe all weather coach specially built for Wilson Haigh was used for the tour. Also a return coach was operated to London for 25/- twice a week. The outward journeys from Holmfirth were made on Mondays and Wednesdays at 6.00am with the returns from London scheduled for 3.00pm on Tuesdays and Thursdays.

The business was registered as a limited company, Wilson Haigh Ltd, in December 1929 with an authorised capital of £7,500 in one pound shares; the directors were Wilson Haigh and his wife Mrs Dorothea Haigh. The assets taken over, listed on 1 October 1929, were as follows:

motorbuses	£6516-3-5
fixed machinery	£200-0-0
office furniture	£60-0-0
petrol pumps & oil cabinets	£267-5-6
loose tools	£29-0-0
petrol, tyres and accessories	£344-11-1
tickets, ticket racks & cash bags	£37-0-0
total	£7454

One unusual accident resulted in driver William Fieldsend being fined £3-7s at Huddersfield Police Court on 6 January 1930. Driving on the Marsden route, he had left his empty bus with the engine running in Meltham Market Place while he delivered a parcel to the Co-op fish shop. Meanwhile, engrossed in conversation, two ladies boarded the bus. Suddenly the bus started moving but fortunately the startled ladies were able to jump off before it gained speed. The driverless bus careered down Station Road and grazed the side of the church wall before knocking down part of the telephone exchange wall. On his return, the astonished driver found the bus a hundred yards away from where it had been left. The magistrate was not impressed.

On 20 January 1930 driver John Hall of Rose and Crown, Holmfirth was fined 42/- for driving in Woodhead Road in a manner dangerous to the public when "overtaking" [i.e., passing] a tram in slushy road conditions at 1.00pm on 9 December. The tram was proceeding to Honley with passengers standing on the rear platform ready to alight at the stop by the steps leading to Taylor Hill. Hall, driving at speed in the opposite direction, passed the tram on the wrong side of the road to the consternation of the tram passengers and conductor. Hall's excuse was that the width of the road was greater on the offside of the tram (13 feet) as against 9 feet on the nearside. This was apparently a common practice of bus drivers at the time.

Haigh's fleet always consisted of single deck vehicles but he did evaluate a Leyland Titan double deck demonstrator during February 1930. Holmfirth council did not favour the use of double deckers on the grounds of poor road conditions while Honley UDC refused to license a double decker for use on the Oldfield route. Around the same time the Corporation evaluated three double deckers on their Holmbridge route.

As well as his timetabled departures Haigh of course ran duplicate buses at busy periods and in particular on Saturdays. He employed an inspector, Lewis Wood of Huddersfield Road, New Mill, and he was on duty from 2.00pm to 11.45pm in High Street, Huddersfield on Saturdays to regulate the deployment of three special buses. If there were insufficient passengers to warrant the use of a duplicate he would turn the bus back into a side street to await the arrival of more passengers. It was also his duty to make sure that short distance passengers did not fill the Holme and Scholes buses and to ensure that longer distance passengers did not board the duplicates which would probably only go as far as Holmfirth. These

Saturday specials often had youthful conductors such as 16 year old Frank Roberts who worked during the week as a junior office clerk.

The parking of these specials in Dundas Street resulted in court cases for Wilson Haigh and the claim that there was one law for the Corporation and another for Haigh. On one occasion in February 1930 after driver Vincent Hicks was reported by the police for this offence, Wilson Haigh and his inspector, Lewis Wood, noted that Corporation buses on the same night were allowed to stand in Market Street for over an hour without any police intervention. Wilson Haigh himself reported the matter to the police but still nothing was done. In court, following the assertion that he was being persecuted rather than prosecuted, the Bench took a very lenient view of the affair. In the same month, when Haigh was prosecuted for allowing passengers without return tickets to board his buses, his solicitor was able to make the Corporation manager look foolish. It transpired that after Haigh had sacked a conductor for embezzlement the same man had no difficulty in obtaining similar employment with the Corporation.

In June 1930 a resident of Wood Nook, Mr JE Lumb, asked Honley UDC to get a bus service provided for that locality. The UDC passed the buck back to Mr Lumb who then personally appealed to Wilson Haigh. Possibly because the Long Lane service was doing so well, a two hourly afternoon Huddersfield to Wood Nook route was licensed by Honley UDC, initially on a trial basis from the beginning of August 1930. This was provided by diverting some existing Long Lane journeys during what had been their layover time via Meltham Road to a terminus at Mount Pleasant. The service was appreciated by shift workers at the Meltham Mills factories who lived in the Honley area. They rode on the bus to the Wood Nook terminus then walked the remaining distance to Meltham Mills.

Earlier, in March 1930, Haigh had applied to Holmfirth and New Mill UDCs for a Scholes-Holmfirth-Huddersfield licence. A 90 minute frequency service was planned via Cross Lane, Cross Heights, Cross, then following the existing Cross-Huddersfield route. Haigh had a petition from over 200 Scholes residents in support of his application. In the meantime he catered for the demand to an extent by duplicating the Cross bus. Leonard Baddeley opposed the application because he feared that such a service would abstract so much traffic from his own Holmfirth-Scholes route as to make it unprofitable; if this service were to be withdrawn, he warned, the residents of Totties and Jackson Bridge would no longer have a bus to Holmfirth.

Nevertheless, after a second application a licence was granted by Holmfirth UDC and the Scholes-Huddersfield service started on Saturday 1 November 1930 with the first bus leaving Scholes at 11.50am. Normal service started at 7.30am from Scholes with a 90 minute frequency, needing one bus. The through fare was 7^1/$_2$d and of course the return ticket system applied within the Huddersfield borough. At the same time Leonard Baddeley started a service from Scholes via Jackson Bridge and New Mill to Huddersfield.

During 1930 two important events took place which were to affect the future of the Haigh concern. In May the LMS Railway acquired a 50% share of the Corporation's motorbus undertaking which was then renamed Huddersfield Joint Omnibus Committee (JOC). To Huddersfield Corporation, one of the advantages of this transaction was the additional financial backing of the railway company which could be called upon in fighting competitors such as Wilson Haigh. Almost at the same time the 1930 Road Traffic Act established the legal framework which from the following year would take licensing powers away from local authorities and vest them in the Traffic Commissioners for the Yorkshire Traffic Area.

Throughout 1930 there was much correspondence between Wilson Haigh and Holmfirth UDC about the "predatory" actions of Huddersfield Corporation/JOC. Haigh pointed out what he felt was erratic timekeeping by JOC buses in Holmfirth. Having arrived from Holmbridge, they tended to stay on the stand for four or five minutes after their scheduled departure time so as to leave just in front of Haigh's bus. Also on Saturdays the JOC was alleged to be running a five minute frequency instead of the agreed ten minute service. In May, Haigh said that he was unwilling to adopt similar tactics as he did not wish to disorganise his services. In December, however, he claimed that the situation was even worse and said that if Holmfirth UDC were still unable to use their powers, he would have to adopt some means of self protection and preservation. As he had spare buses standing in the garage, he did not need to spell out what his tactics would be.

On the weekend of 30/31 May 1931 a special attraction was staged by the Huddersfield Gliding Club at Tinkers Monument. Exhibition gliding flights were given by the German ace Herr Carli Magersuppe. His longest flight lasted 35 minutes during which he cruised about,

twisting and turning with the grace of a bird. He made a number of spectacular dives and, much to the delight of the crowd, he yodelled as he passed by. Three or four thousand spectators turned up each day and many of them were carried to and from Victoria Square, Holmfirth for a 6d fare by a special hourly service of Haigh's buses.

1.3: TRAFFIC COMMISSIONERS' DELIBERATIONS

From June 1931 onwards the traffic commisioners held courts, after which they granted or rejected the applications for licences for bus and coach routes, excursions and tours which Haigh and other local operators had been obliged to make under the new regulations. The first licences granted by the commissioners to Haigh were for summer coastal express services which he operated on Saturdays throughout August and September 1931. Picking up points were in Holmfirth, New Mill, Honley, Meltham and at 11 New North Road, Huddersfield and holidaymakers were brought home the following Saturday. The services were:

Blackpool via Burnley and Preston [actually licensed from April to October]
Scarborough via York and Malton
Bridlington via Leeds and Selby
Morecambe via Bradford, Skipton and Lancaster
Before the 1931 season Haigh had also operated summer Saturday express services to Cleethorpes, Southport and North Wales. Extra coaches were usually hired for the peak of the season – in August 1930 Holmfirth UDC had licensed at least 27 Wilson Haigh buses or coaches, most of which were short term hires.

A stage carriage licence was also granted for a service between Holmfirth and the Isle of Skye Hotel via Greenfield Road, running as frequently as required. This was to operate at Easter, Whitsuntide and during the summer holidays. The Isle of Skye Hotel, closed in 1956, was at the junction of Wessenden Head Road and Greenfield Road and was famous for its ham and eggs teas and as a starting place for walks.

One of Haigh's conductors, Reginald Hirstle of Netherthong, had another use for his pencil besides filling in his waybill. At first passengers did not notice anything unusual about the mild mannered young man who collected their fares but while punching their tickets he mentally recorded their appearances. Then, between stops, using the moving bus as his studio he produced

lightning sketches or caricatures of his passengers. He is said to have astonished his colleagues every day with new examples of his skill. Whether this proved a lucrative sideline for him is not known. His schoolmaster had apparently recommended that he should study at an art college but this was beyond the family's means.

It was well known that the traffic commissioners were keen to reduce wasteful duplication of services on the Huddersfield to Holmfirth corridor. Haigh feared that they would not license some of his routes or, worse still, award them to Huddersfield JOC, who opposed his licence applications. The JOC claimed that since Haigh had started operating in November 1928 the municipal Holmbridge service had become unrenumerative and was failing to meet operating costs of 9d per mile. Previously the fares from Huddersfield to Honley and Holmfirth had been 5d and 6d respectively but since Haigh charged 1d less in both cases the Corporation/JOC had been obliged to reduce their charges to the same level. As Haigh had not been licensed by Huddersfield Corporation under the old system on the grounds that the area was adequately served by the municipal buses the JOC thought that the commissioners should not license his services either.

Haigh claimed that many passengers preferred his more modern vehicles to the older buses run by the JOC. Also, if the JOC really did find their route unprofitable, he suggested this was probably due to the extra buses they insisted on running despite having claimed that the area was adequately served even before the appearance of his buses.

Haigh received many testimonials – whether solicited or not is unknown - to the value of his services which he used to support his applications to the traffic commissioners. Some of these are of interest also for the light they shed on the use made of buses in general in those days. New Mill UDC wrote as follows to the commissioners on Haigh's behalf on 12 November 1931 in support of his application for a licence for the Scholes route. "The district of Scholes is one of the most thickly populated portions of the council's area, having a population in the immediate vicinity of the bus route through Scholes of approximately 600. In addition it is one of the highest parts of the district and is consequently difficult of access, all ways of approach being by steep hills. At present Scholes is served by the omnibus services of Messrs Wilson Haigh Limited - Scholes to Huddersfield via Holmfirth - and Mr Leonard Baddeley - Scholes to Huddersfield via New Mill. In view of your commissioners' decision not to grant renewal of licences to Mr Baddeley in respect of his Scholes service, the continuation of Messrs Wilson Haigh's service becomes doubly important. One of the chief points of this service is its benefit to workpeople who travel daily to Holmfirth, especially early in the morning. If this service were discontinued it would mean that all these workpeople would be obliged to walk to Holmfirth or to Jackson Bridge for the Huddersfield bus, in many cases before 7.00am as a large portion of the passengers are employed in the mills. This would cause considerable hardship when the weather is bad during the winter months. The necessity of this service is proved by the fact that it is so well patronised."

Herbert Warner, who had lived in Holme for 34 years, recalled being frequently drenched as he walked down the hill to the Corporation terminus at Holmbridge in the days before the start of the Haigh route to Holme. He also knew of many workpeople who had had to work all day in wet clothes after walking down from Holme. Children attending the secondary school at Holmfirth also valued the service and in an era before school dinners they were even able to return home at dinner time.

Elihu Leake, a lifelong Holme villager, was a daily passenger to and from his place of work at Holmbridge mill. He thought it would be most unfair and not at all in the public interest if the Holme route should cease to run.

Sam Bower of Liphill Bank used the Parkhead service principally for travelling to Huddersfield and found this preferable to walking down to Bottoms to catch a "Corporation" bus. He frequently saw people waiting at the Parkhead terminus who had walked from Upperthong and from beyond the Ford Inn. The service was also popular with the residents of the housing estates at Boothouse and Parklands. Alfred Battye, a retired representative of Thomas Dysons, Deanhouse Mills, Thongsbridge thought there would be great hardship caused if the Parkhead service was discontinued as it was a great convenience particularly to those who walked in from the outlying farms. He also mentioned Huddersfield ratepayers who used Haigh's buses in preference to the JOC's because of the unfair treatment of Haigh by the Corporation.

Edward Taylor was a farmer of Moorfield House, Oldfield who actually used Haigh's buses for transporting his produce to market at Huddersfield. Without the buses he could not continue his business unless he purchased a car or other vehicle. He thought the whole community would suffer as most people had come to rely on the buses for both work and pleasure; the buses were often crowded with people going to Honley Picture House.

Samuel Beaumont, an accountant with Laycock Dyson and Laycock, solicitors of Huddersfield, had purchased his house at Spinner Gate, Long Lane in June 1930 entirely on the strength of Haigh's bus service to Long Lane and Oldfield. He would never have entertained the idea if it had entailed a walk of nearly a mile in all

weathers. By using the bus, he was even able to save money by coming home at dinner time. He was in no doubt that the withdrawal of the buses would lead to a lowering of property values in the area and, if this were allowed to happen, he would have to sell his property at a loss and move nearer to Huddersfield. He knew of many other business people who would have to make the same sacrifice.

In anticipation of a possible inquiry Haigh was also determined to be in a position to present evidence of the irregularities on the part of the JOC which he had previously brought to the attention of Holmfirth UDC. It was a licence requirement that duplicates had to run within 2 to 3 minutes of the timetabled departure and over the whole JOC route to Holmbridge. In reality Haigh knew that when JOC duplicates dropped off their last passengers at or before Holmbridge they would turn round just beyond the town and reappear on the bus stand in Holmfirth in front of the scheduled departure of one of his buses. Other JOC buses from Holmbridge would arrive late in Holmfirth in order to cream off more passengers who were waiting for a Haigh bus. On Saturday 5 December 1931 a census was taken of JOC buses leaving the Holmfirth bus stand bound for Huddersfield. The many irregularities are shown on the next page.

Also, in an attempt to demonstrate that the JOC were running more buses than necessary to Holmbridge, a passenger census of buses as they left High Street, Huddersfield was conducted over a four day period from 4 December 1931 from about 7.45am (later on Sunday) to 9.00pm. The summarised results are shown below [for each operator, column (1) shows the total number of journeys; column (2) shows the total number of passengers on all the journeys; column (3) shows the average

Haigh's Leyland Tiger TS1/Fielding & Bottomley 12 (WW 8274) was photographed near Holme in heavy snow. Compare the livery treatment in this view with the previous photograph of the same vehicle. 12 passed to Huddersfield JOC as their 28 in 1934. Withdrawn in 1935 it later ran for the Clynnog & Trevor company between Caernarfon and Pwllheli in North Wales. [P.J. Cardno collection]

JOC bus no.	scheduled dep.	actual dep.	in front of HMS bus from:
81	11.55	11.58	Parkhead
70	12.05	12.07	Scholes
62	Special	12.32	Cross
72	Special	1.10	Holme
62	Special	1.40	Scholes
80	1.55	1.57	Parkhead
63	Special	2.02	
76	2.55	2.59	Parkhead
63	Special	3.10	Scholes
72	Special	3.32	Cross
62	Special	3.58	Parkhead
79	4.25	4.27	Cross
72	Special	4.40	Scholes
78	4.55	5.01	Parkhead
80	5.25	5.27	Cross
70	Special	5.57	Parkhead
78	Special	6.08	Scholes
76	6.25	6.27	Cross
41	Special	6.32	
62	Special	7.02	Parkhead
49	Special	7.05	Holme
70	7.05	7.07	
77	7.25	7.29	Cross
76	7.35	7.37	Scholes
79	7.55	7.58	Parkhead

number of passengers per journey]:

Probably little importance was attached to these figures by the commissioners as they failed to take into account passengers boarding at the Chapel Hill stops and on Lockwood Road.

JOC

	(1)	(2)	(3)
Friday	50	465	9.3
Saturday	94	1167	12.4
Sunday	46	292	6.3
Monday	51	485	9.5

On 2 March 1932 Haigh's solicitors wrote to the traffic commissioners to the effect that he was willing to pool his Cross, Holme, Parkhead and Scholes services with the JOC's Holmbridge route. It was suggested that the services could be operated on a 50/50 basis with intera-vailability of return tickets and the receipts pooled and divided in the same proportion. While this offer did not appeal to the JOC it may have influenced the commissioners in the final reckoning.

Meanwhile all the Haigh services continued to operate and at this point it is interesting to examine a selection of Haigh's traffic statistics up to the end of March 1932. The first table is for the year ending 31 March 1931. The

Scholes route had only been in operation for five months so the figures have been extrapolated for comparative purposes (the bracketed figures are the actual statistics for the five month period). Unfortunately figures are not available for the Marsden route. The re-

HMS

	(1)	(2)	(3)
	44	338	7.7
	48	524	10.9
	26	120	4.6
	48	400	8.3

ceipts for the Long Lane group of routes must have been particularly encouraging as this was the shortest by far and also the one experiencing the greatest competition from the trams.

The following financial year saw an increase in the

Route	Miles	Passengers	Receipts	Receipts (pence per mile)
Cross	97,688	342,398	£4138	10.20
Parkhead	86,058	303,108	£3383	9.43
Holme	70,404	269,208	£2714	9.25
Scholes	66,128	224,218	£2116	7.68
Scholes	(27,553)	(93,424)	(£882)	
Long Lane etc	100,516	351,995	£4367	10.43

total number of passengers carried on the above five routes from 1,360,133 to 1,457,804. Not surprisingly the Scholes buses abstracted traffic from the other routes which showed slight decreases in the numbers carried.

The second table (below) shows the total number of passengers carried on each route from the start of operations up to the end of March 1932.

The Marsden figure is an estimate based on the first five years of operation. It can be seen that in six years Haigh had carried almost seven million passengers. His

Route	Weekly Average	Period of Operation	Total Passengers
Cross	5925	3 years	1,249,190
Parkhead	5169	3 years	1,119,090
Holme	4517	3 years	1,012,597
Scholes	3652	1 year & 5 months	318,559
Long Lane etc	6109	5 years	2,075,086
Marsden	3785	6 years	1,217,101

business had developed to such an extent that he was annually carrying about the same number of passengers as were the JOC on their Holmbridge route.

After lengthy deliberations, in April 1932 the traffic commissioners published a very unpopular proposed route network for the Holme Valley based on the use of feeder buses operating from Honley and Holmfirth. Most of Haigh's passengers would have been obliged to change buses in order to complete their journeys. In the 1920s Corporation buses acting as feeders to Huddersfield trams had proved equally unpopular and were soon replaced by through services. There was now a feeling in Holmfirth that what had not been good enough for Huddersfield was apparently to be satisfactory for the Holme Valley.

The JOC and Wilson Haigh departures would have been coordinated, with Haigh running a mixture of through buses and feeders on his Holmfirth area routes. On Monday to Friday Haigh would have had a departure from Huddersfield every 40 minutes to either Holme or Scholes, offering a connection at Holmfirth with a feeder bus for Parkhead or Scholes. In a 4 hour cycle (shown in the following timetable) there would have been a through bus to Holme every 2 hours, connecting at Holmfirth with a feeder bus going to Scholes. The next two departures from Huddersfield would both have been through buses to Scholes with feeders to Parkhead. Scholes was therefore offered a 40 minutes overall frequency but the Parkhead frequency (with no through buses) would have alternated between 40 and 80 minutes.

At 10 minute intervals between the times shown below there would have been JOC departures from Huddersfield for Holmbridge.

Huddersfield	12.00		12.40		1.20		2.00		2.40	
Holmfirth	12.25	12.25	1.05	1.05	1.45	1.45	2.25	2.25	3.05	3.05
Holme	12.38						2.38			
Scholes		12.38	1.18		1.58			2.38	3.18	
Parkhead				1.14		1.54				3.14

Huddersfield	3.20		4.00
Holmfirth	3.45	3.45	4.25
Holme			4.38
Scholes	3.58		
Parkhead		3.54	

Many problems were found with the proposed timetables. Even though Holme retained through buses, frequency was reduced and the bus used by both schoolchildren and business people which arrived in Huddersfield at 9.00am was retimed to arrive at 9.15am, which was too late. Similarly the previous 4.30pm departure from Huddersfield was brought forward to 4.00pm - too early. The departure of the last bus to Holme was also brought forward to 10.00pm.

On the Parkhead route the regular frequency was lost and the need to change buses was thought to be a disadvantage, particularly for the elderly. Because of the relatively short distance involved, it was feared that many passengers, for example those travelling to Elmwood Hospital, would very likely decide to walk from a JOC bus stop in Woodhead Road.

The Scholes timetable was criticised by Haigh for offering too many journeys in the off peak between 9.00am and 1.00pm when the extra mileage was thought unlikely to generate more revenue. Finally with the last bus due to leave Huddersfield at the earlier time of 10.45pm, it would no longer connect with late trains from Leeds and Manchester.

In the Honley area, the separate services from Huddersfield to Long Lane, Oldfield and Wood Nook would have been replaced by one bus operating a circular feeder service from Honley Bridge every 45 minutes. The route was to be via Bradshaw Road (Long Lane turning) terminus and Meltham Road to Wood Nook, then via roads not served by buses to Oldfield, then via the existing Oldfield route back to Honley Bridge, where all passengers wishing to travel further would have to change buses [or onto a tram?]. Haigh ridiculed proposals which would have given Wood Nook residents the luxury of an all day 45 minutes service, when the existing two hourly afternoon service was under patronised and loss making. On the other hand Long Lane terminus and Oldfield would have suffered a reduced service; many people apparently walked to Oldfield from the neighbouring villages of Netherthong and Deanhouse, which were not served at all or not by buses to Huddersfield. The proposed new service would have entailed considerable wasteful mileage over unsuitable country roads which in places were less than eight feet wide. When all these proposals became known there was widespread discontent among the travelling public.

In the summer of 1932 most Holme Valley folk had little money to spend on holidays at the seaside or even on day excursions. Several coach operators competed for the limited traffic and the LMS Railway offered very cheap excursions from Holmfirth. Coach excursion fares were fixed by the traffic commissioners, as were picking up points so that a potential advantage of the coach operators in being able to pick up passengers near their homes was lost. Nevertheless in November 1931 Wilson Haigh had been granted a staggering 95 licences for day and half-day tours, a total far in excess of any other local operator. Haigh's excursions started from four points: Victoria Square in Holmfirth, Honley Market Place, Meltham Market Place and 11 New North Road, Huddersfield. A maximum of five vehicles could operate daily from each point but those starting in the Holme Valley could pick up in Huddersfield only if the direct route of the tour passed through the town.

That trade was slack is illustrated by the fact that in the entire 1932 summer season only 246 day trips were actually run (not including period return trips during the annual holiday weeks). Only 37 out of the possible 95 destinations were reached and, of these, 12 were variations of the popular (and cheap) drives over the moors. Altogether the vehicles ran 16,732 miles and carried 5775 passengers with average receipts of approximately 1/6d per mile.

Holmfirth Chamber of Trade used Haigh's coaches for their annual outing and 14 June 1932 proved no exception. Burlingham bodied Leyland Lion coach YG 852, which had very recently been put on the road, and one other left Victoria Square at midday with 64 passengers bound for Liverpool. Arrangements had been made for the party to inspect the Duchess of Atholl liner of the Canadian Pacific Steamship Company at Gladstone Dock. The "Atholl" was one of four Duchess liners in service between Liverpool and Quebec and Montreal; during the winter they operated cruises to the West Indies. This party, however, only travelled on the ferry across the Mersey as far as New Brighton.

Moving outside the Holme Valley, Haigh failed to obtain licences for what would have been three interesting and innovative routes entirely within the Huddersfield borough boundary. In July 1932 he applied for a circular route around the edge of Huddersfield town centre and through inner suburbs and industrial areas. From Folly Hall it would have run via Longroyd Bridge, Gledholt Bank, Blacker Road, King Cliffe Road, Spaines Road, Bradford Road, Alder Street, Hillhouse Lane, St Andrew's Road and Colne Road back to Folly Hall. This he wanted to operate every 30 minutes from 6.00am to 11.00pm with a maximum fare of 5d. Haigh claimed that the route would not compete directly with any Corporation or JOC route and would save potential passengers having to change trams in the town centre. It would have given a direct service to the many mills and factories on the route and also served both Fartown and Leeds Road football grounds.

At the traffic court Haigh had plenty of evidence of the need for this route as his inspector, Lewis Wood of New Mill, had conducted a survey of the numbers of workmen walking over parts of the route at different times of the day. On 26 July Wood had stood on Gledholt Bank between 6.30 and 9.30am and counted 227 people walking down the bank towards Paddock and another 108 walking up towards Marsh. Later at the same point between 4.30 and 7.30pm he counted 179 people walking towards Paddock and 225 walking in the opposite direction. The following day Wood was stationed in Firth Street, where between 6.30 and 9.30am 581 people walked towards Colne Road and Folly Hall and 171 walked in the opposite direction towards St Andrew's Road. In the afternoon in Colne Road between 4.00 and 6.00pm 592 people walked towards Folly Hall and 467 in the opposite direction. This evidence from a typical working day was interpreted as 2580 potential passengers.

Huddersfield Corporation's opposition to this application was based on three points, although they were clearly also concerned about abstraction of passengers from trams:
(1) Junctions where the route crossed main roads were "dangerous places to negotiate"
(2) There was no need for the service
(3) Nobody had asked for the service

As a result Haigh's application was refused in September 1932. When in October 1933 Huddersfield JOC applied to the traffic commissioners for a licence for an almost identical route, Haigh was furious and resubmitted his application. His solicitor accused the Corporation/JOC of a "bold faced change of front" but failed to win the case. The JOC obtained a licence by using the same arguments that Haigh had used in his application of the previous year and adding the point that since all abstraction of passengers would be from Corporation routes, they were entitled to run the circular. Wilson Haigh's only crumb of comfort would have been that this service, the Inner Circle, turned out to be one of the least successful of Huddersfield JOC's routes, although it lingered on until 1965. During 1932 Haigh had also applied for routes from Huddersfield (Byram Street) via Sheepridge to Deighton and from Huddersfield to Cowcliffe, which the commissioners refused to grant. Again the JOC were soon allowed to start their own Bradley Circular (from Byram Street!) and also to serve Cowcliffe by diverting their Brighouse via Rastrick service. Wilson Haigh and his manager Edward Deakin were clearly men of vision.

The new Holme Valley Grammar School for 450 pupils at Honley opened in September 1932. Haigh advertised his traffic arrangements which, he suggested, would allow pupils to reach school punctually both in the morning and after lunch. It was, however, rather unrealistic to suggest that a pupil could leave Honley at 12.10pm, arrive at Holme at 12.45pm and leave five minutes later at 12.50pm! Contracts were available from any point in the valley; prices from Scholes were 6/6d per month or £3 per annum.

In October 1932 major road works in Lockwood Road caused the diversion of all traffic. Haigh's buses coming into Huddersfield were diverted via Swan Lane and Victoria Road to Rashcliffe; outwards the route was via "Lockwood Old Road" [i.e., Albert Street] and Water Street. Passengers were picked up and set down as required on these roads.

Wilson Haigh Ltd.

REVISED OMNIBUS TIME TABLE,

COMMENCING on SUNDAY, JANUARY 1st, 1933, and until further notice.

Oldfield, Long Lane, Honley, Huddersfield.

[Timetable — Monday to Friday and Saturday Service, with columns: Oldfield Depart, Long L. Depart, Honley (Mkt Pl.) Depart, Hudds. Arrive, Hudds. Depart, Honley (Mkt Pl.) Depart, Long L. Depart, Oldfield Arrive]

Sunday Service commence Oldfield 2-0 p.m. and Huddersfield 2-30 p.m., and continue as above.

Wood Nook, Honley, Huddersfield.

[Timetable — Monday to Friday and Saturday Service, with columns: Wood Nook, Honley, Huddersf'd, Huddersf'd, Honley, Wood Nook]

Sunday Service commence 3-30 p.m. Wood Nook, 3-0 p.m. Huddersfield, and as above.

TABLE OF FARES.

Huddersfield								
4	Lockwood							
4	3½	Cricket Field						
4	3½	3	Berry Brow					
4	3½	3	3	Steppes Lane				
4	3½	3	3	2	Honley Bridge			
4	3½	3	3	2	1	Market Place		
5	4	3½	3	2	1	1	Thirstin	
5	4	3½	3	2	1½	1	1	Long Lane
6	5	4½	4	3	2	1½	1	1 Cross Lane or Bird in Hand
6	5	4½	4	3	2½	2	1½	1 1 Oldfield and Wood Nook

WORKMEN'S RETURN FARES.
Workmen's return tickets shall be issued at one and a half times the single fare on stage carriages departing Long Lane for Huddersfield on or before 8-35 a.m.

CONTRACT TICKETS.

	SCHOOL CHILDREN MONTHLY	ADULTS WEEKLY
From Long Lane to Hudds.	7/-	5/6
From Oldfield to Huddersf'd	8/-	6/-

H. V. DIGHTAM, Printer and Bookbinder, SOUTHGATE PRINTING WORKS, HONLEY.

1.4: LEGAL AT LAST?

Haigh had appealed against the proposed feeder scheme and an inquiry took place in Holmfirth in September 1932. It is hardly surprising that he refused to accept a timetable which effectively gave him only 25% of the traffic between Holmfirth and Huddersfield. He claimed that, out of a current weekly total of 878 departures between Holmfirth and Huddersfield, he operated 393 journeys. The proposals would have cut this to 175 and he would have had to dismiss 27 employees. The whole concept of feeders was unsatisfactory, particularly because of the recent opening of Holme Valley Grammar School at Honley which was going to require extra through workings, not fewer. Holmfirth UDC also objected to the feeder concept because extra buses would have had to turn round in the narrow "congested" streets in the centre of the town. What would they have thought of today's Summer Wine induced congestion? By November Haigh had a petition with over 10,000 signatures to support his appeal as well as many testimonials.

The appeal was successful and on 11 November 1932 the Minister of Transport ordered the feeder proposal to be abandoned and a different scheme drawn up. Finally on 1 January 1933 new timetables were introduced by Wilson Haigh and Huddersfield JOC (Huddersfield-Holmbridge) which did not involve feeder services. Under the new scheme, between Huddersfield and Holmfirth the JOC operated 60% and Haigh 40% of the journeys. Also Haigh was not allowed to run more than 30 journeys on weekdays on his Long Lane/Oldfield/Wood Nook group of services and there was a requirement for all bus fares between Honley and Huddersfield to give protection to the tramway service. Restrictions on picking up by Haigh's buses were swept away, placing his operations on a fully legal footing. This meant that it was no longer necessary for passengers to book returns to Huddersfield and notices appeared, advising passengers already holding return tickets to use them by the end of January or exchange them for cash at the Haigh office.

In the new timetable Haigh's Huddersfield-Holme, Huddersfield-Parkhead and Huddersfield-Scholes routes each ran every 80 minutes on Monday to Friday with one bus on each route. On Saturday they were increased to hourly, interworked with four buses, and an extra bus ran Huddersfield-Cross (a shortworking of Scholes). As previously, the two hourly afternoon Wood Nook service (five journeys) was interworked with the Long Lane (13 journeys) and Oldfield (12 journeys) routes, resulting in a 30 or 60 minute frequency as far as Long Lane, requiring two buses. Haigh's afternoon departures from Huddersfield are shown for a four hour period.

	Monday to Friday	Saturday
2.00	Holme	Holme
2.00	Long Lane	Long Lane
2.20		Parkhead
2.30	Oldfield	Oldfield
2.40	Parkhead	Scholes
2.50		Cross
3.00	Scholes	Holme
3.00	Wood Nook	Wood Nook
3.20	Holme	Parkhead
3.30	Oldfield	Oldfield
3.40		Scholes
4.00	Parkhead	Holme
4.00	Long Lane	Long Lane
4.10		Cross
4.20	Scholes	Parkhead
4.30	Oldfield	Oldfield
4.40	Holme	Scholes
5.00	Wood Nook	Holme
5.00		Wood Nook
5.20	Parkhead	Parkhead
5.30		Cross
5.30	Oldfield	Oldfield
5.40	Scholes	Scholes
6.00	Holme	Holme

The numbers of timetabled Holmfirth corridor journeys, including the JOC Holmbridge service, are shown in the following table [columns marked (1) show no. of round trips]. Wilson Haigh was operating 39% of the total.

Route	M-F (1)	Sat (1)	Sun (1)	Total single trips
Cross	0	12	0	24
Parkhead	13 x 5	17	7	179
Holme	12 x 5	17	7	168
Scholes	13 x 5	17	8	186
Holmbridge	60 x 5	97	36	866

Occasionally the village of Holme enjoyed a 20 minutes frequency, for the annual Holme Sports on the first Saturday in July. On 1 July 1933 the through bus ran from Huddersfield on the hour as usual but the departures at 20 and 40 minutes past to Parkhead and Scholes had connections at Holmfirth for Holme. The sports, promoted by Holme Valley Beagles, were a major event and also featured pony jumping, exhibition classes for cattle and wrestling bouts. The star attraction was a bout between the former Fartown player, Douglas Clark, and "The Masked Wrestler".

For Holmfirth Holiday Week 12-19 August 1933 Haigh is reported to have had over 50 coaches on the road, most of which must have been hired in for that period. During the week in question the number of people leaving Holmfirth and district for one week's holiday was 3585, owing to increased prosperity. Of these, 2235 travelled by train and 1250 bought period return tickets from Haigh to travel to Blackpool, Bridlington, Morecambe or Scarborough. Overall there were 2990 bookings for day and half-day excursions; LMS trains catered for 1350 people whilst 1000 were loyal to Haigh.

To improve the accommodation for his vehicles Haigh had built a new shed, 75 feet long and 50 feet wide, on the site of the old mill yard at his Ribbleden Mills depot. An underground petrol tank of 3000 gallons capacity was a feature under the new concrete floor.

In October 1933 Haigh applied to the commissioners to project his Marsden-Holmfirth route through to Cross. The reasons given were the need to avoid reversing buses in the main street in Holmfirth and also to benefit 300 residents said to be living within a ten minute walk of Cross. It is not clear whether this extension was granted but the application was certainly opposed by the other established operator in Dunford Road, Leonard Baddeley. Two buses would have been needed to provide the hourly service, as was already the case. The first proposed departure from Cross was at 11.00am. A driver was subsequently prosecuted for an offence committed in Dunford Road while driving on the Marsden service but he could have been entering service from the depot.

As prosperity was gradually returning to some of the mills in the Holme Valley, Haigh anticipated a greater demand for his coaches in the following year. For the 1934 season he applied for and was granted licences for a further ten half-day excursions and also a licence for two-day (weekend) excursions to Blackpool Illuminations. The maximum number of vehicles he was allowed to operate from each starting point was increased from 5 to 10 but the extra five in each case were restricted to pre-booked unadvertised private parties such as mill workers' outings. He was also granted permission to increase the number of vehicles used on his coastal express services during the annual Meltham and Huddersfield holidays.

Early in 1934 Haigh's Motor Services was in the news as a result of irregularities which led to a prosecution. Originally crews had operated a split shift system, working up to $5\frac{1}{2}$ hours on either side of a half hour break.

This was not popular with the men and at about the beginning of 1933 it was altered so that crews worked a single shift of 8$^1/_2$ hours; within this shift a break still had to be arranged, to comply with the law, so that the maximum length of driving on either side of the break did not exceed 5$^1/_2$hours. Somehow by November 1933 the Holmfirth police were suspicious that this legal requirement was being flouted. On 21 November they logged the work of five drivers. Leonard Davidson did seven round trips to Holme between 1.30 and 10.45pm. At 3.45pm he had a tea break lasting 15 minutes, therefore his final stint of driving exceeded the limit. Jack Heywood did seven round trips to Parkhead between 1.43 and 11.10pm and also had a 15 minute break at an unspecified time. A third driver, Firth Dawson, drove on the Scholes route between 2.03 and 11.40pm and admitted that his relief man never turned up at all. In February 1934 Haigh was found guilty in all these cases of causing employees to drive buses in excess of 5$^1/_2$ hours without a break and was fined £2 on each count. Two similar cases were dismissed. It transpired that sometimes drivers exchanged parts of their shifts with each other without the knowledge of the firm and there were no proper time sheets. It is also interesting to note that some men started and finished work at Huddersfield. The Bench advised Haigh to make sure that in future he knew what was going on.

This advice turned out to be unnecessary as later in the month it became public knowledge that Huddersfield JOC would soon be taking over Haigh's bus services. He had succeeded in placing Haigh's Motor Services on a fully legal footing within the new regulatory framework so the only way for Huddersfield JOC to obtain a near monopoly on the Huddersfield to Holmfirth corridor now was to buy him out. By February 1934 negotiations were being finalised for the purchase of the business and the assets by the JOC and a price of £13,626-17s-4d was eventually agreed. This did not include the freehold garage, which Huddersfield Corporation purchased separately and later sold at a loss. All was not straightforward as both Baddeleys and Yorkshire Traction initially raised objections about the takeover with the traffic commissioners. As Haigh's express and excursion licences were of no interest to the JOC, these were offered to Yorkshire Traction, possibly in return for the withdrawal of their objections. Yorkshire Traction operated these from the summer of 1935.

Nevertheless Haigh continued to market his services energetically. In an advertisement for what was to be

the final Easter of operations in April 1934 passengers were encouraged to take the Blue Buses to the healthy moorland scenery:

the Holme bus for Brownhill reservoir and Holme Moss, the Scholes bus for Bordhill, Hazlehead and the ruins of Cook's Study the Parkhead bus for Wessenden Valley, Isle of Skye and Wood Cottage, which offered accommodation for ramblers. At 1200 feet above sea level over two miles out of Holmfirth on Harden Moss, this property had at one time been a public house known as Wine Butts and was soon to become a youth hostel. On Easter Monday and Tuesday (2 and 3 April) passengers for these destinations did not need to walk from Parkhead as Haigh ran his occasional service to the Isle of Skye from 9.00am "as required".

On the evening of Thursday 24 May 1934, just a month before the takeover, Jack Payne's band gave a concert in Huddersfield Town Hall. Many Holme Valley people who were in the audience went to catch the last bus at 11.00pm to Scholes via Holmfirth. The importance of the concert had slipped Haigh's mind and a duplicate was not provided. The conductor, Booth Marsden, took pity on the waiting throng and allowed all of them on board but unfortunately the single deck bus was stopped by police at Berry Brow. The police asked the standees to alight and counted twenty of them; together with those seated this totalled 51, well in excess of the legal maximum. The conductor was fined 15/-.

After they had obtained the necessary licences, the JOC took over operation of the former Haigh services on 23 June 1934. The one very slight change was a short extension of the Marsden route to an existing JOC stop nearby, done in case they wanted to link the two routes. It was said that after ten days of JOC operation of the steep Holme route there were more complaints of failures than there had been in five years under Haigh's operation. For a short while after the takeover fourteen of the blue and white buses continued serving the valley with Haigh's fleetname painted out and JOC insignia substituted on the side but the older vehicles were soon withdrawn and newer stock repainted.

Some of Haigh's staff also joined the JOC along with their buses. For a 48 hour week the top rate of pay for a Haigh's driver was £3-7s-6d whereas the JOC paid only £3-3s-6d but a 21 year old conductor transferring to the JOC would have his basic wage increased by 1/6d from £2-5/-. One such driver was John Hall. After war service in Italy, he left the JOC and went to drive for GW Castle but was probably best known later when he ran the Ford

Inn on Greenfield Road, where no doubt he welcomed many coach parties.

Wilson Haigh's son, Walter, worked on the engineering side for Huddersfield Corporation/JOC for four years. He later became deputy manager at Sunderland Corporation and finally, in 1965, general manager for Kingston upon Hull Corporation. Another employee of Haigh's already mentioned is Edward Deakin. Born in 1910 in Sheffield but later moving to Scholes, he attended the old Holmfirth secondary school and on leaving went straight to work for Wilson Haigh. A Jack of all trades and probably master of them all, Deakin is reputed to have worked almost a hundred hours each week in the roles of cleaner, conductor, driver and mechanic in his early days. After the formation of the limited company, at the first meeting held in the offices of solicitors Kidd, Meller and Fletcher on 31 January 1930 he became company secretary. This varied experience was certainly put to good use and at the pinnacle of his career Mr Deakin was appointed general manager of Bradford City Transport from December 1962.

The JOC had still not managed to eliminate all the competition from small independents in the Holme Valley. Apart from Baddeleys who shared Dunford Road, GW Castle also had a couple of competitive licences and within a month of the takeover he was advertising a half hourly service from Victoria Square, Holmfirth to the sheep dog trials at Harden Moss on Saturday 21 July alongside the JOC's ex-Haigh route. Doubtless deliberately echoing Wilson Haigh, he appealed to people to support local enterprise!

When the JOC took over the Ribbleden Mills garage in June 1934 it was announced that Wilson Haigh's offices had been transferred to the rear of his house on the opposite side of Dunford Road. It seems that Haigh continued to run a small private hire business and excursions from this address for some months (still as Wilson Haigh Ltd), hiring in buses and coaches from other operators, including Huddersfield JOC. Unfortunately his operator's licence expired and he did not attempt to renew it. Soon after this he was prosecuted for running a bus without a licence – on an excursion to Blackpool on 20 October 1934, using a vehicle hired from the JOC. In defence he unsuccessfully claimed that he had believed that, as he was hiring buses from another owner with a licence, he did not need one.

Wilson Haigh had been involved with several local charities, particularly Holme Valley Memorial Hospital. He organised Christmas morning charity football matches, the tickets being sold in advance by his conductors and the receipts going to the hospital. The first of these matches took place in 1931 between Haigh's Motor Services and Baddeleys' Green and White Motor Services and ended as a draw - four goals each – with £20 raised for the hospital.

Several of Haigh's staff had formed a male voice choir and since Christmas Day 1932 fell on a Sunday, making a football match impossible on religious grounds, they agreed to sing carols in aid of the hospital. As most of the men were working until midnight the carolling started at 12.30am and continued until 5.00am. Starting at Thongsbridge, they travelled on one of their own buses through much of their operating area. The choir was conducted by Bob Buckley and the bus headlights were used to illuminate the carol sheets. Tickets had already been pushed through the letter boxes of houses on the route bearing the words "HMS Male Voice Choir respectfully wishes you the compliments of the season". Donations were collected afterwards at a more civilised hour.

The last of the football matches was played against the Chamber of Trade on Christmas Day 1933. Haigh's men were victorious by four goals to two in a match which was kicked off by a uniformed nurse from the hospital. All the football kit was loaned to the busmen by Wooldale AFC and after the match it was laundered free of charge by the Holmfirth Sanitary Steam Laundry. There was also a Haigh's Motor Services cricket team.

While Haigh was selling his buses to the JOC, his relative, Hiram Haigh, had died. Hiram had founded the Queen Carriage Company at Shorefoot, Huddersfield and at the time of his death in June 1934 was its chairman. This firm was eventually to become part of the Hanson group. Wilson Haigh himself outlived his bus business by 20 years. In 1954 on his death at Kirkheaton he left the comparatively large sum of £24,753.

Haigh's tickets were of the geographical punch type printed by both Bell Punch and Williamsons. The stages for the Marsden route tended to be on the back whilst those for the Huddersfield routes were on the front. There was a series of single tickets, presumably for use outside Huddersfield borough, and two types of composite tickets with tear off stubs. One type of composite was for workmen only, to be used either as a single or return; the second composite served as an ordinary, child or workman single or return. Unfortunately not many of Haigh's tickets have survived.

1.5: WILSON HAIGH FLEET LIST

Haigh's Motor Services operated a mixed bag of buses and coaches, some purchased new and some secondhand. Livery was blue and white. Fleet numbers were used but not all are known. Ten vehicles actually kept the same fleet numbers when they were taken over by the JOC.

For the three dates shown, (1) is the date first registered, (2) is the date the vehicle passed to Haigh and (3) is the disposal date. An * in column (3) denotes that the vehicle passed to Huddersfield JOC in 1934, with the same or the bracketed fleet number.

No.	Reg. No.	Chassis	Body	(1)	(2)	(3)
	CX 3564	Bethlehem	goods/B-	1921	1921	1927
	CX 3820	Karrier	Chara 14			
	CX 3963		Chara			
	WY 7199	Fiat	Chara 14	1923	1923	1927
2	WT 3556	Karrier CY	B20	1924	?	1930
3	WU 7176	Garner EP	B20F	1926	1926	1932
4	CX 9011	Karrier CL4	B20F	1926	1926	?
5	CX 9100	Karrier CL4	B20F	1926	1926	?
	CX 9101	Karrier CL4	B20F	1926	1926	?
	IJ 7321		B26			
8						
9	WW 5873	Leyland PLSC1	Leyland B32	?	?	1934*(26)
10	WT 3872	Karrier CY	Roe B20	1924	?	1929
11	WW 7439	Leyland PLC1	Leyland C26	1928	1928	1934*(27)
12	WW 8274	Leyland TS1	Fielding & Bottomley B30	1929	1929	1934*(28)
14	WW 8297	Dennis E	B30	1929	1929	by 1934
15	CX 9010	Karrier JH	B24F	1926	1929	1934*
16	WX 568	Leyland LT1	Leyland B30F	1929	1929	1934*
17	WX 856	A.J.S. Pilot 134	Lewis&Crabtree C26	1929	1929	1934*
18	WX 4676	Leyland LT2	Leyland B30F	1930	1930	1934*
19	WX 4394	Leyland TS2	Leyland C30	1930	1930	1934*
20	VA 6188	Leyland PLSC1	Leyland B31	1927	1931	1934*
21	VN 564	Albion PJ26	B20F	1929	1931	1934*
22	YG 852	Leyland LT5	Burlingham C32R	1932	1932	1934*
23	VH 3527	AEC Regal	Burlingham B32F	1931	?	1934*
24	VO 5778	AEC Regal	Burlingham B32F	1931	1933	1934*
25	VO 6841	AEC Regal	Burlingham B32F	1931	1933	1934*
	WW 4097	Karrier CL4	B26	1927	1933	1933
	MY 2276	AEC Regal	B32		1931	
	UW 8656	Gilford	-32-			
	UK 4816		-32-			

2: WALTER BOWER AND THE BLUE AND WHITE

2.1: AN EARLY HOLME VALLEY OPERATOR

Joseph Bower (1846-1936) of Gled Royd, Hinchliffe Mill, Holmbridge was in business as a grocer for 70 years. At the time of his death he was the oldest tradesman in the Holmfirth area and, at his request, the coffin was transported on his own motor wagon instead of by hearse. He had two sons, one of whom, Walter, started a livery business in the days before motor transport as well as helping with the family grocery business. Later Walter and his son (Joseph Edward) ran taxis and from 1913 they operated charabancs to football matches in Huddersfield. Walter's brother died in 1921. From around the summer of that year Walter Bower is believed to have run a bus service intermittently between Honley Bridge tram terminus and Holmbridge alongside GW Castle. Baddeleys and Huddersfield Corporation, however, soon appeared on the scene and, running more frequently, became the major operators on that corridor. On Christmas Day (1923 onwards; possibly earlier as well), when the Corporation trams and buses did not operate, Bower was able to run every 90 minutes between Holmbridge and Huddersfield alongside Beardsells and Baddeleys.

On 2 June 1924 Holmfirth UDC had set up a sub-committee to consider exercising their powers of licensing buses under the Town Police Clauses Act, because of a perceived danger to the public from the "competitive and unrestricted running of buses". This sub-committee recommended that licensing should start from 1 January 1925 and applications for licences were to be received before 10 December otherwise bus owners would no longer be allowed to ply for hire. About the middle of November 1924 Walter Bower, who had by now been appointed as an overseer for the poor for Holmfirth township and was still based at Hinchliffe Mill, restarted running between Honley Bridge and Holmbridge in competition with Huddersfield Corporation and Baddeleys, using his new 14 seater Crossley bus WT 7030, which also saw use as a hearse. He even issued a timetable - but failed to observe it for any appreciable period. On 22 December 1924 Holmfirth Hackney Carriages Committee submitted to the full council their recommendations on the licence applications they had received. This included a rejection of Bower's application. In fact the council delayed the introduction of their licensing scheme until 1 April 1925 but Bower's application was again not

recommended. The Clerk was, however, instructed to tell Bower that his vehicle would be licensed as an ordinary hackney carriage, subject to certain conditions, which would not prevent him from running between Holmfirth railway station and Holmbridge.

Bower continued running "as and when he thought fit" and as a result the council took proceedings against him in July and he was fined. On 5 June one of Bower's drivers, Stanley Chaplin, had been reported for plying for hire contrary to the licence. There was also an accident at Reins, Honley, on the evening of Sunday 12 July 1925 by which time he seems to have started running beyond Honley Bridge into Huddersfield. One of his buses, "proceeding towards Huddersfield" and carrying ten passengers, collided with a taxi and was extensively damaged. Interestingly this took place on the

an unlicensed bus in Albert Street, Lockwood. The police accused him of pirating by carrying three passengers over the Corporation's Holmbridge route. Bower pleaded that the passengers were personal friends who had paid no fares. One passenger swore that this was true and that he sometimes bought the driver a drink in return; the case was dismissed. In January 1926 Bower was refused a licence by Linthwaite UDC for a proposed bus service between Holmbridge and Milnsbridge via Lockwood, Crosland Moor and Park Road West. The application was in the name of his son, Joseph E Bower, and their address was Central Garage, Holmbridge.

In November 1925 Bower had appealed to the Ministry of Transport to have the Holmfirth UDC's licensing decision reversed. His solicitor presented some sound arguments on 14 January 1926 in front of MoT inspec-

The Blue & White Bus

will run the following Service on

CHRISTMAS DAY.

Holmbridge.	Holmfirth	Honley.	Huddersf'd.	Honley.	Holmfirth.	Holmbridge.
10-0	10-15	10-30	10-45	11-0	11-15	11-30
11-30	11-45	12-0	12-15	12-30	12-45	1-0
1-0	1-15	1-30	1-45	2-0	2-15	2-30
2-30	2-45	3-0	3-15	3-30	3-45	4-0
4-0	4-15	4-30	4-45	5-0	5-15	5-30
5-30	5-45	6-0	6-15	6-30	6-45	7-0
7-0	7-15	7-30	7-45	8-0	8-15	8-30
8-30	8-45	9-0	9-15	9-30	9-45	10-0
10-0	10-15	10-30	10-45	11-0	11-15	11-30

Passengers can only return from Huddersfield by having Return Tickets.

last day of operation by Baddeleys between Huddersfield and Holmbridge and it is thought that the impending disappearance of Baddeleys had encouraged both Bower and Castle to restart operations over part or all of the route. During the 1925 September holiday week Bower advertised one excursion daily (Monday to Friday) to the following destinations: Harrogate and Knaresborough, Blackpool, Southport, Scarborough, Doncaster.

Bower continued to run between Holmbridge and Huddersfield from time to time. He was summonsed in Huddersfield in December 1925 for plying for hire with

tor FO Langley. Witnesses - a grocer's manager and a mill worker - supported the view that Huddersfield Corporation's Huddersfield to Holmbridge service was inadequate, a position corroborated by regular contemporary newspaper reports of intending passengers being left behind on this route, but Holmfirth council disagreed and the case was lost. Nevertheless the Minister suggested that Bower should be licensed for a short period until it could be seen whether he would adhere to his promise to provide a regular and reliable service. The committee, however, again rejected the application in

March 1926.

While the Corporation buses were off the road during the General Strike (between 8 and 13 May 1926) Bower's bus was welcomed and he was allowed to run between Huddersfield and Holmbridge every 90 minutes alongside Beardsells and Baddeleys. Bower's last bus operation in the Holme Valley seems to have been his Christmas Day service which in mid 1920s was still offering a 90 minute frequency, latterly starting from Holmbridge at 10.00am with returns from Huddersfield 45 minutes later until 10.45pm.

2.2: COLNE VALLEY VENTURE

Having fallen foul of the Holmfirth licensing committee, Bower decided to try his luck in the Colne Valley. There was considerable potential for buses along the main corridor between Marsden and Huddersfield. He saw that a bus service would be faster than the trams, more convenient than the trains and could be expected to be well patronised. By November 1926 Marsden council were keen to license a bus operator to run between Huddersfield and parts of Marsden beyond the tram terminus. Slaithwaite UDC were, however, loyal to Hansons who already served people in their area living some distance from the tram route and felt that if such a service were really likely to be profitable, Hansons would already have started one. Linthwaite UDC sanctioned the proposed service on 22 November 1926 and finally on 10 December 1926 Slaithwaite followed suit.

Walter Bower's service between Huddersfield and the Moorcock Inn, Hard End, Marsden started on Saturday 1 January 1927 when the first bus actually left his Lord Street terminus in Huddersfield at 12.15pm. Buses ran direct via Manchester Road to Marsden then initially via Brougham Road, Market Place and Fall Lane to the Moorcock. The basic service (on Monday to Friday) ran every 90 minutes from 2.00pm and as the round trip took 90 minutes, just one bus was required. An extra bus was provided on Saturdays and Sundays to give an alternating 30 and 60 minutes frequency. The original through single fare was 9d; a return cost 1/2d. To avoid a dangerous corner, the buses were rerouted in Marsden from 7 January to run direct via Manchester Road to Fall Lane The service was unlicensed by Huddersfield Corporation as it competed with their trams so it had to run on the return ticket system within the borough (only passengers who already had a return ticket could board). Each vehicle displayed a blue light at the front at night so that

Leyland Lioness WW 1661 with 26 seater bodywork by John Taylor of Barnsley was new to Blue & White (Bower) in 1927. It was regularly used on excursions. [P.J. Cardno collection]

"Modern single-deck saloon bodywork" by Taylor of Barnsley in 1927 was exemplified by this additional view of Lioness WW 1661. At this stage Holmbridge was served only on Christmas Day, if then. [S.T. Harling collection]

it could be more easily identified by intending passengers. The timetable claimed that passengers could have a reliable, cheaper and faster ride by supporting the Blue and White, which was Bower's new fleet name, based on his livery. Coach operator (and former bus operator) Frank Harburn of Rugby Garage, Percy Street, Fartown resented Bower trading as Blue and White. Harburn informed the public that he had been using the name since 1921 and had no connection whatsoever with Bower.

Bower's service must have been an immediate success as an improved timetable came into operation on 12 March. This offered a morning service for the first time (the morning journeys always ran between Lord Street and the centre of Marsden only) and a regular 45 minutes headway on Monday to Friday afternoons. On Saturdays and Sundays three vehicles were now required to provide a half hourly frequency. Even so overcrowding

was common and court cases frequent. Walter Bower's son, Joseph E Bower, pleaded guilty to driving with 26 passengers on a 19 seater bus in Manchester Road, Linthwaite on 28 March and was fined ten shillings. Conductor Jack Stead had so many passengers on his bus at Slaithwaite that Constable Feather had to ask some of them to alight before he could count the rest. In all, 45 passengers had been riding on a 26 seater bus. It was a workmen's journey and, as the tram in front had also been carrying 11 passengers illegally standing on the rear platform, the Bench leniently dismissed the case on payment of 4 shillings.

Speeding and dangerous driving were also rife and minor collisions resulted, one incident actually leading to the derailment of a tram outside St Thomas's School in Manchester Road. The bus was being driven towards Marsden by Harry Bradshaw while the tram was return-to the public.

The 42nd annual Marsden Sing, held on Sunday 3 July 1927 in a field off Carrs Road, attracted large crowds and an enhanced frequency (15 minutes) was operated. For the August holiday week Bower advertised his new Leyland Lioness saloon bus which would be running excursions to east and west coast resorts. As the departure time was 7.00am, arrangements could be made to pick up passengers as near to their homes as possible. Seats could be booked with the conductors on the Marsden buses or at the Linthwaite garage that he was now using.

From 22 August 1927 the timetable was significantly improved again. More morning journeys were added and from 12.40pm a half hourly frequency was provided each day. After midday every third bus was rerouted to continue along the A62 as far as the Great Western Hotel, Standedge; the others still ran via Fall Lane and now terminated at the Golf House, Hard End.

ing to Town with Frank Broadley at the controls but neither reached its destination. The bonnet and offside front wheel of the bus were badly damaged and its front axle was bent. Many windows were shattered but fortunately the passengers suffered only shock and minor injuries. The bus had to be towed away and after rerailing the tram was towed to the depot.

In another incident which took place at almost the same location on Sunday 6 March 1927 driver Hubert Burley of Holmbridge had been following a tramcar into Town. No doubt frustrated at being delayed, he tried to pass the tram on the offside and almost collided with another tram coming out of Town. Both trams were fully loaded and a nasty accident was only just prevented by the hasty application of the electric tram brakes. On the following day the court rejected his defence that on a Sunday night he did not expect so many trams to be running. He was fined £5 for driving in a manner dangerous

Eventually from 22 October 1927 Huddersfield Corporation retaliated by reducing tram fares; the maximum fare from Town to any terminus was now 3d and the workman return to Marsden was an absolute bargain at 3½d. To prevent losing his passengers to the slower but cheaper trams, Bower had to cut his fares from 24 October. Huddersfield to Marsden (Centre) return was reduced from 1/- to 9d; the workman return cost 6d and the corresponding single was cut from 7d to 5d. Huddersfield to Slaithwaite return came down from 9d to 7d, with a workman return at 5d and the single down from 5d to 4d.

Bower claimed that despite the reduced tram fares his buses were actually carrying more passengers than before. Workmen certainly continued to use them and conductor Thomas Connelly was fined £1 on 29 December 1927 for having 52 passengers on a 26 seater bus at Marsden. Was this a record for Bower? There were three trams standing at the terminus at the time (5.10pm) which people could have boarded. The bus driver had turned out the saloon lights to try to prevent the police officer from counting accurately. Bower in defence claimed that his duplicate bus had broken down.

Conductor Cecil Donaldson had been frequently reported by the police for carrying far more than the legal maximum number of passengers. On one occasion he had 50 passengers on the last bus to Hard End; the chairman of the Bench regarded this as a particularly bad offence as any passengers left behind could still have travelled to Marsden by tram or train and fined Donaldson 30/-. At the end of October 1927 the unfortunate Donaldson made his fifth court appearance. Constable Wood informed the court that Bower had paid all Donaldson's previous fines and that it was Bower's practice to encourage his conductors to overload the buses on the understanding that if they were caught he would pay their fines. Denying any knowledge of this, Donaldson was fined the increased amount of 40/-.

Drivers too continued to attract the attention of the law as they competed with trams and also rival buses to pick up passengers. Herbert Butterfield was summonsed for driving a motorbus to the danger of the public at Linthwaite on 4 January 1928. Near the Bath Hotel while driving towards Marsden he cut in between a Hansons bus and an oncoming lorry. Catching the rear mudguard of the Hansons bus which was forced onto the pavement, Butterfield narrowly avoided hitting a telegraph pole and failed to stop. He claimed not to have known about the bump until told by his conductor on reaching the Mars-

Photographed before entering service is Blue & White (Bower) WW 3672, a Leyland Lion with Taylor bodywork new in October 1927. The "Safety Coach" lettering reminds us how many buses, charabancs and coaches suffered serious accidents during the 1920s.
[P.J. Cardno collection]

Here Leyland Lion WW 3672 is standing at the New Inn, Marsden, ready to depart for Huddersfield in competition with the Corporation trams. It later passed to Hansons as fleet number 20 and was eventually converted into a van.
[P.J. Cardno collection]

den terminus but was fined £4 10s.

The speed limit for buses and coaches was raised from 12 to 20 miles per hour in October 1928 but that would not have saved two Blue and White drivers. Driver Bray was caught doing 30 m.p.h. over the one mile stretch between the junction with Brougham Road and the Olive Branch. Driver Norcliffe was found to be exceeding 30 m.p.h. between Peel Street turning and Cellars Clough. Both drivers claimed only to have accelerated in order to overtake trams. Their fines were £1 and £2 respectively.

Bower continued to compete effectively with the Corporation trams. In court in December 1928 a police witness had recorded 40 and 42 passengers on buses licensed to carry 26. A "Working Woman" who wrote to the Colne Valley Guardian found the buses quicker and quieter than the trams but was becoming scared at the way in which passengers were crammed into the buses. As soon as one man got off her toes, another stood on them and she was apprehensive about what would happen in a fire. She also referred to the stink of ale and whisky on the buses after 10.00pm.

The Corporation had long since concluded that the only way to remove the competing buses was to buy Bower out but the presence of Hansons on the same road as far as Slaithwaite complicated matters. Eventually, after discussions between all three parties and taking into account the views of the local authorities, an agreement was drawn up whereby Bower would sell his Marsden

route and vehicles jointly to Hansons and Huddersfield Corporation, each paying £2700. The Blue and White buses ran for the last time on 10 January 1929. From the following day a limited coordination scheme was introduced by Hansons and the Corporation which provided for the joint operation of three services in the Colne Valley. Among these was a Huddersfield to Marsden motorbus route, a legacy of Bower which continued the competition with the Corporation trams (and trolleybuses) for a further ten years.

In addition to the 14 seater Crossley mentioned earlier, Bower had used at least the following four vehicles in his Blue and White fleet. The Karrier was new in 1926 and the others in 1927.

CX 9010	Karrier JH	B20-
WW 324	Dennis 30 cwt.	B20-
WW 1661	Leyland Lioness	*B26F
WW 3672	Leyland Lion	*B32F

*Bodywork by John Taylor (Barnsley)

These four vehicles were sold by auctioneer Harold Hanson, the Karrier passing to Wilson Haigh and the Leyland Lion going to Hansons.

For his final venture Bower had used punch tickets printed by Williamson of Ashton, titled "Huddersfield Slaithwaite and Marsden Service", with numerical stages up to 27. The colours of only three values are known: 1/2d white, 1d blue and 1 1/2d salmon

3: GW CASTLE

3.1 FROM BUN VAN TO LIMITED COMPANY

George Willie Castle was a baker and confectioner at Hinchliffe Mill who also started a business as a garage proprietor in 1915 during the First World War. He was said to have rendered a great public service by conveying wounded soldiers from Holmfirth railway station to the military hospital at Bottoms.

Around 1917, along with Joseph Bower, Castle was running small vans to meet the last train from Huddersfield at Holmfirth for the benefit of Holmbridge and Hinchliffe Mill people when they petitioned him to meet the last tram at Honley as well. Castle quickly realised the potential of this and fitted his bakery van with seats. Passengers christened it the "bun van" and were very grateful for the service.

In March 1919 Castle was summonsed for keeping a hackney motor [car] without a licence from the last day of 1918. His excuse was that he had merely had the car on trial and intended to purchase and licence the vehicle only if he was satisfied with it.

The vicar of Holmbridge, JF Beamish, complained in his parish magazine in May 1920 that any journey to Holmfirth still had to be on foot for most people as the fares for horse drawn traps and motor taxis were too high. He travelled to London to give evidence on behalf of Holmfirth UDC in support of Huddersfield Corporation's General Powers Bill before a House of Commons select committee. It was to be 15 April 1922 before the Corporation started their own Honley to Holmbridge service and in the meantime Leonard Baddeley of Huddersfield, Castle and others took the initiative.

By 18 June 1921 Castle was running a "makeshift" bus between Holmbridge and Honley Bridge tram terminus. An hourly service was operated "daily" starting from Holmbridge at 10.00am. Starting Saturday 13 August 1921 he advertised a service from Holmfirth railway station to Hinchliffe Mill from 12.00noon for a single fare of 4d, possibly on Tuesdays and Saturdays only. On Sundays he ran from the top of Victoria Street, Holmfirth, hourly from 2.30pm to 9.30pm to Honley tram terminus, returning 30 minutes after these times.

On 13 August 1921 he advertised a 12 seater charabanc with pneumatic tyres, the "Castle-de-luxe". The first advertised excursions with the new charabanc were:

17 August 1921   Dewsbury, fare 4/-
18 August 1921   Penistone Show, fare 3/6d
21 August 1921   Southport, depart 7.00am, fare 14/-
All the above from Holmbridge

There was already considerable competition from other local charabanc owners. Castle must have had at least two vehicles by this date. In September 1921 he submitted plans to Holmfirth council for a new garage at Hinchliffe Mill but it was to be a year before these were approved. Castle had to appear before Holmfirth UDC on 4 June 1923 to answer some charges and he was then said to be running a daily Honley-Holmbridge service.

Holmfirth UDC started licensing buses and bus routes from 1 April 1925. A 14 seater Ford charabanc C 2332 belonging to Castle was licensed by them but it was not to be used for plying for hire as an omnibus on the part of the Honley-Holmfirth-Holmbridge route within the Holmfirth boundaries. Drivers were listed as George Willie Castle, Herbert Castle and Leslie Castle. Apart from the chara, three landaulettes were licensed and there appear to have been no restrictions on their licences so Studebaker FY 1302, Wolseley KT 1566 and Ford WR 5510 could have been used between Holmbridge and Honley.

Soon afterwards Baddeleys sold out to Huddersfield Corporation and both operators had already been running through services between Holmbridge and Huddersfield. In the circumstances Honley tram terminus had become irrelevant so, apparently not wishing to run through to Huddersfield, Castle seems thereafter to have concentrated resources on his local part of the route in the upper Holme Valley, Holmbridge-Holmfirth. On 1 April 1926, he applied to Holmfirth licensing committee to renew a licence for just this section, which he was said to have been serving for at least a year, but his application was refused.

Nevertheless George Willie Castle was driving a charabanc with 14 passengers on board from Holmbridge towards Holmfirth at 5.00pm on 6 January 1927 when he was dazzled by the lights of a Huddersfield Corporation bus being driven in the opposite direction by Walter Whiteley of Marsh. Castle swerved but could not avoid a collision. The badly damaged chara ended up with its front end through a wall overhanging a 15 feet drop. The chara passengers were shaken and neither driver was hurt.

It was reported to Holmfirth UDC that by 1 April 1927 Castle had failed to observe the conditions endorsed on his charabanc licence and refused to give any undertaking that he would observe them in future. The council communicated with the inspector of police over the matter and eventually refused a licence for 1927/28. By 4 January 1929, however, he was operating 15 seater Chevrolet bus VH 2463 on a 20 minute frequency between Holmfirth and Holmbridge. From 23 January 1930 he was actually granted an "occasional" licence to operate a 20 minute frequency between Holmfirth railway station and Holmbridge on days when Huddersfield Corporation could not cope with the numbers of passengers - market days, Holmfirth Feast day, public holidays and for other special events.

After the change in the licensing system ushered in by the Road Traffic Act 1930, Castle's operations eventually became part of the new framework sanctioned by the new traffic commissioners. From 1 January 1933, when Wilson Haigh's and Huddersfield Joint Omnibus Committee's timetables were reorganised, Castle's Holmfirth-Holmbridge bus service, which he had continued to run, also had a new timetable. On Monday, Tuesday, Wednesday and Friday there was just one journey in each direction in the evening. On Thursday and Saturday there were six evening return trips. The faretable was as follows:

Holmbridge
1 Co-op Lane
1 1 Bottoms
2 1 1 Holmfirth

This infrequent bus service had an additional function for the Hinchliffe Mill based business. Castle's excursions adverts stated that passengers could "book in Holmfirth on our bus in Victoria Street at 9.30 any night". In addition to his coach excursions, Castle also had an occasional service from Holmfirth to Harden Moss for the sheepdog trials. On 21 July 1934 he ran from Victoria Square at 10.15am and every half hour, returning from Harden Moss 20 minutes later; Huddersfield JOC now competed on this route as successors to Wilson Haigh.

George Willie Castle had built up a small fleet of coaches and taxis as a complement to his garage business. One of his last enterprises was the establishment of a sales and service outlet at Upperbridge; despite being seriously ill at the time, he was enthusiastic about its completion. He died at his house "Woodleigh" on 26 October 1935, leaving a widow, Eleanor, five sons and four daughters.

From 4 April 1936 the firm was renamed "Eleanor Castle trading as GW Castle". On Friday/Saturday 18/19 June 1937 the Harden Moss sheepdog trials service was operated, GW Castle running every half hour from Holmfirth at a flat fare of 6d (on Friday between 6.00pm and 9.30pm; on Saturday between 10.15am and 9.00pm). The Holmfirth-Holmbridge bus service probably ceased in September 1939 on the outbreak of war. It was never restarted.

After the war and following the relaxation of the wartime fuel restrictions, during the August holiday week 11 to 16 August 1946 three excursions were operated daily. These were reported as being fully booked up in advance. Regular excursions were run in the season to football matches. The Harden Moss route probably ran for the last time on 21 June 1947. Thereafter Huddersfield JOC had that service to themselves as well. In 1947 a limited company was formed: G.W.Castle Ltd, of Holmfirth.

— CASTLE'S TOURS —

DAY TOURS FOR HOLIDAY WEEK, August 8th to 15th, 1936

SUNDAY	6-0 p.m.—Popular Evening Drive	Fare 2/6
MONDAY	7-30 a.m.—Bridlington	Fare 10/-
	8-0 a.m.—Blackpool	Fare 8/-
	1-30 p.m.—Belle Vue (including admission)	Fare 4/7
TUESDAY	8-0 a.m.—Liverpool, Mersey Tunnel, Chester	Fare 10/-
	8-0 a.m.—Southport	Fare 8/-
	1-30 p.m.—Golden Acre Park	Fare 4/-
WEDNESDAY	7-30 a.m.—Morecambe	Fare 10/-
	8-0 a.m.—Blackpool	Fare 8/-
	9-30 a.m.—Liverpool, for New Brighton	Fare 7/6
	1-30 p.m.—Belle Vue (including admission)	Fare 4/7
THURSDAY	7-30 a.m.—Scarboro'	Fare 10/-
	8-0 a.m.—Liverpool, Mersey Tunnel, Chester	Fare 10/-
	1-0 p.m.—Fountains Abbey and Ripon	Fare 7/6
	1-30 p.m.—Golden Acre Park	Fare 4/-

G. W. CASTLE, Castle Garage, Holmfirth

'Phone 76 and 338.

CASTLE'S TOURS
Easter, 1939

		Fare
SUNDAY, April 9th—		
	5-30 p.m.—EVENING RUN	2/6
MONDAY, April 10th—		
	8-0 a.m.—BLACKPOOL	8/-
	12 noon—WETHERBY (for Races)	4/6
	1-30 p.m.—BELLE VUE	4/6
TUESDAY, April 11th—		
	8-0 a.m.—SOUTHPORT	8/-
	1-0 p.m.—BUXTON AND MATLOCK	7/-
	1-30 p.m.—BELLE VUE	4/6

TAXIS AVAILABLE FOR PRIVATE PARTIES, DAY AND HALF-DAY TRIPS, 4 and 7 Seaters.

Book your Seats or Vehicle Early at Woodhead Rd. or Huddersfield Rd.
Phone 76.

3.2: THE UPPERTHONG BUS

GW Castle continued in coaching on a small scale and by the summer of 1952 had six Bedford, Commer or Leyland coaches in a cream and red livery, all bought new. It was then that the firm became involved in one of the attempts to provide a bus service to Upperthong.

The 280 residents of the village of Upperthong had originally started campaigning for a bus service from Holmfirth to their village as early as 1939. Huddersfield JOC's response had been that [because of impossibly narrow roads] the only practical route involved a long detour via the Ford Inn and could only be operated economically at a fare higher than the residents would be prepared to pay. Towards the end of 1949 the villagers had renewed their demands and Mr James Hugh Hobson of 3 Swallow Lane, Golcar, after first testing the route with a 32 seater bus, offered to provide a service for £2

The first bus from Upperthong was the school bus operated by James Hugh Hobson of Golcar. He ran to St John's School at Parkhead and Holmfirth Secondary School (then at Nabb) for a month's trial from 16 January 1950. Hobson owned only this one vehicle ("Hobson's choice" maybe?), 30 seater Harrington bodied Commer Commando coach HKD 952. New in April 1947 to Toppings of Liverpool, the Commer had passed to Pemberton of Upton near South Elmsall in November 1948 before being obtained by Hobson at the beginning of 1950. It stands outside the shop at the top of the village at the west end of Towngate on the first day. The service ceased after a month and Hobson and his Commer parted company in June 1951.
[Kirklees Image Archive Ke02614]

Leyland Tiger 14 (JWW 438) was bought new by Castle in May 1950. The unusual full front of the Plaxton body was useful at a time when standard half-cab front engined coaches would very soon start to look terribly dated with manufacturers turning out their new streamlined underfloor engined coaches. 14 is parked between Bedford SB 16 and a Midland Red coach. It was sold by Castle in April 1961.
[R. Marshall]

GW Castle coaches were often hired to other, often larger, operators who were short of vehicles on busy weekends. Bedford SB/ Duple 16 (LWR 668) is carrying a party leaving Wembley Stadium.
[R.H.G. Simpson]

per day, which the villagers could raise by any means at their disposal. Fares would not be paid on the bus. Eventually it was agreed that Hobson would run a service just for schoolchildren for a month's trial for 30/- a day. The Leeds petroleum authorities were very tardy in sending the necessary petrol coupons and these were only received one hour before the bus (Commer Commando coach HKD 952) was due to start at 8.30am on 16 January 1950. After the month's trial the service ceased and the children had to walk to school again from 13 February. Hobson wanted to run from the village beyond Holmfirth to Honley and Huddersfield as a means of attracting more passengers but his licence application was opposed by the JOC and finally refused in May 1950 on the grounds that as Hobson only had one bus he was not in a position to do the job properly.

In March 1950 Huddersfield JOC, after surveying five possible routes to the village, concluded that none was feasible so that again they would not be prepared to operate. Eventually GW Castle came to the rescue and made an application to the traffic commissioners for a licence between Holmfirth and Royal Oak Inn, Upperthong. The JOC opposed the application, fearing loss of revenue on their Parkhead service. Nevertheless a licence was granted on 2 January 1953 for a service via Greenfield Road, Ford Inn and Dean Road but with the restriction that local passengers were not to be carried between Holmfirth and Parkhead.

The route was three miles long and the timetable offered eight return trips on Monday to Saturday between 6.10am and 9.45pm, plus three on Sundays. The (single) fares were 3d to Black Syke, 4d to Ford Inn and 6d to Upperthong. The GW Castle secretary, Percy Beardsell, promised that the service would start as soon as the tickets had arrived from the printer. Horace Day, chairman of the campaign committee, said that the best celebration of this new era for the village would be a ride on the first bus. This turned out to be the 1.30pm from Holmfirth on Sunday 18 January 1953 and the vehicle provided was Leyland Tiger coach GWR 790, driven by Sam Wrather of Ribbleden Cottage and sporting a lucky horse shoe on its radiator. In the event so many people wanted a ride that a duplicate was required, with the conductor (Douglas Castle) changing buses en route. Unfortunately once the bus was no longer a novelty, the villagers did not support the service as well as expected.

The Upperthong bus even featured in the BBC Radio programme Woman's Hour on 26 January 1953, when villager Mrs Elizabeth Beardsell spoke about the benefits of the bus service. It was very unusual in those days for any local people to be "on the wireless". 54 years old, Mrs Beardsell had worked as a youthful tram conductress for Sheffield Corporation during the First World War.

Heavy snowstorms soon made the roads impassable and the service was suspended until a way had been cut through. It was not long before the operator warned the campaign committee that the service was not an economic proposition owing to lack of support and was in danger of being withdrawn. From the end of February the timetable was varied for a trial period of two months but with no greater success and the service ran for the last time on 7 May. Williamsons $2^{1}/_{4}$ inches punch tickets printed with stages A to H were used; colours and values were: 1d white, $1^{1}/_{2}$d blue, 2d grey, 3d green, 4d pink and 6d orange (there was no 5d fare).

Douglas Castle, who had conducted on the inaugural Upperthong run, was for some years in charge of the coach side of the GW Castle business. During the 1960s it became evident that car sales and related activities, under the control of his brother Clifford, were doing much better with increasing car ownership. Taxis and funeral hire were also more lucrative so it was decided to close down the coaching business. Latterly the coaches seem to have spent an unprofitably high proportion of their time parked in the garage. Larger bus and coach operator Hebble's Bradford depot manager of the day is on record as saying that if he was ever desperate to hire a coach at the last minute on a peak summer weekend, GW Castle could be relied upon to have one available.

The Castle family and John Steel, manager of Baddeleys, arranged an exchange of business. GW Castle would take over the taxi and funeral side of Baddeleys while Baddeleys would apply for excursion licences similar to those handed in by GW Castle.Therefore in April 1966 on Easter Tuesday the last GW Castle excursions ran, to Blackpool, Harrogate & Knaresborough and Manchester Airport. The five red and cream coaches passed to dealer Stanley Hughes of Gomersal, nowadays part of Arriva. Bedford 21 (HCX 491) was bought by Baddeleys while the Fords (19/20: 5709/10 WX) went on loan to them for the 1966 season. Bedford 18 (RWW 750) became the first full sized coach in the fleet of GB Hirst, an expanding local minibus operator who would eventually take over Baddeleys.

In November 1981, after the receivers had closed down the Baddeleys company, the former Baddeleys head office at Service Garage, Huddersfield Road, Holmfirth was demolished to make way for extended GW Castle car showrooms.

3.3: GW CASTLE FLEET LIST- Information for the period 1921-30 is very incomplete.

No.	Reg'n	Chassis	Body	New	In	Out
1		Ford	? -8-			
2	C 2332	Ford	? Ch12		6/21	
3?	VH 2463	Chevrolet	? -20-	-/29	-/29	?
4?	VH 6346	Bedford WLB	Duple B20	-/34	-/34	7/44
5?	ADK 238	Bedford WLB	Plaxton C21F	- /35	?	5/51
6?	BWX 115	Bedford WTB	Duple C25-	-/37	-/37	11/47
7	EWX 172	Bedford OWB	Duple UB32F	6/45	6/45	1/47
8	FWU 584	Bedford OB	Plaxton FC30F	3/47	3/47	7/63
9	GWR 790	Leyland PS1/1	Plaxton C32F	9/47	9/47	4/56
10?	GWW 624	Daimler CVD6	Yorks Yacht C33F	4/48	4/48	4/52
11	GWW 625	Daimler CVD6	Yorks Yacht C33F	4/48	4/48	5/51
12	EKU 810	Austin K4VT	Plaxton C29F	3/49	3/49	5/52
14	JWW 438	Leyland PS1/1	Plaxton FC33F	5/50	5/50	4/61
15	KWT 221	Leyland PS2	Harrington FC37F	5/51	5/51	1/61
16	LWR 668	Bedford SB	Duple C33F	4/52	4/52	4/66
17	LWR 863	Commer Avenger	Plaxton C33F	4/52	4/52	1/61
18	RWW 750	Bedford SBG	Yeates C41F	3/56	3/56	4/66
19	5709 WX	Ford 570E	Plaxton C41F	1/61	1/61	4/66
20	5710 WX	Ford 570E	Plaxton C41F	1/61	1/61	4/66
21	HCX 491	Bedford SBG	Plaxton C35F	1/54	6/63	4/66

4: BEARDSELLS

The brothers Luther and Harold Beardsell were the proprietors of Station Road Garage, Holmfirth from December 1923; Luther had earlier worked for the Holmfirth Motor Company Ltd who also ran a charabanc. From April 1925 the Beardsells' Crossley chara CX 3859 was licensed by Holmfirth UDC. On 20 August 1925 they ran an hourly service to Penistone Show for 2/6d return and on the holiday period Saturdays in August and September 1925 they conveyed train passengers and their luggage to and from Holmfirth railway station from the outlying districts for 1/-.

Beardsells applied to Holmfirth UDC for a licence for a circular route through Wooldale, Totties and Scholes to connect with trains at Holmfirth but this was rejected in November 1925; a similar licence was obtained by Baddeleys. The Beardsells were, however, granted a licence by Holmfirth for a route between Netherthong and Jackson Bridge via Holmfirth but it is unclear whether this service was ever operated.

From 1923 (or earlier) both Bower and Beardsells had operated Christmas Day services between Holmbridge and Huddersfield, a day when neither buses nor trams were run by the Corporation. As a result Luther Beardsell was summoned for plying for hire without a licence in Market Street, Huddersfield on Christmas Day 1926. He was well represented by his solicitor Mr JH Fletcher and the case was dismissed; he claimed to have applied to the Huddersfield chief constable for temporary licences which were never granted. It was suggested that in future the chief constable should obtain authority from Huddersfield Corporation to issue temporary licences to proprietors who were willing to provide a public service on any day when Corporation staff were given a holiday. Beardsells ran again on Christmas Day 1927 [and 1928] when their timetable was as follows:

Holmbridge	dep. 9.15am and every 90 minutes
until 10.45pm	
Holmfirth	dep. 9.30am and every 90 mins until
11.00pm	
Huddersfield	dep. 10.00am and every 90 mins
until 11.30pm	

The terminus in Huddersfield was at the top of High Street and fares were 1¹/₂d per stage.

A similar situation but in very different circumstances had arisen during the General Strike. In the absence of Corporation buses between 8 and 13 May 1926 Beardsells - and Baddeleys and Bower - were each allowed to run without fear of prosecution every 90 minutes between Huddersfield and Holmbridge.

By January 1927 HL 1741, a Gotfredson with B20F body new in 1923 to J Bullock & Sons Ltd of Featherstone as their no. 17, was licensed by Holmfirth UDC and the two vehicles were certainly licensed until mid 1929. Barnsley & District Traction had complained in June 1927 that Luther Beardsell was running without a licence over the Holmfirth end of their routes (Holmfirth-New Mill-Shepley-Huddersfield or Barnsley). In April 1928 Beardsell Bros. offered to operate the Baddeleys Holmfirth-Scholes circular route, a service they had been refused a licence for in 1925, if the existing operator was compelled to withdraw it because of maintenance problems but nothing came of this.

It is likely that the Beardsells were one of the many small bus operators who disappeared from the scene after the implementation of the Road Traffic Act's provisions in the early 1930s.

5: HORSE DRAWN OMNIBUSES FROM HOLMFIRTH AREA 1849

8.00am from Elephant and Castle to Dunford Bridge
11.00am from Duke of Leeds [New Mill] to Hazlehead
8.00am, 8.45am, 2.00pm and 3.30pm Hayleys omnibus from Elephant and Castle to Huddersfield
9.00am from the George to Huddersfield
4.30pm from Duke of Leeds [New Mill] to Huddersfield

6: OTHER CHARABANC OPERATIONS IN THE HOLME VALLEY

The first charabanc to be driven over the Holme Moss road – in 1914 - is reputed to have belonged to the Huddersfield General Carrying Company (J Haigh and J Mosley), whose main business was road haulage of wool. A 4-ton Commer, CX 978 was given a 32 seat chara body at weekends for excursions but it was requisitioned by the War Department for service in France during the First World War. Also owned was Straker-Squire charabanc CX 2176.

During the "roaring twenties" there was considerable competition between various small businesses which advertised their charabanc excursions in the Holmfirth Express, particularly during holiday weeks. Apart from the more substantial firms such as Baddeleys and Wilson Haigh, the following operators were active in the Holme Valley in the 1919-29 period before the need to comply with more stringent legislation discouraged many from continuing in this line of business. The names of their vehicles are shown where known.
Fred H Beaumont of Honley
Beaumont Bros of Meltham
Kilner and Brooke of Bridge Garage, Honley (two Karriers)
Herbert Booth of New Mill
Joe Middleton of Midlothian Garage, Holmfirth (30 shillings excursions in "Holme Valley")

In the spring of 1914 this 34 seater Commer charabanc was delivered to Kilner & Brooke of Bridge Garage, Honley. The firm ran excursions before and after the First World War. [Omnibus Society collection]

100

John A Littlewood of Newtown Garage, Honley (14 shillings excursions in "Velvet Coaster")
Heeley Bros of New Mill
Wooldale Cooperative Society ("The Pioneer")
Hirst Bros of Hepworth ("Pride of the Valley")

Fred H Beaumont Ltd, Far End Garage, Honley was operating chara excursions from Holmfirth, Honley Bridge and St George's Square, Huddersfield for Whitsuntide 1919. There was one trip per day and the Blackpool fare of 22/- included lunch at the Tower. Beaumont was already offering holiday tours:
16-20 June 1919, five day Scottish Mystery Tour for 8 guineas
21-25 July 1919, five day Welsh Tour for 8 guineas
18-22 August, five day West of England Tour
8-13 September, six day South of England Tour for 10 guineas

Among the many road accidents regularly reported by the Holmfirth Express during the 1920s was that of a Beaumont Bros (Meltham) charabanc (29 October 1927). Halfway down the hill from Dunford Bridge [Dunford Road, Underbank] at 11.30pm on the Saturday night a "luxury" 18 seat chara caught fire and was completely burnt out. The flames reached a great height and the heat was intense, closing the road for some time. The passengers were a private party of tennis players from Wilshaw tennis club; they had been the guests of the Dunford Bridge tennis club. Another bus had to be requisitioned to bring them home.

7: BADDELEYS REVISITED

Since the publication of Baddeleys of Holmfirth in 2002 some additional information has come to light and it is convenient to include it here.

Percy Baddeley was the older half-brother of Jesse and Leonard Baddeley. Their father Hiram Baddeley was born into a coal mining family in Smallthorne, north Staffordshire in 1867. By 1881 he was working as a driver in a pit at Sharlston, east of Wakefield and on 3 February 1890 he married Hannah Stafford at nearby Warmfield. Hiram Baddeley and his first wife had two sons, Percy (born in December 1895 at Flockton) and Herbert, and a daughter Elizabeth. Meanwhile, having obtained mining certificates (1st class in 1894), Hiram had become a colliery manager and by 1896 was working for the Jaggar (or Jagger) family, farmers who also owned mines in the Emley, Flockton and Grange Moor areas. As the first Mrs Hiram Baddeley did not enjoy good health, Florence Jaggar (born 1870), a daughter of one of the colliery owners, who is recorded in the 1891 census as a dressmaker, helped Mrs Baddeley with the housekeeping. After the early death of Hannah Baddeley in December 1896, Hiram married Florence at Emley in September 1897 and they also had three children: Jesse (born March 1899), Leonard (born June 1901) and Florence Adella (born 25 June 1903 at Emley Moor). Both Percy and Herbert initially followed in their father's footsteps by finding work in the local pits. It seems that Percy did not get on well with his stepmother and he went to live with an aunt.

Following the death of Hiram Baddeley in the colliery accident in 1908, his widow Florence would have had some money of her own from her family's colliery and farming interests and probably also an insurance or compensation payment. It was part of this money – and possibly also some finance from her brother - that she later used to set up her sons Jesse and Leonard in business as motor engineers and charabanc proprietors in 1919.

Florence's sons were partners whereas half-brother

Percy was only employed as a driver and when the limited company was formed in 1925 he did not become a director. Despite this unfairness the good natured Percy continued to drive for the firm, working very long hours. Percy married Annice and their son Joseph James Baddeley was also later associated with the family firm, as a driver; before he was old enough to drive, he used to fill the buses up with petrol. Percy's daughter Evelyn [Mrs Evelyn Harrison, who kindly supplied most of these details] remembers boarding a "yellow peril" double decker driven by her father and riding from Lockwood to Meltham and back.

During the early years of the business Jesse, who is thought to have been educated at Almondbury Grammar School, appears to have been the engineer and only occasionally took the wheel whereas Leonard drove regularly. Jesse was unlucky in love as his intended bride failed to turn up at the church on the wedding day. It is believed that this preyed so much on his mind that he took an overdose to end his life in November 1931.

After Leonard Baddeley's appointment of Guy Levison as manager in 1935, Both Percy and his son Joseph parted company with the family firm and went to work for Yorkshire Traction at their St Andrew's Road depot. Percy and his wife were also at one stage licensees of the Castle Hill public house.

It is thought that Leonard Baddeley might actually have died while on holiday on the French Riviera and that his body was brought home prior to the funeral.

In later years Percy Baddeley's side of the family became even more indignant about their exclusion from the family business which had been set up with Hiram Baddeley's compensation money. They saw Miss Florence Adella Baddeley giving away more and more money to the church, money which rightly should have been theirs. Miss Baddeley died on 20 December 1982 at "Glenthorpe", her Station Road (Honley) bungalow.

The Beaumont Bros. of Meltham business was also mentioned in Baddeleys of Holmfirth (it was eventually taken over by Baddeleys), where there is a reference to their 1/- football specials from Meltham (p.31). In fact this facility had earlier attracted the attention of Huddersfield JOC, whose traffic superintendent WT Richards had opposed the Beaumonts' application on 3 November 1933 for renewal of their licences to take football supporters from Meltham to the Fartown and Leeds Road grounds. The Beaumonts admitted charging only 1/- return from Meltham when the combined bus and tram fare was 1/2d. They subsequently agreed to charge 1/6d

and pick up only at their garage, which seems to have satisfied the JOC.

The following story reminds us that irregularities did not disappear with the old licensing regime in 1930. On 8 October 1934 Leonard Baddeley himself drove a one man 20 seater vehicle on the Huddersfield-Deepcar route and, unluckily for him, a traffic examiner from Leeds, Reginald Blythman, was a passenger. As will be remembered, a condition of the licence was that the same passenger could not both be picked up and set down between Huddersfield and Jackson Bridge. A passenger boarded at Honley and did not wait to get a ticket before sitting down; he said that he had placed his 1d fare on the seat next to the driver (later denied by Leonard Baddeley in court). Baddeley claimed that he had intended to collect the fare when he stopped at New Mill - but the passenger alighted at Brockholes. The law had been broken and Baddeley was fined £1.

In Baddeleys of Holmfirth there is a reference (p.32) to an accident which resulted in a bus being rebuilt as a breakdown tender. The accident occured on 22 September 1938 when Irvin Pogson of Cowlersley Lane, Huddersfield was taking his PSV test. Also on Leyland Lion bus CK 3733, besides the examiner, were a Baddeleys mechanic and another driver who was to take his test following Pogson. After Pogson had been instructed to stop on the steep part of Dog Kennel Bank, the brakes failed and the bus ran backwards out of control. The 'passengers' jumped clear before the bus ran through a wall, scraped between two trees and finished up wedged against a third. Pogson suffered cuts from the broken glass and was treated at a nearby house. The Ministry of Transport examiner was Harold Thomas. When the bus regained the road, tests showed that both footbrake and handbrake were working normally. Consequently the driver was summonsed for driving without due care and attention; he denied the charges but the outcome is not known.

8: HOLME VALLEY PARISH COUNCIL, MINIBUS PIONEER 1980-88

8.1: A RURAL BUS PROBLEM AND A LOCAL SOLUTION

Around the time of local bus deregulation in 1986 minibus routes, often using roads which larger buses had been unable to serve, became fashionable in many parts of Britain. Yet Holme Valley Parish Council, in partnership with SKJ Motors, had been offering such a network

of minibus services in the Holmfirth area since 1980.

In the 1920s Huddersfield Corporation's determination to operate buses only along the relatively flat main road through the valley as far as Holmbridge had been the impetus for Wilson Haigh to serve the higher villages. Similarly fifty years later their successors West Yorkshire Passenger Transport Executive (trading as "Metro") were using large buses on a route network developed in the 1920s and 1930s by Huddersfield and Wilson Haigh while residents of more inaccessible hamlets pressed for bus services closer to their homes. Interestingly the Huddersfield municipal undertaking had considered the possibility of using 12 seater minibuses to operate feeder services into Holmfirth among other places in 1968, when the legislation eventually used by the parish council was newly on the statute book, but the idea had been rejected.

Holme Valley Parish Council was established as a result of the 1974 local government reorganisation. The council's response in connection with a February 1976 West Yorkshire Transportation Study meeting was prophetic: "existing bus services … should be maintained … and supplemented by a midi or mini-bus service operating within the parish in conjunction with existing services and serving particularly those parts not at present served by public transport".

West Yorkshire PTE had been asked to run a bus service to Cinderhills, a district at the top of a very steep hill out of Holmfirth. In September 1976 at a public meeting in the town the PTE informed Cinderhills residents that they would be prepared to operate a 20 seater bus between Holmfirth and Cinderhills. [This service would presumably have been run by their recently acquired subsidiary, Baddeleys; their garage was conveniently located a short distance from Holmfirth Bus Station.] Unfortunately only two return journeys in the mornings plus two in the afternoons were proposed, with no trips convenient for people travelling to and from work. Also the PTE were not prepared to subsidise the route. Brian Eastwood, the PTE's Kirklees District manager, was to estimate the costs of operation; the onus would then be on residents to put pressure on their parish council or district council or the county council to find the cash to subsidise the route. Once financial backing had been established, it was hoped that after a month's trial the service could be extended to similar areas such as Upperthong (unsuccessfully and briefly served by GW Castle in 1953) and parts of Wooldale (where Baddeleys had run until 1939).

A different solution was proposed in December 1977 when Yorkshire Traction expressed interest in providing "community minibuses" for the Denby Dale and Holmfirth areas; Cinderhills was one of the districts identified as requiring public transport. The Barnsley based company, whose predecessor had started running into Holmfirth in 1924, would have supplied a vehicle and trained local volunteers to drive it without payment. Such community minibus schemes were being provided in this period by fellow National Bus Company subsidiary Eastern Counties in sparsely populated parts of Norfolk but the Holme Valley needed more frequent services which could not have relied on a rota of volunteer drivers, so attention was again focussed on the PTE's proposals for more conventional bus services.

Progress was very slow. Local MP Richard Wainwright (Liberal, Colne Valley) had said that the Cinderhills people had already been too patient and that many similar isolated villages in Calderdale had enjoyed a reasonable bus service for years. He could have added that many existing bus routes in West Yorkshire ran at a loss yet the communities they served were not being asked by the PTE to justify their subsidies.

But even in Calderdale the existing bus network did not satisfy all needs. From 2 October 1978 Hebden Royd Town Council sponsored three new experimental minibus routes in Hebden Bridge to areas unserved by full size buses, mainly housing estates, using vehicles from Gledhill Bros. of Todmorden. One of the routes ran to the nearby Dodd Naze estate, built in a windswept location at the top of a steep hill; there was a close parallel with Cinderhills at Holmfirth.

By March 1979 the PTE had made no discernible progress with the projected Cinderhills route. At this stage Joyce Wainwright, political assistant and wife of the MP, arranged for a speaker from Hebden Bridge to give a presentation on their minibus scheme one Friday night in Meltham. Fortunately Tony Garrood, Liberal parish councillor since January 1978 for [Holmfirth] North Central ward, which included Cinderhills, braved the sleet to turn out for the talk and was very impressed by what he heard.

In March 1980 Tony Garrood placed proposals before Holme Valley Parish Council for the introduction of a similar minibus network, funded and planned by the parish council, radiating from Holmfirth. The following month, after receiving reassurances from their counterparts in Hebden Bridge, the council accepted his proposals and agreed to support an experimental service for

12 seater Ford Transit BCP 124V, bought new by SKJ in March 1980, was used to inaugurate the Holme Valley Parish Council minibus services in November 1980. Waiting in Holmfirth Bus Station after the deregulation of local bus services, it displays the SKJ blue, gold and yellow livery to good effect. [A.D. Hanson]

three months at a cost not exceeding £2500. The route network was to be much more extensive than Hebden Bridge's, serving outlying and isolated villages and hamlets as well as housing estates. The forthcoming scheme was described by Richard Wainwright as "an excellent example of the sort of self-help project that is championed by the Liberals". Tony Garrood was to remain very much the champion of the minibus services as they were expanded and consolidated.

The parish council then obtained a permit to operate local bus services from the traffic commissioners under Section 30 of the 1968 Transport Act (and Section 8 of the 1980 Traffic Act), which enabled a minibus carrying no more than 12 people to operate a service without recourse to full licensing by the traffic commissioners. Tenders were invited from local private firms to provide a minibus and driver to run the service on the basis of an hourly rate (to include all costs of operation). Four operators tendered to run the services and, after an inspection of some of the vehicles by councillors, the quotation of £5.30 per hour from SKJ Motors (Shelley) Ltd of Kirkburton was accepted; there were initially 36 hours of operation per week. The council's financial support for the services was based on Section 137 of the 1972 Local Government Act; the minibuses were beneficial to the community.

SKJ was a relatively new company, established in 1973 by three printing workers, Stuart Clarkson, Keith Bedford and John Buxton, whose initials gave the business its name. Unfortunately Mr Clarkson had died soon afterwards but a minibus was then acquired, followed by a taxi; their interest in minibus operation had apparently been stimulated by a television programme about a Scottish postbus. After the purchase of the Springfield filling station in Penistone Road, Kirkburton, SKJ began to employ full time mechanics and built up a fleet of coaches, garaged at Springfield. Day trips in summer and British and continental tours were offered; the first continental trip (to Amsterdam) had taken place in 1979. SKJ soon established a network of agents to sell their excursions and tours in the Skelmanthorpe, Denby Dale, Holmfirth and Meltham districts. John Buxton was the company secretary and Keith Bedford was general manager, while other directors were chairman Kenneth Asquith, who also ran the firm's Shelley grocery business, and Dora Hardcastle. The Holme Valley Parish Council contract was to provide valuable all year work. By 1983 SKJ had about 20 employees and 12 coaches (DAFs, Leylands and a new Plaxton bodied Ward Dalesman with chassis built in nearby Shepley by Ward Motors), in addition to the minibuses. The dark blue livery (with gold fleetname) was later relieved by gold bands or blocks.

Meanwhile there was some discussion between the council and the PTE in relation to preparation of schedules. They were also asked to supply timetable cases and bus stop signs free of charge; the parish council would pay the PTE to erect them. Prominently sited bus stop signs were regarded as an important element of publicity and originally bore the HVPC logo. The actual timetable leaflets were produced and issued by the parish council (Don MacRae, a councillor who was an architect, drew the maps) and made available in outlets such as shops and community centres. An Almex ticket machine (then standard in their Huddersfield depots) was to have been purchased from the PTE at a cost of £70 but this does not seem to have taken place. Instead tickets which were torn off a pad were used initially; these were adequate in view of the simple fare structure. Tony Garrood himself had devised the routes, checking their suitability by car accompanied by his two young children and noting suitable stopping places and timings.

8.2: THE MAIN HOLMFIRTH NETWORK

The trial started on Monday 17 November 1980 after an official launch on the previous Saturday afternoon. A brass band had given the minibus a rousing send off from the bus station after Richard Wainwright had cut a yellow ribbon in the presence of a film crew from Look North.

There were three routes:
1: Holmfirth Bus Station to Hepworth School via Cinderhills Road, Scholes, Chapel Gate and Dean Bridge
2: Holmfirth Bus Station to Wooldale via Town End Road, then in an anti-clockwise circle via Wooldale Road, Totties, Greenhill Bank Road, Kirkroyds Estate (Royds Avenue) and Lower Town End Road
3: Holmfirth Bus Station to Upperthong (circular) via Hill, Binns Lane, Five Lane Ends, Upperthong Lane, Town Gate, Broad Lane, Ashgrove Road and Greenfield Road.

Just one vehicle was needed to run all three routes in turn in the order suggested by the route numbers. There were two round trips on each service on Monday, Tuesday and Wednesday (mornings only) and four on each on Thursday, Friday and Saturday (mornings and afternoons); there was no Sunday service. The dark blue SKJ 12 seater Ford Transit minibus BCP 124V bought new in March carried a board inscribed "HOLME VALLEY P.C. COMMUNITY BUS SERVICE" attached to its radiator and general manager Keith Bedford drove regularly.

[This was not of course a community minibus service in the legal sense of one run by unpaid volunteers.] The simple farescale was 20p for up to three stops or 30p for longer journeys (half fare for children and pensioners). The council were prepared to operate at a loss, especially at the outset, but hoped to be able to recover at least 50 per cent of costs from revenue.

On the Upperthong route no passengers were picked up in Greenfield Road. Officially this restriction was implemented "in interests of safety" but it was also necessary to avoid abstracting more passengers (in addition to Upperthong residents) from the PTE's Parkhead bus route.

The routes were soon reported to be popular with children, the elderly, part time workers and shoppers; Thursday (Holmfirth market day) was especially busy and 4089 passengers were carried in the first eight weeks. There was actually some concern about the loads being carried up some of the horrendously steep sections, especially South Lane up to Cinderhills and Cooper Lane on the outward loop of the Upperthong route. [Many Holmfirth people still remembered the tragic accident of 1947 when a coach belonging to Rowe of Cudworth, Barnsley (AEC Regal HL 5033) had careered out of control down Dunford Road, killing nine members of a male voice choir and injuring most of the rest.] The network had been advertised to operate until 14 February 1981 to assess demand but, as it was judged to be a success, the initial timetable was continued beyond this date until the council had finalised plans for a revised service.

In the light of operational experience and requests for bus services from further communities, an improved network was introduced from 20 April 1981, still mornings only from Monday to Wednesday and mornings/afternoons on Thursday to Saturday. Running times on all routes were speeded up to allow a new service to Thongsbridge and Woodlands to be operated, still using the one bus. Some extra journeys were added on 1 (Hepworth) and 2 (Wooldale) while 3 (Upperthong circular) was renumbered 4. The new 3 - route numbers again reflected the order in which the minibus served each route - ran between Holmfirth and Woodlands Estate via existing route 2 as far as Wooldale Road then covering new territory via Little Lane, Robert Lane, Sycamore, Springwood Road and Woodlands Avenue. The new timetable was again advertised as a three months trial operation but the minibuses were in fact already established as a permanent element in the Holme Valley's public transport system. On the first anniversary of the network,

payments to the operator were increased by 65p per hour to £5.95 per hour from 17 November 1981. Although it was planned to increase fares to raise 50% of the difference, in the event this was found to be unnecessary.

From 1 March 1982 routes 4 (Upperthong) and 3 (Woodlands) exchanged route numbers because the Upperthong journeys were now run between the 2 (Wooldale circular) and Woodlands trips to give a more evenly spaced timetable for the common section of those routes between Holmfirth and the central part of Wooldale. The new 4 was also extended beyond Woodlands via Luke Lane to Brockholes, which was initially served in an anticlockwise loop via Oakes Avenue, Oakes Lane and New Mill Road. To give protection to existing PTE bus routes, there were no stops in New Mill Road. The provisions of the legislation under which the services operated had by now been relaxed to allow the use of 16 seater minibuses and from this month larger Ford Transit HNB 847N was sometimes used to relieve overcrowding, particularly on Thursdays (market day) and Fridays. The council was also about to introduce additional minibus networks, described below, on those days for which the 12 seater would be needed. From 9 August 1982 the Brockholes loop working was abandoned when outward buses started to run via New Mill Road, Oakes Lane and Oakes Avenue; they turned round at the top of Oakes Avenue and returned to Holmfirth by the outward route reversed. This change, typical of the way the network

HOLME VALLEY PARISH COUNCIL
MINI-BUS ROUTES
NOVEMBER 1983

--------- CINDERHILLS-SCHOLES-HEPWORTH
———— WOOLDALE-KIRKROYDS CIRCULAR
-·-·-·- UPPERTHONG CIRCULAR
– – – WOODLANDS-BROCKHOLES-THURSTONLAND

Visiting the Holme Valley? Why not ride round on our Minibus Service?

If you are visiting the Holme Valley you have probably been attracted by the superb scenery as seen on 'The Last of the Summer Wine'. Why not take a ride out of the centre of Holmfirth on our **Parish Council Minibus Service.**

This service was organised by the Holme Valley Parish Council in an effort to meet the needs of residents in areas which are are not fully served by the West Yorkshire P.T.E. The dark blue minibus of S.K.J. Motors climbs the hills and penetrates the most scenic parts of the valley where no double deckers go and which many tourists do not find.

The service runs on MONDAY, TUESDAY and WEDNESDAY MORNINGS ONLY and ALL DAY on THURSDAYS, FRIDAYS and SATURDAYS. We regret there is NO SUNDAY SERVICE. For a scenic route we would particularly recommend Route 1 to Hepworth leaving at 8.30, 10.30, 12.15, 1.30, 3.30, and 5.30 or a quick trip on the UPPERTHONG CIRCULAR leaving at 9.30, 11.30, 12.30, 2.30, 4.30 and 5.15.

ALL BUSES leave from the bus station by the G.P.O.

FARES ARE 40p for a complete OUT and BACK TRIP (half for OAP's and children.)

was fine tuned to users' needs, allowed pensioners living in Oakes Avenue to travel both to and from the centre of Brockholes. From the same date extra journeys ran on the 3 to Upperthong.

The only other route alteration on the main Holmfirth minibus network before deregulation took place from 28 November 1983 when route 4 (Brockholes) was extended from Oakes Avenue via Thurstonland Bank Road to Thurstonland.

Holmfirth routes 1 to 4 continued to be the backbone of Holme Valley Parish Council's public transport operation in terms of mileage and patronage but the council also introduced a further two groups of routes for communities unserved by the main bus network and it is to these that we will now turn. The fares already mentioned were also charged on all these services.

8.3: MARKET DAY ROUTES

One of the newer networks was a group of four market day routes run by another SKJ minibus which visited some very remote settlements. After a six months trial at an estimated cost of £500 (assuming a 50% return from takings) had been recommended in November 1981,

these were introduced on 11 March 1982 and ran on Thursdays only as follows (four round trips on each):

A: Holmfirth Bus Station to Austonley via Greenfield Road and Burnlee Road, then in an anti-clockwise circle via Liphill Bank Road, Booth House, Mellor Lane, Flush House, Yew Tree and Shaw Lane
B: Holmfirth Bus Station to Cliffe (circular) via Cinderhills, Stake Bank Lane, Cliffe Road, Hey Cliffe Estate, Cliffe Road and Town End Road
C: Holmfirth Bus Station to Cartworth (circular) via Rotcher, Cartworth Road, a double run via Cartworth Bank Road to Wellhouse (Rising Sun), then Choppards Lane, Choppards Bank Road, Cross, Upper Bank End Road and Cinderhills
D: Holmfirth Bus Station to Sude Hill (Bellgreave Avenue) via Town End Road, Wooldale, Springwood Road, Stoney Bank Lane, New Mill, Sude Hill and Fulstone Hall Lane

Routes A and C ran through particularly scenic districts. While the A served bleak areas on the edge of uncultivated moorland, the C featured sweeping green hills, woods and some particularly picturesque hamlets along the narrow lanes lined with drystone walls which the minibuses almost scraped. A few people in Cartworth using the new minibus route had not been down to Holmfirth for five years or more.

Market day route receipts were at first disappointing

but they did improve. To increase its patronage, from 12 August 1982 route D was altered to run more directly between Wooldale and New Mill via Kirkroyds Estate (Royds Avenue), usefully supplementing route 2 on its busiest day; minimal use had been made of the service in the Stoney Bank area. This rerouting also provided enough spare time to extend D beyond Sude Hill to the small village of Fulstone in an anticlockwise loop, out via Horn Lane, Snowgate Head and Ebson House Lane and back via Fulstone Hall Lane. A change was also made to route C from 4 June 1984 when it was rerouted via Cote Lane, Hade Edge and Longley instead of direct via Choppards Bank Road, to serve scattered housing between Choppards and Hade Edge. Passengers were not picked up at Hade Edge, to protect the PTE.

8.4: MELTHAM AND HONLEY LINKS

After the success of the Holmfirth based routes, councillors were under pressure to introduce services elsewhere in the valley; hence this last group of routes was centred on Honley. Their story is complex as they attracted fewer passengers and the council had to make more changes in response to often conflicting demands.

In December 1981 Meltham Town Council were persuaded by one of their councillors, David Haigh, a bus enthusiast and preservationist later involved with

Fares will be the same as before. 20p for up to 3 stops. 30p for 4 or more stops.
Children (Age 5-16 incl.) and pensioners – half fares.

— — — —	AUSTONLEY CIRCULAR
– – – – –	CLIFFE CIRCULAR
· · · · · · ·	CARTWORTH CIRCULAR
– · – · – ·	SUDE HILL – FULSTONE

Are you visiting the Holme Valley on a Thursday? Why not ride round on our Market Day Minibus Service

If you are visiting the Holme Valley you have probably been attracted by the superb scenery as seen on 'The Last of the Summer Wine'. Why not take a ride out of the centre of Holmfirth on our **Parish Council Minibus Service**.

This service was organised by the Holme Valley Parish Council in an effort to meet the needs of residents in areas which are not fully served by the West Yorkshire P.T.E. The dark blue minibus of S.K.J. Motors climbs the hills and penetrates the most scenic parts of the valley where no double deckers go and which many tourists do not find.

The market day service runs ONLY on THURSDAYS. As it runs to the very outer most areas of the Holme Valley the scenery on all four routes is very impressive, as these areas are probably even more remote than those served by the everyday minibus. The minibus on the AUSTONLEY CIRCULAR leaves at 8.55, 10.55, 1.55 and 3.55 (journey time 35 mins.); the CLIFFE CIRCULAR at 9.30, 11.30, 2.30 and 4.30 (20 mins.). The CARTWORTH CIRCULAR leaves at 9.50, 11.50, 2.50 and 4.50 (25 mins.), and the FULSTONE CIRCULAR at 10.15, 12.15 and 3.15 (30 mins.).

ALL BUSES leaves from the bus station by the G.P.O.

FARES are 40p for a complete OUT and BACK TRIP (half for OAP's and children.)

the Town Bus business, to contribute 45% of the costs of an experimental (six months trial) Friday only route between Thurstonland and Meltham. Minibuses were to run via Oakes Avenue, Brockholes, Hall Ing, Honley, Wood Nook, Knowle Lane and Thick Hollins Estate; two short circular routes in Meltham were also to be operated by the same bus. Holme Valley Parish Council would bear the rest of the financial support and Tony Garrood had suggested to David Haigh that a through service between Meltham, Honley and beyond could attract more passengers than a Honley local route. After objections from a private individual to the traffic commissioners had been assuaged, this jointly sponsored SKJ route started on 2 April 1982 with four round trips between Thurstonland and Meltham on Fridays which were also meant to connect with trains at Brockholes Station. The two Meltham local services were the Mill Moor circular (serving Wessenden Head Road, Leygards Lane, Mill Moor Road, Matthew Grove, Bracewell Road and Colders Lane) and the Sunny Heys circular (serving Golcar Brow Road, Red Lane, Highfields, Sunny Heys, Broadlands and Mean Lane).

Unfortunately in August residents were being warned that usage of the minibus had been disappointingly low; the message was "use it or lose it". Unacceptably high losses - it was needing an 83% subsidy – were in part attributed to poor publicity but it was hoped that suggestions from the public might enable the councils to introduce improvements which would attract more passengers, as had happened in Holmfirth.

As a result of a review which concluded that it was "completely unviable" in its existing form, the route was continued for a further month (October 1982) on a revised basis. The number of journeys was reduced to two, in the morning only, but the route was extended from Thurstonland to Holmfirth via Brockholes and Thongsbridge. Passenger numbers did improve towards the end of October. Meltham council then decided to continue their financial support provided Holme Valley also maintained theirs. To the embarrassment of Tony Garrood, who had persuaded Meltham to get involved in the first place, Holme Valley voted by a narrow margin (on the casting vote of the chairman) against continuing the service but then SKJ announced that they would run without subsidy until the licence expired, since loadings appeared to be improving. The operation had been costing £25 per week, shared between the two councils. Conservative parish councillor James McKenna, one of the Holme Valley councillors who wanted the route withdrawn, pointed out that the minibuses were taking up one third of the council's expenditure. While conceding that most of the other minibus routes fulfilled a "substantial social need", he described the Thurstonland-Meltham route as a "good initiative taken too far".

It soon transpired that the parish council had paid for an extension of the licence for this route at a time when, according to some councillors, they had already irrevocably decided to withdraw financial support. Although SKJ had agreed to run without subsidy from November, so far they had been running (as a mere contractor) on the council's licence, which only the council could renew. From November SKJ continued running on the council's licence, even though the Meltham-Honley-Thurstonland-Holmfirth route now had no connection with the council and SKJ were operating it in their own

SKJ's Reeve Burgess Reebur bodied Bedford 17 seater OGV 250W entered the fleet in March 1984 and was allotted fleet number 6. Like BCP 124V it lasted until the closing down of SKJ's operations in January 1988 and is also seen in Holmfirth Bus Station towards the end. [A.D. Hanson]

right. The service seems, however, to have been finally withdrawn at the end of January 1983, while Meltham council were still considering how it might be continued.

Holme Valley Parish Council's minibus services were not seen again in Honley until 5 December 1983 when what was to become a more successful Honley Minibus Service network was launched; this also served one of the areas earlier covered by the ill fated Thurstonland-Meltham route. A three month trial at an estimated cost of £3120 (assuming a 50% recovery of costs) had been recommended in June. The new routes ran on Monday to Friday mornings only, using a 17 seater SKJ minibus - a second 17 seater, 1977 Bedford CF YVH 220R, had been acquired by SKJ in March 1983. At first the services

were advertised as running for the three month trial period but they became a permanent fixture. There were two routes between Holmfirth and Honley:
Holmfirth Bus Station-A6024-Miry Lane (Longlands)-Woodlands-Oakes Avenue-Oakes Lane-Brockholes Centre-Brockholes Station-Hall Ing-Honley Centre
Holmfirth Bus Station-Netherfield Estate (Leas Avenue)-Netherthong-St Mary's Estate-Oldfield-Cross Lane-Bradshaw Avenue-Croft Drive-Grasscroft Road-Scotgate Road-Honley Centre
plus two short circular routes in Honley:
Roundway Circular via Roundway and Stoney Lane
Magdale Circular via Thirstin Road, White Gate, Magdale, White Gate and Church Street

The Honley-Holmfirth sections were covered twice each way while the Honley circulars each enjoyed four round trips. On the Roundway route there were many elderly people living in flats while estate roads in the Grasscroft area were too narrow for conventional buses. The short Magdale "figure of eight" route combined minute lanes, awkward bends and

difficult cambers and gradients. Route numbers between 1 and 6 were shown in publicity for the Honley services but were not applied consistently and are omitted from this account to avoid confusion.

From 1 August 1984 the Holmfirth-Netherthong-Honley route was diverted via Deanhouse instead of St Mary's Estate. The circuit of the estate had been little used but there had been requests from elderly residents in the Deanhouse area who wanted to use the minibus to do their shopping in Holmfirth or Honley. The Holmfirth-Brockholes-Honley route was altered in Brockholes to run via A616, the village centre, double run to Oakes Avenue, then Brockholes Lane. There was also a proposal for both Honley routes to be rerouted to leave Holmfirth via Station Road and Bridge Lane to avoid traffic congestion in Victoria Street but this did not take place.

New ground was covered from 15 April 1985. The Roundway and Magdale services were reduced, which allowed an additional route of two round trips Monday to Friday mornings to Netherton Moor to be slotted in. This meant that the minibuses were for the first time penetrating one of Huddersfield's southern suburbs. The Netherton Moor buses followed the existing Magdale route to White Gate then ran via Netherton Moor Road before describing a very large clockwise terminal loop through acres of new housing via Coppice Drive, Moor Lane, Hawkroyd Bank Lane and Falconers Ride. At this stage the three groups of parish council minibus routes were together carrying about 5000 passengers per month.

From 3 March 1986 the separate Roundway service was withdrawn and replaced by diverting the Honley-Netherthong-Holmfirth route via Roundway and Stoney Lane; the Scotgate, Grasscroft and Westcroft areas, which had produced very few passengers indeed, were no longer served. The remaining Magdale journeys were also withdrawn but the Netherton Moor service, which covered most of the Magdale route, was doubled to four journeys and Magdale passengers now had to walk to and from Sandbeds junction. Presumably some residents of Netherton Moor had been tempted to ride by bus to Honley (or through to Holmfirth?) and were finding it convenient to do their shopping there. The Honley-Brockholes-Holmfirth service reverted to its earlier route in Brockholes direct between Brockholes Lane and Luke Lane via Oakes Lane and Oakes Avenue. Finally the Holmfirth-Honley and Honley-Netherton Moor routes were improved to run until mid afternoon but still only on Monday to Friday.

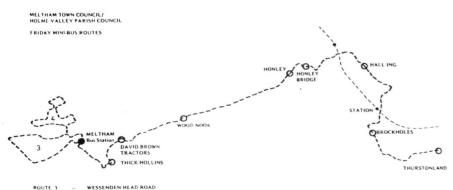

MELTHAM TOWN COUNCIL/
HOLME VALLEY PARISH COUNCIL

FRIDAY MINI-BUS ROUTES

HONLEY • HONLEY BRIDGE • HALL ING • STATION • BROCKHOLES • WOOD NOOK • MELTHAM Bus Station • DAVID BROWN TRACTORS • THICK HOLLINS • THURSTONLAND

ROUTE 3 — WESSENDEN HEAD ROAD
LEYGARDS LANE
MILL MOOR ROAD
COLDERS LANE

ROUTE 4 — GOLCAR BROW ROAD
RED LANE
HIGH FIELDS
SUNNY HEYS

Holme Valley Parish Council

HONLEY MINIBUS SERVICE

NEW TIMETABLE   3rd MARCH 1986

The new timetable has been organised by Holme Valley Parish Council in an effort to meet the needs of local residents in areas not fully served by West Yorkshire P.T.E. The Dark Blue and Gold Minibuses of SKJ Motors will serve the following routes from 3rd March 1986

1   Holmfirth/longlands/Woodlands/Brockholes/Hall Ing **Honley Bridge/Honley** Centre
2   Honley/Magdale/Netherton/Magdale/Honley
3   Honley/Roundway/Oldfield/Deanhouse/Netherfields Holmfirth
4   Holmfirth/Netherfields/Deanhouse/Oldfield/Roundway Honley Centre
5   Honley/Honley Bridge/Hall Ing/Brockholes/Woodlands Holmfirth

The service will run every day (Monday to Friday) between 9.15am and 3.15pm. This will be for a trial period to assess demand, so encourage your friends and neighbours to use it as much as possible

USE IT OR LOSE IT

Comments on the service are welcome and should be made to any Parish Councillor or sent to **The Clerk to the Parish Council,** Council Office, HOLMFIRTH Telephone Holmfirth 684992 or 686882 OR Huddersfield 605111

Fares will be: Adult   **25p up to 3 stops**
                                       35p 4 or more stops
                    Child (5/16incl) **15p up to 3 stops**
                    O.A.P.   **20p 4 or more stops**

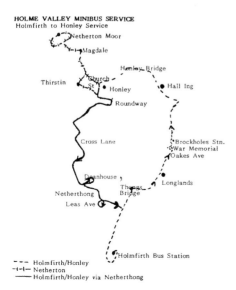

HOLME VALLEY MINIBUS SERVICE
Holmfirth to Honley Service

- - - Holmfirth/Honley
–·–·– Netherton
——— Holmfirth/Honley via Netherthong

8.5: GENERAL DEVELOPMENTS UP TO DEREGULATION

Meanwhile in the spring of 1982 with the minibus services costing about £5000 per annum, the council had considered and rejected the possibility of a post bus operation in the Holme Valley. This option had been looked into before the Section 30 operation with SKJ had been established and the conclusion was unchanged: that it would provide only a minimal service more suited to a much more remote rural area (and would therefore offer no material improvement on the services already operated).

A committee of inquiry was set up in November 1982 to examine the circumstances in which the licence extension had been paid for which allowed SKJ to continue the Meltham-Thurstonland route after the council had withdrawn financial support. As a result general discussion of operational problems led to the establishment in 1983 of a parish council Minibus Sub-committee. This sub-committee was to liaise with SKJ and report regularly to the council on the financial position and operation of the services.

In June 1984 there was a fares increase on all routes to 25p (up to three stops) or 35p (four or more stops) with the usual reductions for children and pensioners, still very reasonable prices. A 40p "complete out and back" ticket for tourists was also advertised. The farescale revision resulted from a 12% increase in the hourly rate paid to SKJ from 1 April. The council were keen to offset costs by introducing advertising on the backs of tickets and on and inside the buses but nothing came of this.

SKJ was supposed to send waybills to the council every month but there were complaints in July 1984 that this was not happening. There were also complaints from time to time that waybills were not being completed properly. This was important because SKJ kept all the fares income and the council paid them the difference between that and the hourly rate. Fuel tax rebate was passed on by SKJ to the council; in 1984 this was worth

about £300 per quarter.

In December 1984 complaints were made by the council about unsatisfactory arrangements for cash handling by drivers. When taking fares, drivers put the cash in their jacket pockets as they were not supplied with cash bags. This was remedied when drivers were given a box or plastic container in which to keep the cash but the council would still have preferred a bag system. Councillors also wanted the painted destination boards displayed in the bus windows replaced by more conventional roller blinds but SKJ never used these; route numbers or letters were not shown on the buses either.

A tachograph was installed on the bus working the Honley routes on 7 December 1984 to monitor late running. In January 1985 it was reported that tachographs had been installed on all the vehicles.

Holme Valley Parish Council had developed a substantial route network in areas not served by the PTE. From 1983 three SKJ minibuses were needed on Thursdays, two on Monday, Tuesday, Wednesday and Friday, and just one on Saturdays. By the beginning of 1985 SKJ had only three minibuses licensed as psvs (public service vehicles): the 12 seater Ford Transit BCP 124V, the 17 seater Bedford CF YVH 220R and another 17 seater Bedford, OGV 250W with Reeve Burgess Reebur body acquired secondhand in March 1984. If one was unavailable on a Thursday a minibus without a psv licence was used and passengers travelled free of charge.

By now Holmfirth was being overwhelmed by visitors, as people who had seen Last of the Summer Wine on television turned up in their cars or in coach parties. Whereas the minibuses had been introduced to bring residents of outlying villages into town, in 1985 the council advertised the routes to tourists as a means of "getting out of the centre of Holmfirth and into the wonderful countryside that made the BBC choose this valley to film". The parish council minibus was said to reach "other parts of the valley other large coaches cannot reach". Like many of their kind, however, the minibuses were not ideal for sightseeing and their small capac-

S.K.J.
MOTORS LTD.
Holme Valley P.C.
Single Fare
35p

06624

Issued subject to the companies
terms and conditions

SKJ MOTORS LTD
Holme Valley Parish Council
BUS TICKET
SINGLE JOURNEY
30

Issued subject to the companies
terms and conditions

SKJ MOTORS LTD
Holme Valley Parish Council
BUS TICKET
SINGLE JOURNEY
35

Issued subject to the companies
terms and conditions

ity meant that they were able to make only a limited contribution to shifting the hordes from the pavements of Holmfirth. There was also the possibility of crowding the locals off - in publicity tourists were asked to give them priority. Requests to SKJ to apply "Holme Valley Parish Council Summer Wine Bus Service" lettering to the buses were never acted upon. A park and ride facility for tourists was considered but not proceeded with while another scheme which never materialised was a proposed day rover ticket.

In March 1985 new "roll off" tickets ("cloakroom style") were introduced, replacing the more flimsy tickets which had been torn off a pad. Councillors were disappointed that no advertisements appeared on the back but apparently no advertiser could be found.

From early 1985 (until December 1986) John Ros-

tron, the former Huddersfield Corporation Passenger Transport general manager who had retired as Director of Operations with West Yorkshire PTE in 1976 and lived in Holmfirth, acted as a consultant to the Minibus Sub-Committee. He advised on the fares structure (left unchanged) and on effects of the Transport Bill which would soon usher in the deregulation of local bus services.

The sub-committee held quarterly meetings with the operator and regularly examined performance analyses for six month periods. Fairly typical figures were those for October 1984 to March 1985, which show the percentage of costs recovered from income:

Holmfirth Mon-Sat routes 1 to 4	63.62
Holmfirth Market Day rtes A to D	52.16
Honley routes	38.31
Overall	55.28

The services were particularly popular with senior citizens, who paid half fare. Had all passengers paid the full fare, some routes would actually have shown a profit. Although there were regular calls from some councillors for the Honley routes to be abandoned, the council to their credit persisted with them.

From March 1986 the hourly rate paid to SKJ was reduced to £6.20 but fuel tax rebate applicable to the increased hours worked was to be retained by the operator at the rate of 75p per hour. The rest of the fuel tax rebate was still paid to the council.

All three networks, Holmfirth routes 1-4 and A-D and the Honley minibuses, were continued largely unchanged by SKJ on the deregulation of local bus services from 26 October 1986, a fate enjoyed by few British bus routes outside London at the time. The only alteration was that Monday and Wednesday afternoon journeys were at last added on Holmfirth routes 1 to 4 from 27 October 1986. This timetable enhancement had been suggested and costed as early as June 1983. Only on Tuesday (early closing) did these buses still finish at midday. The routes were actually registered by SKJ as commercial services which meant that no tendering process was required. Another operator later wrote to the council, asking to be "considered on tender lists". Timetable leaflets, previously the responsibility of the parish council, were now produced by West Yorkshire PTE but did not at first mention the support provided by the parish council or include their phone number. SKJ incidentally also took over West Yorkshire PTE route 319 (Huddersfield-Waterloo-Storthes Hall) under contract to the PTE, for which the company was paid £8200 per annum. The

parish council now participated in the PTE's concessionary fares scheme but soon found that they were not being reimbursed to the expected extent because of the way in which generation factors were assessed.

8.6: EXIT SKJ

The SKJ business had been expanding for several years (by October 1984 the company was running a filling station on the A1 at Ferrybridge) but from mid 1986 onwards was experiencing financial problems, the full extent of which did not become apparent for some time because of "incorrect accounting". In Summer 1987 the tours programme was less profitable than expected and by August the parish council was finding it difficult to communicate with SKJ to the extent that the chairman planned to visit their premises to find out what was happening. At the same time the traffic commissioners served prohibition notices on several vehicles which did not meet maintenance standards and at the resulting inquiry in September, the SKJ operating licence was cut from 15 to 10 vehicles for three months.

On 18 December 1987 West Yorkshire Passenger Transport Authority announced their intention to revoke the 319 (Huddersfield-Storthes Hall) contract owing to unsatisfactory maintenance standards. Hours later, in a separate development of which the PTA/PTE were allegedly unaware, it was disclosed that Peat Marwick McLintock had already been called in as receivers at SKJ on account of the severe financial problems. The receivers advertised the company for sale as a going concern on 22 December, which resulted in at least 30 expressions of interest.

The PTE reassigned the 319 contract on an emergency basis to Yorkshire Rider from 29 December 1987 but for a short period SKJ continued to operate their registration commercially in competition with their subsidised replacement. Clive Swindell, the manager running SKJ on behalf of the receivers, claimed that the route was still profitable without the PTE subsidy. Christmas and New Year coach trips also went ahead as planned.

Unfortunately a buyer for the whole business could not be found so it was to be sold off in parts. SKJ officially ceased trading on Friday 15 January 1988, after which a Mirfield school contract was abandoned and other school contracts in the Shelley, Kirkburton, Scissett and Cumberworth areas were reassigned to Yorkshire Traction. Nevertheless the receivers had guaranteed the operation of the Holme Valley minibus services until 31 January

1988 so John Buxton was allowed to continue running them under the SKJ licence, even though SKJ itself had ceased trading. By the end of January some councillors wanted to select a different bus operator (three companies had already expressed interest in submitting tenders to run the service) or call in West Yorkshire PTE to advise them but after last minute negotiations with Bill Oldham, chairman of the Minibus Sub-Committee, Buxton established a new company (Wanderama) to operate the minibus services and was given a 12 months trial. The new arrangement from 1 February was slightly more expensive for the council but it was envisaged that the existing route network would only be maintained until Easter, after which a scaled down version needing less financial support would be introduced. Wanderama

seems to have used the minibuses latterly used by SKJ (Ford Transit BCP 124V and Bedfords YVH 220R and OGV 250W), which Buxton had earlier been reported as trying to buy back from the receiver. What the council did not realise was that Buxton was continuing to operate under the old (SKJ) licence. Early in March the traffic commissioners pointed out that the operator's licence was not transferable and insisted that Buxton apply for a new one. When he failed to do so, the commissioners withdrew the operator's licence, which meant that fare paying passengers could not be carried. On Friday and Saturday 11-12 March 1988 passengers were allowed to travel free but on the Monday they found that there were no buses running and Wanderama was no more.

With some misgivings about future loss of local control the parish council accepted the PTE's offer both to share the financial support and to find an operator to run the services unchanged at the existing level of subsidy (£275 per week) while a new route network was planned and put out to tender. After a week without the minibuses, from 21 March 1988 Yorkshire Rider took over on this short term contract. The minibus routes had become part of the mainstream bus network and were run as ordinary tendered services with subsidy payments now shared between the council and West Yorkshire PTE on an approximately 50-50 basis. It is beyond the scope of this account to include full details of the changes that have taken place to the Holme Valley minibuses since then but here is an outline.

Towards the end of Yorkshire Rider's tenure, the council received an apparently unsolicited petition, praising their operation. The services had, however, been won on

retendering by Yorkshire Traction who took over on 4 July 1988, when the routes were extensively altered and relaunched as the "Summer Wine Minibuses". Yorkshire Traction painted some minibuses in a blue and cream livery (with the long requested appropriate lettering) approximating to the old colours of County Motors, the Waterloo, Huddersfield based company absorbed by them in 1969; it was from County's old Penistone Road depot that the minibuses were now operated, by a curious coincidence situated on the same road as SKJ's Penistone Road, Kirkburton premises. For two seasons (1989 and 1990) summer Sunday routes were operated, in 1990 marketed as "Summer Wine Country Tours 1 and 2". Finally on 4 September 1995 a new contractor took over in the shape of the present incumbent, Milnsbridge based Stotts Coaches, who also now run the Marsden route started in 1926 by Wilson Haigh.

The PTE had been scarcely enthusiastic about the prospect of running to Cinderhills in 1976 and had more or less ignored the parish council's minibuses for as long as was possible – their existence was not even acknowledged in PTE "comprehensive" area timetables before October 1986. For their part Holme Valley Parish Council, feeling that "local decisions [were] more effective than those made far away in Wakefield or Whitehall", had also been content to remain separate, constantly reviewing services, listening to local people and learning as they went along. The PTE have recently admitted that their involvement with the parish council and their minibuses since 1988 has influenced the development of other rural minibus networks in West Yorkshire and elsewhere.

YORKSHIRE TRACTION

HOLMFIRTH SUMMER WINE TOURS

★ NO NEED TO BOOK ★
★ JUST HOP ON ★

DEPARTS:
EVERY SUNDAY & BANK HOLIDAY MONDAY
FROM 27TH MAY UNTIL 27th AUGUST 1990

New to London operator Fox, Hayes in March 1977, SKJ Bedford YMT/Duple 53 seater 8 (SLO 513R) had been used on newly gained tendered route 319 on "deregulation day" 26 October 1986. Here it is standing near the entrance to Huddersfield Bus Station on 28 October 1987 and was sold to Kenmargra of Linthwaite after the collapse of SKJ. [H.J. Black]